NEW YORK
CHARTER
COMMISSION

REPORT
1923

ARTES
SCIENTIA
VERITAS
LIBRARY OF THE
UNIVERSITY OF MICHIGAN
TUEBOR

REPORT

OF

THE NEW YORK CHARTER COMMISSION

TO THE

LEGISLATURE

WITH A

DRAFT OF CHARTER

FOR THE

CITY OF NEW YORK

APPROVED BY THE COMMISSION ON
MARCH 5, 1923

REPORT

OF

THE NEW YORK CHARTER COMMISSION

WITH A

DRAFT OF CHARTER

FOR THE

CITY OF NEW YORK

1923

THE NEW YORK CHARTER COMMISSION

HENRY DE FOREST BALDWIN, Chairman

JOHN F. HYLAN, Mayor
CHARLES L. CRAIG, Comptroller
EDWARD RIEGELMANN, President, Borough of Brooklyn
JOHN J. KELLER, Alderman
HOWARD LEE McBAIN, Secretary
EDWARD M. BASSETT
GEORGE CROMWELL
LEWIS L. DELAFIELD
JOSEPH M. LEVINE
HERMAN A. METZ
WILLIAM BARCLAY PARSONS
FRANK L. POLK
ARTHUR S. SOMERS
H. PUSHAE WILLIAMS

FRANKLIN W. M. CUTCHEON, Counsel

CONTENTS

LEGISLATIVE AUTHORIZATION

From Chap. 343, Laws of 1921.

Section 1. Within thirty days after this act takes effect, the governor shall appoint a commission consisting of fifteen persons, residents of the city of New York, to be known as the New York charter commission, to inquire into the local government of the city of New York, and the counties contained therein, with power to investigate the manner of conducting and transacting business in the several departments, boards and offices thereof, the effect and working of the charter of Greater New York, and the acts amendatory thereof and supplementary thereto, and of any and all other acts relating to such city, and to suggest such legislation as it may deem advisable with respect thereto. Such commission shall draft and submit with its final report a new charter and, within its discretion, an administrative code or other body of supplementary local law for enforcement within such city. The governor shall include among the persons appointed as members of such commission the mayor and the comptroller of the city of New York, the president of one of the several boroughs thereof, and a member of the board of aldermen thereof, to serve respectively during the periods of their incumbency of such offices, and such appointment shall not affect in any manner the title to any such office which any one of the said persons is holding. The governor shall, in like manner, fill by appointment such vacancies as may at any time occur in the membership of such commission.

§ 2. Within ten days after the commission shall have been appointed, its members shall meet and organize by the election from their number of a chairman and a secretary. It shall be the duty of such commission from time to time to report the progress of its work to the legislature of nineteen hundred and twenty-two; but if it shall not be practicable to report finally thereto, it shall submit its final report to the legislature of nineteen hundred and twenty-three, together with bills to carry out its recommendations in the premises. The commission may, in and for the performance of its duties, employ counsel and such and so many clerks, stenographers and other persons as it may deem necessary, and fix their compensation. It may hold its meetings at any time or place within the city of New York. Any examination or investigation by the commission may be made by or before any one or more of its members, pursuant to the order of the commission duly made and entered on the minutes of any meeting thereof at which a quorum may be present, and the proceedings of or before such commissioner or commissioners shall be deemed to be the proceedings of or before the commission as a whole, when approved and confirmed by it.

(§§ 3 and 4 contain the customary grant of power to subpoena, administer oaths, and otherwise conduct investigations for the purpose defined.)

§ 5. For the purpose of carrying out the provisions of this act, the sum of twenty-five thousand dollars ($25,000) is hereby appropriated out of any funds in the hands of the comptroller not heretofore appropriated. Payments of or on account of the expenses of the commission shall be made by the comptroller from the sum so appropriated upon vouchers, in form to be approved by such comptroller, when certified by such commission, or by such officer or officers as it may designate, by proper resolution, for that purpose.

§ 6. This act shall take effect November first, nineteen hundred and twenty-one.

Approved April 30, 1921.

REPORT *of*

The New York Charter Commission

To the Legislature of the State of New York:

The New York Charter Commission, appointed by the Governor pursuant to the provisions of Chapter 343 of the Laws of 1921, submits to your Honorable bodies its report, together with a draft of an Act designed to constitute a new charter of the City of New York (Appendix A).

Organization.

The Commission was organized as required by the Act providing for its appointment and elected as its Chairman Hon. Francis M. Scott. Of his services and counsel, which would have been especially valuable by reason both of his conspicuous ability and of his unusually wide experience as Corporation Counsel and as Justice of the Supreme Court, the Commission and the public were deprived by his untimely death in February, 1922. Subsequently to the death of Judge Scott, Mr. Henry de Forest Baldwin was appointed a member of the Commission and was elected and remains its Chairman. Mr. Howard Lee McBain, one of the members of the Commission, was elected, and at all times has been its secretary. The Commission in the first instance appointed as its counsel Hon. Edward J. McGoldrick, and, after his resignation upon becoming a Justice of the Supreme Court appointed in his stead Mr. F. W. M. Cutcheon.

Procedure.

During the earlier months of the Commission's existence it held a considerable number of public sessions, which were devoted almost wholly to the formulation of certain basic principles to be observed in the later work of charter revision. Subsequently, in November, 1922, the Commission, desiring to expedite the actual work of formulating a draft of charter held many executive sessions as a committee of the whole.

The Commission has had the benefit of numerous conferences with a number of the present as well as several of the former officials of the City and has received many communications of value from individual citizens as well as from numerous civic bodies. The accompanying draft of charter has been printed in considerable numbers and has been widely circulated. Criticisms and suggestions have been freely offered and not a little of the value of the Commission's work should be attributed to the information and suggestions thus received. A majority of the members of the Commission are or have been associated, in official capacities, with municipal or closely related activities and therefore have a not inconsiderable familiarity with the organization and operation of the City Government. The Commission has had the benefit not only of the report of the Joint Legislative Committee appointed pursuant to your joint resolution of April 15, 1921, but also of the reports of the other legislative committees and of the various Commissions which have preceded it in the work of revision of the Greater New York Charter.

Principles.

The formulation of the draft of charter submitted with this report has been governed largely by the following considerations:

First, and not the least important, the desirability of reducing the needlessly long, redundant and complex Greater New York Charter to manageable volume and of substituting a reasonably simple and compendious enactment.

Second, the inauguration of a system under which the City, through the medium of its legislative bodies and administrative officers, will control its own affairs, within the limitations imposed by the letter and purpose of the State Constitution, thus rendering unnecessary and unwarranted those continual appeals to the Legislature which, upon one hand, result in mandatory legislation that robs the City of the power to direct its own expenditures and, upon the other, affords an excuse, not often a justification, for inaction or unwise action upon the part of City authorities.

Third, the regulation of the financial administration of the City in such manner that the injunctions of the Constitution concerning that subject may be observed and that there may be definitely established a "pay-as-you-go" policy which, in the opinion of the Commission, is requisite, not merely for the maintenance unimpaired of the City's credit, but as an assurance that the measure of home rule afforded by the proposed charter can be granted safely,—at least in the first instance.

Revolutionary Innovations Avoided.

No attempt has been made to introduce into the charter revolutionary or even especially novel features. The existing charter, cumbersome as it is, has, in the opinion of the Commission, provided a form of government which has worked extraordinarily well, particularly when one considers the magnitude of the experiment which it represented, the divergence of interests which have demanded recognition and the difficulty of securing for the administration of City affairs the same quality of ability and experience which are secured by private enterprise through the medium of greater continuity of tenure and more brilliant opportunity for advancement and reward. It should be clearly understood that, subject to the reservation that it does not permit local control of the City's affairs, the Greater New York Charter, as amended, far from being a failure in practical operation is, except in form, a highly creditable monument to those who first devised and those who gradually have moulded it into its present substance. The Commission, therefore, believing that progress in the science of government rarely is made through the abrupt substitution of a device wholly experimental for an instrumentality which, even if defective, has proved itself workable, has contented itself in the main with providing for the increase of the City's powers of self-government, the protection of its credit and the simplification and improvement of detail in charter structure.

January 1, 1926, the Effective Date.

The Commission recommends that the draft of charter submitted, if enacted and if accepted by the City, shall not come into force in its entirety until 1926. In its opinion there exists no emergency which demands haste in making the changes proposed. It is plain that no revision of the existing charter should be imposed upon the City against the will of its inhabitants. Therefore the submission of the charter to the electors of the City for their acceptance or rejection at the election of November, 1923, has been provided for. If the proposed charter is enacted and accepted, time must be afforded for an examination by the City authorities and a reorganization, at least to some extent, of official and departmental functions and for the preparation of ordinances covering many subjects which, although regulated in detail by the present charter, are not so regulated in the proposed charter. It is also desirable that the legislative policy with respect to public-service regulation and public-utility operation, with which the Commission has not felt at liberty to deal except in very general ways, shall be established before this organization of departments and official functions shall be undertaken. The Commission, moreover, has recommended various changes with respect to the assessing and collection of taxes which should not be inaugurated except after a considerable period of notice to taxpayers. For all of these reasons the Commission would deprecate an effort to put the proposed charter into force as a working scheme at a date earlier than that which it has selected, January 1, 1926, at which time the next city administration will commence.

Attention is now invited to the concrete terms of the proposed charter.

The Proposed Powers of the City.

Extremely broad powers of local self-government and control of municipal affairs are conferred upon the City as such. Supplementing the general grant of powers, but not in derogation therefrom, a very large number of specific powers are conferred. This course has been followed in an endeavor to avoid litigation for which an undefined grant of power offers tempting opportunities. The specific grants are intended to, and it is believed do, include all powers with respect to local or municipal matters which are now possessed by the City or by any of the authorities of the City or its counties, as well as such additional powers as are essential to complete local governmental and administrative autonomy with the exceptions enumerated below:

1. The school-system, not including the College of the City of New York or Hunter College of the City of New York, is left, except with respect to taxation, to be dealt with by the Legislature as a part of the state educational system.

2. Certain boards, officers and departments may not be abolished or stripped of essential powers. These include the Board of Aldermen, the Board of Estimate and Apportionment, elective and constitutional officers, the Municipal Civil Service Commission, the departments of Police, Pensions and Taxes and their respective Commissioners, the Board of Review (dealing with taxes and assessments), judges, the Corporation Counsel, Chamberlain and Commissioner of Inquiry.

3. The regulation of the rates and practices of public service corporations is restricted to such services and matters as shall not be regulated by State or Nation.

4. While the powers to construct and acquire revenue-producing improvements and to lease them for operation by others are not limited, the power of the City directly to operate such improvements is limited, substantially, to the exercise of such powers as it now possesses and such as hereafter may be conferred upon it by the Legislature.

5. The powers to contract and refund long-term debt are limited and a pay-as-you-go policy is otherwise enforced by numerous provisions with respect to the budget, the collection of taxes, the administration of pension funds and the constitution of the sinking funds.

6. The method of exercising the powers of taxation, eminent domain and assessment of benefits, severally, is prescribed as to essentials.

The City's powers are distributed, for purposes of exercise, between various officers, boards and departments, as indicated below, but, except as stated, all such powers may be exercised, redistributed or assumed by the Board of Aldermen or the Board of Estimate and Apportionment, or by the two Boards acting in conjunction.

Distribution of Powers.

In the matter of governmental organization, the Commission has adhered to the somewhat illogical, but practically successful, scheme of the present charter, modifying it in detail but retaining its principle. One set of powers, including the power of taxation and, it is believed, all powers which are purely legislative in their nature, is confided to the Board of Aldermen. Another, confined almost wholly to those pertaining to administrative routine or requiring essentially sound business judgment and promptness of decision in their exercise, is conferred upon the Board of Estimate and Apportionment, the composition of which remains unaltered. Administrative powers of unusual importance, particularly those the exercise of which is likely to involve considerations of political expediency and, as well, the making of the appropriations (a function which vitally affects both ordinary administration on the one hand and taxation upon the other) are to be exercised by the two bodies conjointly. City powers, not expressly or by necessary intendment entrusted to the Board of Estimate and Apportionment or to the two boards, acting in conjunction, or specifically vested in other City agencies, are vested in the Board of Aldermen, which thus becomes the repository not only of many specified powers but also of all of the undefined and residuary powers of the City.

Powers of the Board of Estimate and Apportionment.

The powers conferred upon the Board of Estimate and Apportionment, acting alone, comprise:

1. Control of the official and departmental organization and the transfer of powers from one municipal authority to another; the transfer of unused budgetary appropriations to other purposes sanctioned by the budget.
2. Authorization of all street-openings and improvements and of all other public, including local, improvements, except such as may cost, severally, more than $500,000; authorization of the condemnation of excess lands.
3. Control of the routine of assessment proceedings and awards in connection with improvements.
4. Authorization of stock and bond issues, except any

such as may exceed $50,000,000 for a single purpose; authorization of refunding operations.

5. Control and management of city property, including water-front property, and of the sinking funds.

6. Control of the operation of such revenue-producing improvements as the City is empowered to operate.

7. The granting of franchises; control of the use of streets by public service corporations; unless the subject has been taken over by the State or Federal government, the regulation of their rates and practices.

8. Regulation of zoning and control over the city map.

9. The auditing and compromise of claims and the initiation, defense and settlement of legal proceedings.

Conjoint Powers of the Board of Aldermen and the Board of Estimate and Apportionment.

The powers which are to be exercised by the Board of Aldermen and the Board of Estimate and Apportionment in conjunction are the following:

1. The creation and definition of the constitution and powers of local improvement boards.

2. The authorization of public, including local, improvements (except street improvements) costing in excess of $500,000, severally; the establishment and maintenance of street and park opening and other reserve funds.

3. Cession of city property to the State or to the United States.

4. The determination of the number and the salaries of officials (with a few specified exceptions) and of all employees to be maintained by the City Treasury.

5. Authorization of stock and bond issues, in cases in which the issue (for any single purpose) exceeds $50,000,000.

6. The authorization, subject to prescribed safeguards, of the operation or lease by the City of revenue-producing improvements.

7. Supervision of pension, retirement and similar funds and the inauguration of a consolidated system.

8. The adoption of annual budgets for city and educational purposes; the making of appropriations otherwise.

The Board of Aldermen.

The draft of charter reported herewith does not deal with the constitution of the Board of Aldermen or with the apportionment of aldermen. The matter of apportionment should be dealt with by the Legislature or by the City, under legislative authority, after the method of electing aldermen shall have been determined.

Enough has been said in the preceding paragraphs of this report, to demonstrate that the accompanying draft of Charter contemplates investing the Board of Aldermen with very far-reaching powers. Not only does the proposed Charter aim at conferring upon the board very numerous legislative powers, under which it may direct the exercise of the police power of the State in many respects of the utmost importance, but it requires the participation of the Board of Aldermen, with the Board of Estimate and Apportionment, in the determination of many of the most important administrative decisions of the municipal government. The Commission is of the opinion that it is desirable that the importance, and therefore the power, of the Board of Aldermen shall be thus increased, (first) in order that the electorate of the City may have imposed upon it a constantly recurring sense of responsibility for the conduct of the municipal government and the necessity of informing itself concerning and of interesting itself in municipal affairs—that is to say, in order that a genuine, and not a make-believe, system of home-rule may exist—and (second) in order that all of the elements of the electorate may have an immediately effective medium of expressing their opinions and exercising their influence upon the decisions of particular municipal problems. It is a trite statement, but one which expresses a fact that cannot be too frequently recalled, that the citizenship of New York is composed of many diverse elements, that it is divided not only into dissimilar geographical districts but into groups, distinguished by origin, occupation, living conditions and other characteristics which socially and economically have distinct and sometimes divergent interests. In a body such as the Board of Estimate and Apportionment, which is most often controlled by the votes of officials who have been elected by the City at large and in which no member ever represents any district smaller than a borough, it may often become difficult to obtain proper representation for, or appreciation of, the needs of relatively minor groups of citizens, which, nevertheless, are entitled to, and in the interest of the City at large should, receive most serious consideration. The Board of Aldermen, with a membership representing relatively small and more numerous constituencies, and comprehending the entire city, is a natural medium for the expression of the views and the exercisé of the influence of such smaller groups.

The proposal to transfer such large powers now exercised by the Legislature to the local City government, and particularly the proposal to increase the powers and importance of the Board of Aldermen, will be more readily accepted and approved by many, if such transfer of power could be accompanied by provisions which will give some hope that the Board of Aldermen may become more completely representative of the people than it is at present. We may expect that the important city officers who sit in the Board of Estimate and Apportionment will always be selected by the organizations of the two great national parties, and that all of them, since they are elected together at one municipal election for four years, may quite usually be selected by the same national party. Those voters who may feel that they are not adequately represented by the party in power (and not infrequently they amount in the aggregate to a majority), cannot very well be given representation in the local city government elsewhere than in the Board of Aldermen. And this is the place where all the elements of a political opposition properly should be heard. But under our present election machinery no group of citizens in an aldermanic district, other than the organizations of the great national parties, can run candidates for aldermen with any hope of success. We all know that there are many citizens who are very loyal in national and state affairs to the political parties of their choice who, if they could unite to some extent irrespective of the precise location of their residences and be given a hopeful opportunity to be represented, would act independently of the national party organizations in local matters. It seems to a majority of the Commission that these citizens should be given a hopeful opportunity to secure representation in the city government. The fact that they could be so represented might very well react upon the national party organizations and tend to cause them, to a greater extent than has heretofore been the case, to select their aldermen with reference to the more important local problems which demand solution.

Proportional Representation.

The Commission has considered various suggested solutions of the problem thus presented and a majority of its members are of the opnion that, of all possible expedi ents that have come to their attention, the system of proportional representation is the most promising. The entire draft of charter has been prepared, and, in particular, the very broad authority vested in the Board of Aldermen has been provided for, upon the assumption that the Legislature may deem it wise that some system of proportional representation shall be required or permitted in the selection of aldermen. Regardless of the wisdom of applying such a system to the election of Members of Congress or Members of the Legislature or to the election of any body in which it is primarily desirable to maintain the two party system, a majority of the Commission believes that in a body, the duties of which are or ought to be discharged in a spirit almost wholly non-partisan, from the point of view of National or State politics, the most important functions of which are to decide administrative, financial and other business problems, a system of proportional representation not only should operate unobjectionably from a political point of view but may well assure much more general and attentive consideration of the views of the people as a whole and much more scrupulous examination of the City's problems than is possible under the system of party government now in vogue.

A majority of the Commission believe that a system of proportional representation, if applied to the election of aldermen in the City of New York, may tend to improvement in at least the following respects: (1) representation in the Board for any group of voters, adhering to some common program of municipal action, provided it is so numerous that its views should be afforded an opportunity for expression in the determination of the policies of the community, even though it may not be sufficiently powerful to prevail in an election under the present system as against either of the established political parties; (2) a *fair* representation, and no more, for each group; (3) hopeful candidacies sponsored by groups independent of the control of the organizations which ordinarily direct the activities of established parties; (4) selection by the minority groups of their best available candidates, chosen solely with relation to municipal issues, which in time, almost necessarily, should force like selections by the major parties; (5) closer relations between an alderman and those who have elected him, between whom in the case of a minority group no national political organization will intervene; (6) a vigilant and an active-minded criticism by every group in opposition to the party in power in the Board of Estimate and Apportionment; (7) vastly increased public interest in the selection of members of the board and in its debates and decisions; and, consequently, (8) a greater security against hastily conceived, unconsidered, or one-sided, enactments.

The question whether a system of proportional representation should be *imposed* upon the City of New York or should be tendered to it for voluntary adoption or rejection is one the decision of which the Commission does not believe to be within its province. The Commission is advised by its counsel that, under the State Constitution, as it now exists, the inclusion in the charter of provisions for proportional representation in aldermanic elections would in all probability, if attacked in the courts, be held to be unconstitutional. A copy of Counsel's opinion upon this subject is appended hereto as Appendix B. The Commission accordingly will submit a draft of a concurrent resolution, for adoption by your honorable bodies, if they approve, which provides for an amendment of the State Constitution by the addition to Section 2 of Article X of the Constitution of provisions which would empower the Legislature either to require the adoption of proportional representation in City elections to such extent as it may deem wise or to provide that cities at their own option may adopt the system by such method of decision as the Legislature may prescribe.

Reasons for Withholding and Granting Certain Powers—Checks Upon the Exercise of Certain Powers.

1. The School System.

The best opinion of those who have had adequate opportunity to observe the management and operation of the educational system of the City appears to favor the incorporation of the school system, proper, in the State system, rather than the maintenance of a separate city system. The Commission has adopted this view and has provided in the proposed charter that the territory of the City shall constitute a school district, distinct from the City considered as a public corporation. This accords with the policy of the present law which, the Commission may assume, represents the considered judgment of the Legislature. On the other hand, the proposed charter provides for the support of the schools by the City, except for contributions which may be made by the State. It is required that each annual educational budget (which in the first instance is to be prepared by the Board of Education) shall provide for the necessary expense of maintaining the City schools upon at least the same level of service as that then currently existing but leaves to the discretion of the City authorities additional and emergency appropriations. Funds appropriated for existing service are to be subject to the unrestricted control of the Board of Education. This does not differ in substance from the present arrangement.

The accompanying draft of charter does provide, however, that the educational budget shall at all stages remain separate from the City budget proper and that the school tax shall be extended and shall appear upon tax-bills and tax-receipts in distinct, segregated amounts. This is for the purpose of compelling not only the city authorities but the Board of Education, the Legislature and the public to recognize the precise extent of the provision made and of the burden assumed for ordinary school purposes.

The Commission recommends that the College of the City of New York and Hunter College of the City of New York be left, so far as appropriations and taxation therefor are concerned, under the jurisdiction of the City. These institutions are not in a true sense parts of the public school system for which the Constitution imposes responsibility upon the Legislature; nor has the State any peculiar interest which dictates the assertion by it of control over them. Upon the contrary, they are peculiarly the concern of the City and in the opinion of the Commission the City should be permitted to determine for itself the extent to which their usefulness justifies their cost or warrants increasing it. The City is filled with their graduates, many of them occupying positions of influence, and no apprehension need be felt that these institutions will not be justly or adequately cared for.

2. Permanently Established Offices, Departments and Procedure—Administrative Reorganization—Transfers of Powers.

Except as stated above (under the heading, "The Proposed Powers of the City"), the accompanying draft of charter authorizes the City, through the Board of Estimate and Apportionment and with the Mayor's approval to establish and define the powers of offices, departments and other agencies (both city and county) and to transfer powers and functions from one officer, department or agency to another. The proposed charter does not attempt to establish any officers, boards, departments, bureaus or commissions except such as the Commission believes should be regarded as essential and therefore should be permanent. No explanation need be given of reasons for giving a permanent character to the two great City boards—the Board of Aldermen and the Board of Estimate and Apportionment—to elective (including all constitutional) offices, to judges, to the Municipal Civil Service Commission or to the Corporation Counsel.

The Police Department, considered both from the standpoint of the public's dependence upon it for the maintenance of order and the enforcement of law and from the standpoint of its natural susceptibility to political interference and the influence of other interests, occupies a unique position of importance and peril. In the opinion of the Commission, the interest of the State in its proper organization and discipline and in its protection from political or other interested interference is so great that the State itself should prescribe the conditions which it regards essential to its efficiency and integrity. By making the Mayor solely responsible for the administration of this department, as is the case under the existing charter, we believe we are insuring a continuance of what has proved, after many experiments in dividing responsibility, the most successful solution of a most baffling municipal problem.

The Constitution of the State requires the Legislature to restrict the City's "power of taxation, assessment, borrowing money, contracting debts * * * so as to prevent abuses in assessments and in contracting debt." (Sec. 1, Article XII.) This, in the analysis, means that the Legislature is to determine the City's financial structure and organization, for in no other way can it effectually give vitality to the constitutional mandate. It must also define the processes of taxation, condemnation and assessment of benefits, both because the Constitution enjoins the duty (see also Sec. 7, Article I) and because reasonable protection of the taxpayer and the property owner is incompatible with leaving these vital matters to the unrestricted discretion of the City, which must exercise the requisite powers for its own ends and often in hostility to individual interests. The Commission, therefore, has incorporated in the proposed charter articles prescribing the methods to be observed in making assessments, both for taxes and benefits, in levying taxes and in exercising the power of eminent domain. In addition to other reasons for specific definition of procedure in these matters, the Commission is advised that certain of the provisions with respect to them, which authorize and define judicial jurisdiction and procedure, involve the exercise of legislative power which cannot constitutionally be delegated to the City but must proceed from the Legislature itself.

Accordingly, on the one hand, the proposed charter defines the financial powers of the two great City boards, the powers and duties of the Comptroller, establishes, as independent officers, the Chamberlain (to be the collector and custodian of the public funds) and the Commissioner of Inquiry (now the Commissioner of Accounts) and creates the Department of Pensions, all of which the Commission regards as essential parts of a proper municipal financial organization. On the other hand, it establishes the Department of Taxes, the Board of Assessors and the Board of

Review as necessary components of the City's taxing and assessment system.

The Board of Standards and Appeals, which exercises certain powers which the Commission is advised should possess direct legislative sanction, is continued, with somewhat enlarged powers.

Neither the Board of Standards and Appeals nor the Board of Assessors is protected against disturbance by action of the municipal authorities.

As to the remainder of the administrative officers, departments and other agencies which may be deemed necessary to a proper municipal organization, the City is left free to establish, to abolish and, as to powers and functions, to alter them as the Board of Estimate and Apportionment may deem best, although administrative functions of borough presidents are not to be transferred except by unanimous vote of the members of the Board.

Pending January 1, 1926, the existing Board of Estimate and Apportionment is authorized and directed to establish an *interim* organization (to become operative on that date), as to which it is left a free hand, except that it must permit the powers of the Department of Health for the protection of life and health to reside, without disintegration, in a single department or officer and must leave intact the obligations now imposed upon citizens with respect to these subjects.

3. Ownership and Leasing of Revenue Producing Improvements—Their Operation—Regulation of Privately-Owned Public Utilities.

The proposed charter grants to the City practically unlimited power to construct and otherwise acquire revenue-producing improvements. The cost and earning capacity of the improvement, nevertheless, must be ascertained as nearly as possible and corporate stock or bonds may be issued to finance it (within the constitutional limits) only to the amount upon which the estimated annual earnings of the improvement will suffice to pay interest after providing for the estimated expense of operation, maintenance and other proper charges and an amortization charge to be so calculated as to amortize the investment within its life (not exceeding fifty years). The Commission is of the opinion that, considering the legal limits of the City's debt-incurring power (even if enlarged to the extent suggested in this report), and the effective limitation thereof imposed by its practical ability to borrow money, a great municipality such as New York City should be permitted to exercise its own discretion as to what it must or should provide in the way of public utilities—for which private capital not infrequently cannot be found.

On the other hand, a majority of the members of the Commission, in view of the strong probability that your honorable bodies will deal at their present session with the subject of municipal operation at least of transit facilities, have deemed it wise to confine the grant of power to operate revenue-producing improvements to such as now exist or may hereafter be granted specifically by the Legislature. The proposed charter, however, contains checks upon the exercise of all such powers whether heretofore, or hereafter granted. It seems reasonable, considering the difficulties under which a municipality labors in the operation of public utilities and the opportunity for political abuse which is inherent in any such undertaking, that, before the City shall have the right to enter upon any such enterprise upon a very large scale, the consequences shall be ascertained as far as practicable and that there shall be ground for believing that the undertaking will not be disastrous. For these reasons, the accompanying draft of charter provides that before the operation of any revenue-producing improvement involving an investment of more than $50,000,000 for a single purpose shall be entered upon, it shall be judicially determined, after investigation by a competent commission of disinterested citizens, that the proposed enterprise probably will be self-supporting, taking its entire life into consideration, and that both the Board of Estimate and Apportionment and the Board of Aldermen shall determine that the proposal is wise. Provision is made also for the submission of such proposals to popular vote. With respect to improvements of less magnitude, it is provided that the ability of the improvement to be self-sustaining shall be determined by engineers of, or appointed by, the Board of Estimate and Apportionment and that the project shall be authorized by concurrent action of that board and the Board of Aldermen. An attempt, also, to assure the financial soundness of enterprises undertaken by the City, after they come into operation, will be found in the section which provides for a readjustment of rates in such manner as (if possible) to avoid deficits and which gives taxpayers and creditors the right to enforce the performance of its duties by the Board.

The City is given broad power to lease municipally-owned revenue-producing improvements, subject to provisions for the reservation of adequate rental and for recapture.

4. Stock and Bond Issues.

Aside from corporate stock or bonds issued to finance revenue-producing improvements (a subject already dealt with), long term obligations may be issued for the following purposes only:

(1) Those for which specific authority already exists, to the extent to which it has not been exercised;

(2) Sites for schools, colleges, museums, etc., and the construction and equipment of buildings therefor;

(3) Assessment bonds, in anticipation of the collection of assessments for benefits—to mature in not more than ten years;

(4) General Fund bonds;

(5) Refunding bonds, issuable only to refund issues which might be lawfully made at the date of the refunding;

(6) Upon the establishment of a consolidated pension system, bonds to provide for making good then existing deficiencies in pension and retirement funds consolidated in the new system.

Bond issues may be serial and complete amortization of every issue of stock or bonds within the life of the issue must be provided for.

The Comptroller is authorized to issue and sell revenue and special revenue bonds and tax notes substantially of the descriptions now authorized.

It is required that each annual budget shall provide not only for special revenue bonds issued during the preceding year but for revenue and special revenue bonds issued after January 1, 1926, which have not in fact been redeemed out of the taxes levied therefor.

Other Details.

1. Taxes.

It is proposed to abolish the Board of Taxes and Assessments and that its functions shall be discharged by a Commissioner, to be the administrative head of the Department of Taxes and by a number of non-permanent tax-boards, to be appointed by the Commissioner, as needed, from the entire number of deputy tax-commissioners, of which boards the Commissioner and his Assistant Commissioner, also, may be members.

It is also proposed to establish a Board of Review, independent of the Tax Department, by which all applications to review decisions of tax-boards must be heard in the first instance and from whose orders, made upon formal applications, appeals will lie to the Appellate Division of the Supreme Court. Provision is made for informal applications to this Board, but without right of appeal from orders made thereon. Certiorari in tax matters is abolished. The Board of Review is also given jurisdiction to review assessments not confirmed by a court of record.

By far the greater part of the city's revenue is derived from the tax on real estate which in 1922 yielded over $280,000,000. The Tax Department apportions this huge annual tax levy by an assessment of real estate in accordance with its actual value. It is of the greatest importance not only to the individual property owner but to every member of the community that these taxes be levied fairly and that the community have confidence in the operation of the Tax Department. The economic burden of the taxes collected is increased by inequality in assessment. People pay more willingly taxes which they believe to be fairly apportioned. Lack of confidence in the fairness with which the tax is apportioned creates unprofitable and unnecessary dissatisfaction and lessens, insofar as any inequality exists, the amount the city can collect. Therefore any improvement in the procedure which will facilitate the correction of errors in assessment must be of advantage to the city.

The methods at present in use in the City of New York for the assessment of real property conform to the best modern practice; but of course there must always be cases of difference of opinion between the Tax Department and the property owners.

The chief defect of the assessment machinery in this city is that the property owner must appeal for the correction of assessments to the officials who are responsible for the valuation, and that he has no further appeal except by court proceedings. The values of properties are fixed by Deputy Tax Commissioners and appeals are heard by members of the Board of Tax Commissioners who do not themselves make original valuations. The members of the Board, however earnestly they may endeavor to review appeals impartially, are obliged to work hurriedly and must always be somewhat influenced by a natural tendency to uphold the work of their subordinates; and even if they successfully overcome that tendency the property owner is apt to feel that he is a victim of it if his appeal is rejected even for the best of reasons. Where the property owner's appeal to the Tax Commissioners is denied his only remedy is to apply to the Supreme Court for a writ of certiorari to have the assessment reviewed by the court. This necessitates the employment of counsel and real estate experts and all the expense and delay incident to court proceedings and the preparation of expert testimony. Competent authorities estimate that in this city unless a reduction of one hundred thousand dollars on the assessed valuation can be obtained, the expenses of certiorari proceedings are likely to be in excess of the relief to be obtained by a successful litigation. This practically deprives the large mass of property owners of an adequate remedy.

In order to afford a simple and less expensive method of tax appeals the Commission has adopted the plan briefly outlined above.

The first appeals which will be referred as now to Boards composed of Tax Department officials, should have the result of correcting obvious errors and ought to work as satisfactorily to the property owners as under the present system.

After the taxes are levied, the property owner who is dissatisfied with the decision of the Tax Department will still have the right of an appeal to the Board of Review, provided his appeal be seasonably taken. He can present a complaint informally to the Board of Review, which is empowered to hear and decide summarily and to order any adjustment or refund of taxes that may be necessary. No appeal will be allowed to the courts from a decision on such an informal complaint but whether or not an informal complaint has been made or decided, the property owner is given an additional right of submitting a formal and detailed complaint, and if this is not decided to his satisfaction an appeal can be taken directly to the Appellate Division. Although such a formal complaint would require careful preparation, as is now necessary in certiorari proceedings, the procedure before the Board of Review would be much simpler than in the Supreme Court and the case would be reached with much less delay. Moreover an appellate body which gives its attention exclusively to questions of taxes and assessments should be in a far better position to decide appeals equitably than a court of law.

The present head of the Tax Department is a Board of seven members. The President of the Board usually exercises supervisory power, although this can be exercised by a majority vote of the Board. The need of having such a large Board under the present system is chiefly to hear appeals. The change proposed in the method of determining appeals makes a large Board superfluous. It is proposed therefore to have one Commissioner as head of the Tax Department so as to concentrate the responsibility for routine administration.

A first tax-payment of one per cent. of the tax assessments is required to be made, beginning in 1927 (that is to say, nearly four years hence), on the second day of January; the balance becomes due May first but payment in either case may be postponed for four months by paying interest at the rate of six per cent. per annum; thereafter defaulted taxes are to bear interest at the rate of three-fourths of one per cent. per month. This arrangement should obviate in part the necessity of issuing revenue bonds and as compared with the present arrangement should mean a large annual saving to the City in interest (paid and received).

Such provision is made that the Board of Aldermen, in its discretion, may reasonably classify taxable property and may provide for its assessment upon differing bases of valuation or for its taxation at different rates.

2. Condemnation and Assessments of Benefits.

The existing law upon these subjects has been completely revised, redundant provisions have been eliminated and provisions rearranged so as to bear logical relationship with one another. The laws which are applied in practice, however, have been retained with immaterial alterations.

The proposed charter provides that all forms of public improvements, except public buildings, may be provided for, in whole or in part, if in the judgment of the City authorities the conditions justify such course, by the assessment of private property especially benefited thereby.

Upon the Board of Review has been conferred the power to review the work of the Board of Assessors, in place of the present Board of Revision of Assessments as under the existing charter.

3. Pension Funds.

Provision is made for a single agency to administer, investigate and report upon pension and retirement funds, through which a very great and only partially appreciated city obligation (moral if not legal—probably legal in part) is gradually accumulating. The Board of Pension Fund Trustees, which is proposed, is to be composed of City officials, three of whom are already directly interested in the management and protection of existing funds. The remaining members of the Board are to be the most responsible among the possible representatives of the City. Pending a consolidation of all pension systems (which is authorized to be made by joint action of the Board of Aldermen and the Board of Estimate and Apportionment, pursuant to a plan which the Board of Pension Fund Trustees is directed to formulate and report), the existing funds are to be kept distinct but not extended. Permanent provision is made against the impairment of accrued benefits but the proposed charter contemplates the incorporation of all funds, from the date of consolidation, in a single fund to be maintained upon an actuarial basis which will properly protect the beneficiaries and will assure the City against the future discovery of obligations that may not have been provided for. Retirements which entitle the persons retired to pensions or like benefits are to be made by the Board of Pension Fund Trustees. The beneficiaries of the various funds, actual and contingent, are afforded wide supervisory privileges, to be exercised through the medium of an Advisory Committee.

4. The Budgets.

The proposed separation of the city and educational budgets already has been explained.

The proposed charter provides for the appointment by the Board of Estimate and Apportionment of a Commissioner of the Budget, whose duty it shall be to gather materials for and to prepare a proposed city budget for submission to that board. He is given full authority to secure information from city officials at any time and official and department estimates, including a very full statement by the Comptroller, are required to be transmitted to him not later than the first day of September of each year. The Commission is of the opinion that in a city, the affairs of which are of the magnitude of those of the City of New York, the work of budget-making should go on continuously. This is particularly true because supplementary appropriations must constantly be considered and acted upon. It is appropriate that the Commissioner of the Budget shall be a subordinate of the Board of Estimate and Apportionment, both because as such he will be supported by the authority of that body and because, by making him a part of its organization, the duplication of an established machinery may be avoided.

In making up the annual budget, the Board of Estimate and Apportionment, in effect, is left with full discretion as to all except contractual and quasi-contractual obligations, except that provision must be made for the state courts and any boards, if any, that in substance serve only the City or one or more of its subdivisions. It is also provided that *all* taxes and assessments levied after January 1, 1926, and in default for more than four years shall be deemed "uncollectable" and that provision for an equal revenue be made in the next ensuing budget. Tax-liens now are subject to sale after three years and it has been assumed that this period will not be extended.

The initiative of the Board of Aldermen in the formulation of the budget is greatly increased, but its action thereon is subject to the approval of the Board of Estimate and Apportionment to be given within a limited period.

5. Borough Presidents.

Each of the Borough Presidents is required to appoint a Commissioner of Public Works who is authorized to exercise all of the administrative powers of the Borough President, irrespective of the latter's absence or disability. It is believed that the power of the Board of Aldermen over appropriations, together with this provision for Commissioners of Public Works, who should quickly become the executive heads of the Borough Presidents' offices in routine matters, may be regarded as a reasonably sufficient answer to the criticism that the power that spends is the power that appropriates. (As a matter of fact, the Borough Presidents do not, either in theory or practice, control the Board of Estimate and Apportionment.) The system provided for, in practical effect, does not differ from the British governmental system under which taxation, appropriation and expenditure are all controlled by Ministers, subject only to the necessity of obtaining the approval of the House of Commons. That system certainly has stood successfully the test of experience.

6. The Chamberlain.

In deference to the opinion that the principal auditing officer of the City should not be also the collecting agency of the City or the custodian of its funds, the Commission has recommended that the Chamberlain be made the independent head of the city treasury proper and that bureaus for the collection of (1) taxes, (2) interest, rents and water-rates, (3) arrearages of taxes, assessments and water-rates, and (4) license fees, shall be maintained in his department.

7. The Board of Water Supply.

The Board of Water Supply is not abolished but the Board of Estimate and Apportionment is empowered (a) to leave it in existence, (b) to consolidate it with the department charged with the control of water distribution in the

City, or (c) to convert it into a department of the city government.

8. Commissioners of the Sinking Fund.

It is proposed to abolish the Board of Commissioners of the Sinking Fund and confer its powers upon the Board of Estimate and Apportionment.

9. Reports—Audits—Publicity.

The proposed charter contains numerous provisions for reports by officers, departments and the executive officials of revenue-producing improvements, for the examination and audits of their accounts (both by the Comptroller and the Commissioner of Inquiry), for the investigation of methods of administering the City's affairs, for public hearings, for the furnishing of information to citizens, for publicity through the publication of notices of proposed action and of data and for tax-payers' actions.

10. Appointments and Removals.

All departmental heads and all independent appointive officials (except the Commissioner of the Budget and subordinates of borough presidents) are to be appointed and may be removed by the Mayor. All elective officers, except Aldermen, and also the Police Commissioner, may be removed by the Governor.

11. Repeals.

In an ordinary case, the repealer clause incorporated in this draft would probably be sufficient and the wisest form of effecting the necessary modification of existing laws. But in this case, where the purpose is to eliminate, to the utmost extent possible, the mandatory effect of existing legislation, and particularly since the City, if it be not repealed, may attempt to supersede much of it by enactments of its own (with resulting confusion), a very careful examination of the existing Charter, the Consolidation Act and all statutes now in force which affect the City should be made to determine whether the specific repeal of acts which may not be affected by the repeal clause proposed is not desirable. The proposed charter provides that the existing Board of Estimate and Apportionment shall transmit to the Legislature, with a report of its action in creating an interim official and departmental reorganization, its recommendation as to desirable specific repeals.

In this connection the Commission desires to call attention to the *Digest of Special Statutes Relating to the City of New York,* which was prepared by a legislative committee pursuant to Chapter 530 of the Laws of 1914, and was published in 1922 under the direction of this Commission pursuant to a special appropriation therefor made by the legislature in 1922. This Digest will be of great service when this whole problem of specific repeals is taken in hand. The Commission also calls attention to a study made by Mr. Arthur W. Macmahon of the *Statutory Sources of New York City Government* which will also be of service in this connection. This study, published in pamphlet form by the Commission, is an able discussion of the difficult legal problems that are involved in proposals to simplify the statutory sources of the City's government.

New Policies.

Sinking Funds.

The City maintains a number of sinking funds from which provision is supposed to be made for the payment at maturity of its funded debt, other than serial bonds and short-dated paper. These sinking funds are the following: (1) The Sinking Fund for the Redemption of the City Debt (i.e., that of the old City of New York), which at the end of 1921 secured about $24,000,000 of debt all outstanding in the hands of the public, and should cease to exist in 1929; (2) The Sinking Fund for the payment of Interest upon the City Debt (the debt of the old city), which has practically been absorbed in The Sinking Fund for the Redemption of the City Debt; (3) The Sinking Fund of the City of New York, which secures the funded debt of Greater New York not secured by special revenues and not including serial bonds, water bonds and short-dated paper, amounting at the same date to about $565,000,000 of publicly held debt; (4) The Water Sinking Fund of the City of New York, which secured at the end of 1921 about $180,000,000 of publicly held obligations; (5) The Rapid Transit Sinking Fund, which at the same date secured more than $193,000,000 of obligations in the hands of the public; (6) and (7) two sinking funds of the old City of Brooklyn and (8) one of Long Island City, the three last mentioned funds at the date mentioned securing less than $8,000,000 of obligations in the hands of the public.

With negligible exceptions, the sinking funds of the City are invested in its own obligations and the revenues of these funds, as they accumulate, are invested and by ordinance are required to be invested in the same way. The surplus revenues of the Sinking Fund for the Redemption of the City Debt, which amounted for the year 1921 to about $34,000,000, are withdrawn in exchange for so-called "General Fund Bonds," which in effect are merely receipts for the payments of the money thus returned to the City but which nevertheless draw interest. The money thus obtained is used as if general revenue and its return to the City operates to reduce current taxation. This, under the existing law, will continue in a generally accelerating volume (by reason of the increase of the City's special revenues pledged to the sinking fund and of the regularly increasing volume of General Fund Bonds upon which the City pays interest to the sinking fund) until 1929. After that date, the surplus and revenues of this Sinking Fund for the Redemption of the City Debt will be transferred to the "Sinking Fund of the City of New York," a sinking fund for the amortization of such of the City's funded debt as is not otherwise provided for. The revenues of the other sinking funds and the amortization installments (raised by taxation outside the two per cent. tax limit, as permitted by the Constitution), so far as they are not used for the extinguishment of the debt secured, are invested, as a rule, in new obligations of the City which are purchased from the City for the sinking funds as they are issued. In this way in 1921 about $10,000,000, net, of sinking fund revenues were invested in city obligations (exclusive of General Fund Bonds) upon all of which interest is paid into the sinking funds.

The result of this process is two-fold:

(1) The surplus revenues of the Sinking Fund for the Redemption of the City Debt, becoming, as they do, a part

of the general city resources, enables the City to spend for general purposes just that much more money than it could spend otherwise; for as the City taxes its property up to the full constitutional limit otherwise than for the debt service and possesses substantially no other means of raising revenue for current expenses, it would be compelled, but for this recaptured sinking fund revenue, to confine its expenditures for general purposes to the amount that would be produced by a two per cent. tax upon the assessed valuation of its taxable property. The vice of this system, from the point of view of sound financing, is that, as the greater part of these transferred revenues are derived from property which the City has acquired through the medium of outstanding issues of corporate stock and bonds, at least an equivalent should be applied to retiring or amortizing the City's funded debt, which as things are arranged is cared for in much the larger part by taxation outside of the two per cent. tax-limit.

(2) So far as the money paid by the City as interest upon General Fund Bonds and reinvested in bonds of that issue is concerned, it is merely paid out of the General Fund upon a fictitious debt owed by the City to itself and reabsorbed into current revenues. The whole thing is an "in-and-out" account and amounts to a more or less frank withdrawal of the large surplus revenues of the Sinking Fund for the Redemption of the City Debt and their use in the same way in which they would have been used had not that sinking fund been over-served.

But with relatively minor exceptions, the interest upon city obligations held in other sinking funds is raised by taxes in addition to those comprised in the fixed two per cent. levy. In 1923, the amount of interest thus to be paid upon bonds held in the various sinking funds, other than General Fund Bonds, and to be raised by taxation outside the two per cent. limit, is fixed in the budget at more than $6,460,000. In addition, there will be raised by like taxation in order to pay the amortization installment due to the Sinking Fund of the City of New York (the new fund) $7,100,000. There will be other revenues falling into the sinking funds other than the Sinking Fund for the Redemption of the City Debt, which in 1921 amounted to more than $3,200,000. Except as these sinking fund accretions are used to redeem or by cancellation to extinguish the City's funded debt secured by sinking funds—less than $15,000,000 of which falls due from 1923 to 1927, inclusive—the moneys thus raised (most of it by taxation outside of the two per cent. limit) are invested in city obligations (principally new) for the interest upon which a new tax not included in the two per cent. limit is levied during succeeding years; the proceeds of this tax and pre-existing taxes are used to pay interest to the sinking funds, the amortization installments and miscellaneous revenues are added and all these again, except as secured debt is retired, are invested in further city obligations. And so the process goes on progressively. When the revenues of the Sinking Fund for the Redemption of the City Debt fall into the Sinking Fund of the City of New York (in 1929), this process will be greatly accelerated, unless some device, similar to the vicious practice with respect to General Fund Bonds, be adopted.

According to present practice, these sinking fund moneys which are invested in new city securities (other than short-dated obligations) are paid out, when re-taken by the City, for various forms of improvements, some of which, like docks, may be prospectively revenue-producing and some of which, like school sites and buildings, are unproductive from the standpoint of revenue. The money thus raised and so invested does not represent, in any real sense, an amortization of existing debt, much of which—in excess of the ten per cent. debt-limit—has been incurred upon the assumption of its annual amortization, but merely enables the City to keep down the amount of new obligations which otherwise it would sell to the public. It is in reality raising a part of the cost of improvements by taxation in excess of the two per cent. limit. This it would be doing, also, if it sold these new bonds to the public and afterwards paid the principal and interest by means of taxation. But it is not amortizing the debt secured by its sinking funds and in particular it is not amortizing those portions of its debt which it has been permitted to incur upon the strength of its obligation to amortize them.

To the extent that this process maintains (theoretically) the reserves required for amortization of the debt secured by the sinking funds and held by the public, the practice may be justified in its legal aspect, but, inasmuch as the

City's obligations held in the sinking funds are not real additions to its ability to redeem its debts, this justification is theoretical rather than real.

It must not be thought that there is anything new about what has been described. All of it dates back as far as 1903, when Mayor Low's administration secured the passage of the General Fund Bonds Act and the practice of investing sinking fund moneys in newly issued city obligations goes much further back.

Now, sinking funds have very well-defined legitimate functions. Their primary purpose is to secure to the creditor the prompt payment of his claim. They constitute savings-funds which assure the debtor the means to pay his debt or some part of it. In cases permitting such retirement, they permit obligations to be retired before maturity and thus save interest charges. They may assure or facilitate the amortization of the cost of an improvement which has been financed by means of the principal issue and thus automatically convert it into a real asset. By furnishing security for payment and providing a market for the issue secured, they maintain the market price of the issue and enhance the prices which the debtor may obtain or restrict the rates which he must pay with respect to other loans. In the case of the City, they are intended, in large part, to constitute the justification under the Constitution for exempting various large corporate stock and bond issues from the constitutional debt-limit by assuring the accumulation of special funds for their amortization.

Only in indirect ways are such purposes served by the City's sinking funds. It is plain that the mere accumulation in a sinking fund of the City's own obligations, unsecured by lien, cannot add anything to the debtor's security. Nor does it increase the City's ability to pay the debt at maturity, except as it supplies a reserve of the City's own obligations which theoretically may be sold in the case of an issue that the City is not authorized to refund or cannot conveniently provide for in the budget. The sinking funds, however, may be said to afford, indirectly, a real security to creditors and a real resource to the City in that the annual income of the funds, and particularly the surplus income of the Sinking Fund for the Redemption of the City Debt, has become so large that it practically assures the City's ability (sometimes in a round-about way) to pay almost any installment of the existing funded debt as it matures. But this resource would have existed if the sinking funds had not been created. The other purposes ordinarily served by sinking funds are not satisfied except indirectly and incidentally. By the use of sinking fund revenues for the purchase of new issues of city obligations and particularly by assisting temporary financing (the carrying for a time of revenue and special revenue bonds, tax-notes and corporate stock notes), they doubtless operate, if wisely utilized, to save interest-charges and at times to maintain the City's credit. They certainly do not serve, but their administration rather results in evasion of, the purpose of the Constitution to compel the current accumulation of real assets for the retirement of existing debts.

In view of the possibility that large increases of city debt will occur in the immediate future for the purpose of financing enterprises which may produce no surplus revenue for several years, it seems highly desirable that the sinking funds shall be placed upon a footing at least resembling that which the Constitution unquestionably contemplates. This will be even more desirable if the constitutional debt-limit be enlarged. Unfortunately, the City's financial operations have so long been founded upon the existing laws and practice that to inaugurate a complete reform of the sinking fund system does not seem presently practicable or wise.

If the draft of charter submitted herewith be enacted, the Comptroller will be required to calculate periodically the reserve which must be maintained in each sinking fund in order to amortize each issue secured on or before its maturity. This reserve will be required to be made up, eventually, of or from (1) obligations of the issue secured, (2) revenue or special revenue bonds, (3) other city obligations having maturities earlier than that of the debt secured, and (4) obligations of the United States, the several States and municipalities other than the City which are qualified investments for savings banks in the State of New York. The investment of revenues or moneys of any sinking fund in obligations of the City, other than those specified, unless the required reserves have been established and are being maintained, is prohibited. When that condition exists, such investments may be made. Securities held in the sinking funds are to be kept alive and interest thereon collected. Obligations held in a sinking fund may be sold for the purpose of paying or redeeming the debt secured or for reinvestment within the limitations in that respect summarized above. Obligations, other than those of the City, comprised in reserves are to be valued for actuarial purposes at their true market value.

The Board of Estimate and Apportionment is authorized to apply any surplus sinking fund assets and revenues to the retirement of the principal issue secured and of course, if invested in refunding bonds or exchanged for assets of other sinking funds applicable to the purpose, they may be applied to the retirement of other city debt.

Taxation, outside of the constitutional tax-limit, for the payment of interest upon city obligations held in sinking funds, except to the extent necessary to maintain the reserves for amortization, is forbidden.

Constitutional Debt and Tax Limitations

The demands upon the current resources of the City are constantly and necessarily increasing. It is extremely likely that these demands will greatly increase in the near future. Even with the exercise of the most rigid economy, the revenue necessities of the City will in the very near future exceed the yield of a 2% tax. Bridges, tunnels, water-front improvements, schools and other public buildings must be constructed; streets must be opened, enlarged and repaved; a great variety of other public improvements must be provided; in each instance, large expense that cannot be recovered through assessments upon private property must be met; constantly enlarging demands for educational facilities must be met; the administrative staff, the police and fire force, and the operative employees of the City must be increased as the City grows in numbers and in occupied territory and as its communal activities are extended. It is only at this price that its development as a great metropolitan business center can be continued and its prosperity and usefulness to the State and Nation assured. The State of New York, outside of the City, shares largely in the benefits, direct and indirect, of the City's prosperity and development, and has an evident interest that they shall not unnecessarily be checked. Aside from the fact that the City comprises one-half of the population and more than one-half of the wealth of the State, the fact that its commerce, its enterprise and its wealth, create, furnish the facilities of, and stimulate in so large a degree the business of the entire country, including the remainder of the State, renders the City's prosperity the prosperity of the State. The State should see to it that in the City of New York business may be done more easily and in greater proportionate volume than anywhere else in the world. A substantial proportion of the taxes for City purposes paid by the inhabitants of the City are, in truth, merely a part of the business expense of those who prosecute their enterprises with the help of the facilities it affords.

Already the City's educational system absorbs about one-third of the budgetary appropriations. In 1923, the City must raise by taxation for the service of the public school system approximately $80,000,000, out of a total of about $250,000,000 raised by that means—or 31.9% of its entire tax-levy for city and county purposes. Fully to meet the requirements of the public schools, in a city of heterogeneous and largely of unassimilated foreign population, is an imperative and a paramount necessity. Until this obligation has been discharged, subways, street and water-front improvements, bridges, tunnels, parks and public buildings must wait. Only police, fire and health protection stand on the same plane. Much of the care given to the instruction, discipline and hygiene of the City's school children is given, however, not merely to render them more efficient economic units, or individuals better equipped for life, but to prevent the growth of elements hostile or unadapted to American institutions and laws, and in that sense is given for the benefit of the State and the Nation.

It must be quite evident to any observer of reasonable intelligence and detachment that the City's present resources of taxation cannot long support the growing needs of normal administration, of its educational system and of its physical development. It is axiomatic and susceptible of verification that, in a community situated as is New York City, the public requirements must increase more rapidly than does the value of its taxable property, for the increase of value is the product of the increase of business, which cannot occur beyond narrow limits without provision in advance for the facilities which are necessary to the expansion of population and territory which in turn are essentials of the expansion of business. We see an example of this in the existing need of transportation facilities which demand investments so much greater than any probable early returns will justify that private capital declines to provide them.

Accordingly, we find that the City has reached the limit of its constitutional power to tax property within its limits. If the Commission's recommendations with respect to the sinking funds and taxation therefor should be adopted, the legitimate pressure for an enlarged tax-limit would be somewhat further increased.

The City's debt almost has reached the constitutional limit, if indeed, including all charges which (morally, if not legally) are unescapable, such as the provision of pension reserves, that limit has not been passed already. Evidently, some relief soon must be given.

There seem to be only two practicable methods of affording immediate relief:

First: The State, if it will, can provide relief in the matter of the schools. Education is and by the Constitution is declared to be a state function. The State can assume financial responsibility for its support as well as responsibility for its administration; it can determine for itself, through its own agencies, what in its interest as a whole shall be supplied to the City in the way of schools, teachers and administrative staff, and then, by direct taxation, it can provide the means to sustain the schools, to acquire sites and construct buildings for them and to pay the interest upon the indebtedness which in the past has been contracted to supply and maintain them, levying its taxes proportionately throughout the State or upon the New York City school district, as may be deemed just and wise. This would leave the City free to apply such part of the moneys which it now raises for school purposes as may be necessary to its other rapidly increasing needs.

Or the State can by constitutional amendment free the hands of the City to some less extent by establishing a separate tax-limit for service of the educational budget, placing the power to determine and allocate the gross amount to be raised by taxation for such purposes, within the prescribed limit, in the hands of the Board of Education or other body administering the city school district. In that event, the tax to be imposed for all educational purposes, including the acquisition of sites and the construction of buildings, except as the City may elect voluntarily to aid therein, might perhaps be placed at 8 mills per dollar of assessed valuation ($100,000,000 upon the basis of 1923 tentative assessments).

If this expedient were adopted, the tax-limit for proper city purposes (other than service of the city debt) might be placed at 1.70 cents per dollar of assessed valuation, which would result in increasing the aggregate tax-limit by one-half of one per cent, and the limit of taxes available for new or additional city purposes by about 34/100 of one per cent.

The Commission commends these alternative suggestions to the consideration of the Legislature. If either of them should be adopted, it would be reasonable and wise to insert in the City Charter a provision requiring all net revenue derived from revenue-producing improvements to be applied, whether after or without withdrawal from the sinking funds to the retirement or to provision for the amortization of the principal of the City's funded debt.

Second: The Commission has recommended the judicial ascertainment, in advance of authorization, of the probable cost and earning power of any proposed revenue-producing improvement to cost more than $50,000,000 and the granting to the City of power to issue bonds (within constitutional limits—whatever they may be) for the purpose of financing the improvement to an amount proportionate to the ability thus determined of the improvement to provide for interest upon its investment after providing for all other proper charges, including amortization. This is an attempt to grant to the City approximately the same discretion (within constitutional limits) and to compel it to exercise the same foresight and prudence which a well-managed private corporation possesses and exercises. It would seem not imprudent, considering the real necessity for permitting the City to regulate and meet the demands of its own development and considering the practical limitations which the market for securities imposes, to permit bonds to the extent thus defined to be issued irrespective of the constitutional ten per cent. debt limitation, not, however, permitting them to be excluded in calculating the City's debt-incurring power for other purposes except as and to the extent that they actually may become "self-supporting." The Commission will submit in connection with this report, a draft of amendment of Section 10 of Article VIII of the Constitution, which provides (1) for such exemption, (2) applies to the entire existing debt contracted for revenue-producing improvements (so far as not already wholly exempt) the same rule of proportionate exemption which is already applicable to the debt incurred for revenue-producing improvements incurred prior to 1910, and (3) codifies the provisions of Section 10, Article VIII, which apply only to the City. The Commission submits this as a not unreasonable suggestion for consideration by the Legislature. As a matter of fact, unless some such expedient be adopted, the gift to the City of home-rule in the matter of rapid-transit construction and operation must for a long time remain in large part merely illusory.

The Commission's Appropriation and Accounts.

The Commission believes that it will complete its work within the limits of its original appropriation. This it could not have done if Mr. Cutcheon had not preferred to serve the commission as its counsel without compensation. It will annex an account of its expenditures.

Conclusion.

While the Commission has given to the draft of proposed charter submitted herewith a very great deal of consideration and labor, it is fully conscious that errors and incongruities may have crept into it—conscious also that concerning many of its recommendations more than one view may be urged and supported by reasonable argument. It asks that the Legislature, in reviewing its work, accord to it some reasonable measure of indulgence and the same open-minded consideration of its recommendations which the Commission has conscientiously endeavored to give to all aspects of the interests of the City and State with which it has been called upon to deal.

It would be impossible for the Commission to exaggerate its debt to its counsel, Mr. F. W. M. Cutcheon. He has given his time prodigally to the work of the Commission; and on almost every page the proposed charter bears the results of his profound study of, and reflection upon, the facts and problems of our municipal life and government and the impress of his clear mind.

Respectfully submitted,

HENRY DE FOREST BALDWIN, *Chairman*
HOWARD LEE MCBAIN, *Secretary*
JOSEPH M. LEVINE
J. J. KELLER
GEORGE CROMWELL
HERMAN A. METZ
ARTHUR S. SOMERS
EDWARD M. BASSETT
H. PUSHAE WILLIAMS
LOUIS L. DELAFIELD
WM. BARCLAY PARSONS

Dated, New York, March 5, 1923.

APPENDIX A

CHARTER

OF

THE CITY OF NEW YORK

(1923)

TABLE OF CONTENTS

ARTICLE I.

Corporate Status and Rights; Boundaries; Boroughs.

ARTICLE II.

Elective Officers.

ARTICLE III.

Board of Aldermen.

ARTICLE IV.

Board of Estimate and Apportionmment.

ARTICLE V.

Conjoint Jurisdiction of the Board of Aldermen and the Board of Estimate and Apportionment.

ARTICLE VI.

The Mayor.

ARTICLE VII.

The Comptroller.

ARTICLE VIII.

President of the Board of Aldermen.

ARTICLE IX.

Borough Presidents.

ARTICLE X.

Departments, Officers and Employees.

ARTICLE XI.

The Corporation Counsel.

ARTICLE XII.

The Chamberlain.

ARTICLE XIII.

The Commissioner of Inquiry.

Section 74. Appointment of deputies; designation of deputy as acting commissioner by Mayor.
75. Examinations to be made by commissioner; reports.
1. Financial condition of city every three months.
2. Operation and organization of all parts of administration and revenue-producing improvements.
3. Reports to Mayor and Board of Aldermen.
4. Limits of examination of certain officers.
5. Power to compel testimony.

ARTICLE XIV.

Police Department.

Section 76. Police commissioner: removal by Mayor or Governor.
77. Power of police commissioner.
1. General.
(a) Appointment of deputies; designation of acting commissioner.
(b) Assignment of captain or inspector as chief inspector; power of chief inspector.
(c) Assignment of captains as inspectors.
(d) Detailing of officers as detectives.
(e) Details to duty; leaves of absence.
(f) Rules and regulations.
2. Subject to powers of Boards of Estimate and Apportionment and Aldermen.
(a) Appointment of members of force.
(b) Establishing of ranks and grades and so forth.
(c) Uniforms and so forth.
(d) Special patrolmen; park police.
(e) Stations and patrols.
(f) Rewards for information.
(g) Control of traffic.
(h) Supervision of certain occupations.
(i) Conduct investigations; power to compel testimony.
78. Special detail not to affect promotion.
79. Duty of inspector or captain.
80. Duties of members of department.
81. Powers of members of force.
82. Absence from duty; resignations.
83. Board of Aldermen to specify causes for discipline; trial; court review limited.
84. Present force and rules continued.
85. Exemption from military or jury duty or arrest.

ARTICLE XV.

Department of Pensions.

Section 86. Definitions.
87. Powers of commissioner.
88. Members of board; rules; powers.
89. Board to manage pension and retirement funds.
90. Pension funds to be kept separate until consolidated fund established.

Section 91. Powers of board.
1. Make investments and manage funds.
2. Appoint actuary.
3. Fix payments into funds.
92. Duty of Actuary.
93. Publication of statement of funds.
94. Board to prepare plan for consolidated pension fund; to protect participants in existing funds.
95. Audit by Comptroller.
96. Chamberlain custodian of funds.
97. Pension Fund Advisory Committee.
98. Powers of Advisory Committee.
1. Designate member of committee to attend board meetings.
2. Examine books and records.
3. Make independent audit.
4. Meeting of participants.
5. Advice to board.
99. Board to have sole right to retire officers and employees.

ARTICLE XVI.

Department of Taxes.

Section 100. Commissioner of Taxes; duties.
1. Control of officers and employees.
2. Duties of deputies: records and maps.
3. Office in each borough.
101. Enter upon real property and examine buildings; compel testimony.
102. Commissioner to appoint deputies.
103. Commissioner to appoint boards for the correction of tax assessments.
104. Duties of department.

ARTICLE XVII.

Municipal Civil Service Commission.

Section 105. Mayor to appoint and remove on charges.
106. Organization and action of commission.
107. Power of commission.
1. Classification; rules.
2. Appointments; change of status; discharge.
3. Enforcement of civil service rules.

ARTICLE XVIII.

Board of Standards and Appeals and Board of Appeals.

Section 108. Organization of board.
1. Members.
2. Qualification of appointed members.
3. Chairman and secretary.
4. Compel testimony.
5. Board of Appeals.
6. Official members.
109. Powers of board.
1. Test materials; make investigations.
2. Rules and regulations generally.
3. Rules and regulations in respect to certain buildings.
4. Certain powers over buildings.

ARTICLE XIX.

The Public School System.

ARTICLE XX.

Interim Provisions for the Administrative Organization of the City and County Governments.

ARTICLE XXI.

The Budget.

ARTICLE XXII.

Assessment and Levy of Taxes.

ARTICLE XXIII.

Board of Review.

ARTICLE XXIV.

Acquisition of Title to Real Property for Public Purposes.

Section 191. Purchase of property under condemnation or awards therefor.
192. Vesting of title.
193. The title to be acquired by the city.
194. City entitled to compensation and liable to assessment.
195. Contracts of landlord and tenant or other contracting parties; how affected.
196. Corporation Counsel to represent interest of city before the court and provide clerks and offices; expenses.
197. Board of Estimate and Apportionment to direct who shall furnish maps, etc.
198. Cost of maps, etc., to be certified to the Corporation Counsel.
199. Costs and charges; taxation thereof.
200. Damages for real property taken; when to be paid.
201. Instruments assigning or pledging awards to be filed in the office of the Comptroller.
202. Moneys of persons under disability, how disposed of; moneys paid to persons not entitled thereto.
203. Sums assessed to be liens; provisions of Article XXV of this act not applicable.
204. Notice of filing the final decree of assessments.
205. Interest to be charged on assessments if not paid in sixty days.
206. Assessments may be set off against award.
207. How notices shall be posted.
208. Publication of notices where property is without the city.
209. Order of court granting application to condemn to be filed in the office where instruments affecting real property are required to be recorded.
210. Procedure in case property to be acquired is situated in two or more counties; filing of orders, reports and decrees in such cases.
211. Discontinuance of proceedings by Board of Estimate and Apportionment.
212. Discontinuance of a proceeding by the court.
213. Amendment of defects, etc.

ARTICLE XXV.

Assessments for Local Improvements and Awards for Damages Caused by Grading Streets.

Section 214. Board of Assessors.
215. Award of damages to land and buildings by reason of grading streets.
216. Certificates; description of property.
217. Notice of completion of assessments or awards to be given.
218. Confirmation of any award final and conclusive.
219. Awards for intended regulation.
220. Assessments after registration of contract.
221. Assessments to be transmitted for entry and collection and awards certified for payment.
222. Awards; when to be paid.
223. Remedies.
224. Comptroller's power.
225. Petition to the Supreme Court in case of fraud or error; power of court limited.
226. Assessments not to be set aside for certain irregularities and technicalities.
227. Re-assessment.
228. All claims may be embraced in one proceeding.
229. When proceedings to be brought.

ARTICLE XXVI.

Miscellaneous Provisions.

Section 230. Definitions.
231. Inferior courts continued.
232. City Record.
233. Preparation of registry of voters; publication in City Record.
234. Publication of record of assessed valuations of real estate in City Record.
235. Expense limited to unexpended balance.
236. Officer or employee not to have interest in transactions with the City; penalty.
237. Officer or employee not to influence election or appointment to office; penalty.
238. Officer not to appoint or retain in any office or employment any person dismissed on charges; penalty.
239. Penalties to this act in addition to other penalties.
240. Court to compel testimony required by city official.
241. Access of public to books, accounts and papers.
1. Copies to be furnished.
2. Open to inspection.
3. Court order to compel compliance.
242. Court order for examination of public officer.
1. Ground for issuing order.
2. Procedure.
3. Costs.
243. Tax payer's suits against officers.
244. Suits against the city.
1. Service of papers.
2. Place of trial.
3. Execution on judgment.
245. Unexecuted contracts to be performed.
246. Seals of city and its departments.
247. Acts repealed.
248. Constitutionality.
249. Time of taking effect.
250. Act a public act.

AN ACT

To Provide a Charter for The City of New York

The People of the State of New York, represented in Senate and Assembly, do enact as follows:

ARTICLE I

Corporate Status and Rights; Boundaries; Powers

Short Title

SECTION 1. This Act shall be known and may be cited as the "Home Rule Charter of The City of New York."

Corporate Status and Rights

SECTION 2. The City of New York as heretofore constituted shall continue to be a body politic and corporate, having a common seal and perpetual succession, with all of the grants, rights, properties, estates, interests, claims, demands, powers, functions, privileges and jurisdictions heretofore held or exercised by it.

The grants of franchises, properties, estates, interests, privileges, rights of any nature, and all other grants made by the Nicolls Charter, the Dongan Charter, the Cornbury Charter, the Montgomerie Charter, by the confirmatory act passed the 14th day of October, 1732, and by any other charter or act made by the State of New York or any of its predecessors in sovereignty to any of the municipalities or public corporations heretofore united and consolidated into The City of New York as heretofore constituted by Chapter 378 of the Laws of 1897, entitled "An act to unite into one municipality under the corporate name of The City of New York the various communities lying in and about New York Harbor, including the City and County of New York, the City of Brooklyn and the County of Kings, the County of Richmond, and part of the County of Queens, and to provide for the government thereof," as amended by Chapter 466 of the Laws of 1901 and as amended from time to time and last amended by Chapter ... of the Laws of ...., are, and each of them is, hereby ratified and confirmed in and to the said The City of New York.

Boundaries and Boroughs

SECTION 3. The boundaries of the City of New York shall remain as at present established, and the City of New York shall continue to be divided into five boroughs to be designated respectively: Manhattan, The Bronx, Brooklyn, Queens and Richmond; the boundaries whereof shall be as follows:

First: The Borough of Manhattan shall consist of all that portion of the City of New York, as now constituted, known as Manhattan Island, Nuttin or Governor's Island, Bedloe's Island, Bucking or Ellis Island, the Oyster Islands, and also Blackwell's Island, Randall's Island, and Ward's Island in the East or Harlem Rivers.

Second: The Borough of The Bronx shall consist of all that portion of the City of New York, as now constituted, lying northerly or easterly of the Borough of Manhattan, between the Hudson River and the East River or Long Island Sound, including the several islands belonging to the municipal corporation heretofore known as The Mayor, Aldermen and Commonalty of the City of New York, not included in the Borough of Manhattan.

Third: The Borough of Brooklyn shall consist of the territory known as Kings County.

Fourth: The Borough of Queens shall consist of the territory known as Queens County.

Fifth: The Borough of Richmond shall consist of the territory known as Richmond County.

Powers

SECTION 4. Subject to the limitations and conditions in this Act, in the Constitution of the State of New York and in the Constitution of the United States of America prescribed, the City of New York shall possess, and it is hereby authorized to exercise in any and every appropriate manner, all and every power, authority and jurisdiction requisite to regulate, manage and control its property and to administer the government of the City and its inhabitants with respect to all municipal and local matters and affairs, including, among others, power to enforce the laws and punish violations thereof, maintain order, protect property, suppress vice, abate nuisances, enforce honest dealing, and preserve and care for the safety, health, comfort and general welfare of the inhabitants of the City and sojourners therein, and as well any and every power of the several boards of the supervisors of counties comprised in the City which heretofore have been vested in any of the officers, boards, departments, commissions or other authorities of the City; and in furtherance of the aforesaid grants and powers, but not in derogation or restriction thereof nor to the exclusion of any power not expressly enumerated, the City of New York, except as above provided, is expressly authorized and empowered:

1. **Ordinances.** To make ordinances consistent with this Act, to execute or provide for the execution of, or give effect to, all or any of the powers of the City, and to provide for the enforcement of ordinances as well as to prescribe penalties, forfeitures and imprisonments to punish violations thereof.

2. **Assessment and taxes.** (a) To classify and determine the valuation of and to assess private property within the City for purposes of taxation;

(b) To levy taxes, which in the reasonable discretion of the City may be levied at differing rates upon different classes of property, and in particular to assess and levy taxes upon personal property or improvements on land upon a basis of assessment or at a rate different from the basis or rate employed with respect to the land itself;

(c) As justice may require to add to and omit from assessment rolls property erroneously omitted therefrom or included therein; to correct assessments and abate or remit taxes on real or personal property;

(d) To assess and levy taxes upon businesses and occupations conducted in the City;

(e) To collect and enforce the payment of and to compromise taxes; to determine the date as of which any tax shall become a lien upon property; to enforce such liens by the sale thereof or otherwise; to reduce and discharge liens;

(f) To allow rebates upon taxes paid in advance of due dates and to charge and collect interest and penalties with respect to deferred installments or delinquent payments.

3. **Apportionment and assessment of costs of improvement.** (a) To determine whether any, and if so how much, of the cost of any public or local improvement, including, among others, public works and facilities, shall be borne by the City as a whole, and unless the whole thereof is to be so borne by the City, to apportion the cost thereof, as may be just and reasonable, among the boroughs of the City or to allocate the same, in whole or in part, to any particular borough or boroughs or any part or parts of any thereof;

(b) To determine whether the cost of any thereof in whole or in part, and if in part what portion thereof, shall be assessed and levied upon property within the City deemed to be benefited thereby, provided, however, that no part of the cost of any public building not constituting part of any public work or facility, shall be assessed upon property;

(c) To make awards and payments in consideration of the taking or destruction of or injury to property or rights or interests in property occasioned by any such improvement;

(d) If it be determined so to do, to make assessments of all or any part of the cost of any such improvement (with the exception aforesaid) upon property within the City deemed to be benefited thereby; to collect, enforce payment of, correct, compromise, reduce or discharge such assessments; to provide for the payment of assessments on property owned by the City for local improvement; to determine the dates upon which liens upon property to secure payment of assessments shall become effective; to enforce such liens by sale or otherwise and to reduce and release the same;

(e) No assessment of benefits for a local improvement shall ever exceed fifty per cent. of the value after such improvement of the land assessed, without the improvements, if any, thereon;

(f) To subdivide the City and its boroughs into local improvement districts; to create and define the powers and functions of local improvement boards.

4. **Assessments and taxation for local improvements.** To determine, consistently with and in execution of the

provisions of this Act, the procedure for the assessment, reassessment, levy, abatement, remission and for the collection, in installments or otherwise, with or without abatements, interest or penalties, of taxes and of assessments for local improvements and for the creation, enforcement, reduction and release of liens upon property to secure payment of the same and for the review of such assessments and taxes at the instance of property owners aggrieved thereby.

5. **Appropriations, accounts, special funds.** (a) To appropriate and apply moneys to any city or county purpose, whether specifically or by appropriation in gross for the expenditures of any department, bureau, board, commission, corporation or office or for the accomplishment of a specified object, and to revoke any appropriation or in whole or in part to transfer an appropriation already made from one purpose or object to another;

(b) To provide for the manner of and to regulate the keeping and auditing of accounts;

(c) To establish, maintain and provide against the depletion of street-opening, improvement, administrative and reserve funds and accounts.

6. **Contracts and suits.** (a) To contract and be contracted with, under seal or otherwise;

(b) To institute, maintain, defend, appeal, discontinue and otherwise control any action or proceeding in any court and to compromise and settle controversies.

7. **Acquisition of property, excess condemnation, cession to U. S. or State.** (a) For any city or county purpose, to determine the necessity for and to purchase, acquire by condemnation or otherwise acquire real property within or without the limits of the City including estates, interests, easements and rights in land or improvements thereon;

(b) To take by deed, cession, gift, grant, devise or bequest, absolutely or in trust for any city or county purpose, or by lease, real and personal propery within or without the limits of the City;

(c) In connection with the acquisition of land for any park, highway, street or other public place, and as a part of the same transaction or proceeding, to acquire in fee, by purchase, condemnation or otherwise, lands additional to those required for such purpose but suitable for building sites to abut upon such park, highway, street or other public place or upon already existing and directly intervening streets upon which any such park or public place also shall abut;

(d) To cede to the State of New York or to the United States of America any property of the City or interests or rights in or with respect to the same.

8. **Public improvements and facilities.** (a) To determine the necessity for and the nature and location of and to authorize, construct, lease or acquire by purchase, gift, devise, bequest, and consistently with the Conservation Law of the State by condemnation; (1) improvements of navigation and facilities of water-borne commerce, including among others boats, docks, piers, wharves and warehouses; (2) improvements consisting of or comprising public works and facilities and property, real or personal, and interests in and rights and easements with respect to property required for use in connection therewith, whether any of said works, facilities or properties be within or without the limits of the City, for supplying itself and the inhabitants and industries within its limits with water, light, power, heat, transportation of persons and property (whether by land or water), telephones, telegraphs and other means of communication, markets and market facilities, garbage and sewage-disposal plants; and (3) other public improvements of every description, including among others, all such improvements as are enumerated or referred to in Subdivisions 9, 10, and 12 of this Section, as well as all kinds of local improvements;

(b) Peaceably to enter upon private property for the purpose of making surveys, maps, soundings and borings for or in connection with public or local improvements;

(c) To safeguard, make regulations with respect to and acquire property, interests or rights for the protection of the safe, sanitary, efficient and convenient operation of any such improvements, works, facilities or properties;

(d) To provide itself with any of the services or facilities above-mentioned by contract with public or private corporations or with individuals.

9. **Public buildings.** To determine the necessity for and the nature and location of and to authorize, acquire

sites for, construct or lease and to equip and maintain, within the City, municipal or public buildings, (including, among others, buildings wherein to conduct the government and business of the City, court-houses and court-rooms, armories, drill-halls, police-stations, firehouses, prisons, jails and other correctional institutions, hospitals, sanatoria, clinics, dispensaries, day-nurseries, public baths, lodging houses, almshouses, work-houses, reformatories, comfort stations, and buildings for other charitable institutions maintained by the City).

10. **Educational and welfare institutions.** (a) Except as otherwise provided by law with respect to educational service under the control of the Board of Education, to determine the necessity for and to establish and maintain, assist to maintain or contribute to the support of, to provide for the management of and regulate schools, academies, colleges, technical and vocational institutions, libraries, museums, art-galleries, and such other institutions and instrumentalities for the instruction, enlightenment, improvement, entertainment, recreation and welfare of its inhabitants as shall be deemed appropriate or necessary for the public interest or advantage;

(b) To determine the necessity for and the location of, and to authorize, construct, equip and maintain buildings and other facilities for the purposes thereof or to provide sites therefor;

(c) To make and perform or carry out any and all contracts between the City and any institution of the character aforesaid for, or to assist in, the maintenance or operation thereof or the construction or equipment of buildings and other facilities or the provision of sites therefor.

11. **City property: vesting title, payment of awards, management; supplies for courts; improvement of navigation; inalienable property.** (a) To fix the date as of which title to property or any interest therein condemned at the instance of the City shall vest in the City and the time for the payment of any award of compensation or damages made on account of or in connection with any such condemnation or the making of any public or local improvement;

(b) To hold and otherwise manage and deal with real and personal property of the City within and without the limits of the City and to provide for and regulate the custody and care of City property;

(c) To provide accommodations and supplies for any of the courts of the State or City or any of the counties therein held within the City and accommodations for and the maintenance of jurors serving therein;

(d) To take out or acquire patents and patent rights and copyrights;

(e) To sell and convey if not required for any public purpose, or (if not required for any public purpose) to lease for a term of years not exceeding ten years, or to grant permits for the temporary use of, any of the property of the City or interests or rights or easements in or with respect to the same and to exchange for other property and to devote to other public or municipal use any property of the City determined to be no longer required for the purpose for which it was acquired or had been used;

(f) To agree with respect to or, in the absence of such agreement, to prescribe the compensation to be paid for and the terms of, and to regulate, the use of property of the City by the public or by private corporations or individuals;

(g) To maintain, operate, control, regulate the use of, alter and discontinue improvements of navigation and facilities of water-borne commerce (including among others boats, docks, piers, wharves and warehouses);

(h) To establish highwater, bulkhead and pierhead lines, and to restrict, regulate and control the water-front of the City and the improvement, filling in and use thereof;

(i) Generally to exercise all of the powers and dominion of ownership over any and all of the property and interests of the City, but the rights of the City in and to its water-front, wharf property, public landings, wharves, docks, land under water, streets, avenues, parks, playgrounds and all other public places, whether now owned or hereafter acquired, are hereby declared to be inalienable, except (1) streets, parks and other public places which shall have been closed or discontinued and (2) that a sale to or exchange with an upland owner for other lands may be made of lands under water inside the highwater mark when established by the City in front of the property of said upland owner, and (3) that the City's interest in a public easement in or with respect to real estate, if the same amount merely to a cloud thereon, may be released, with or without compensation;

(j) Moneys derived from the disposition of property, whether real or personal, or of any estate or interest therein or easement thereon, shall be applied to the reduction of the City debt, either directly or through the medium of one or more of the sinking funds as the Board of Estimate and Apportionment may direct.

12. **City plan; approval of maps; regulation of buildings on unopened streets; opening, closing and use of streets; agreements with other municipalities.** (a) To make and change the map or a plan of the City and of each borough therein and to take measures to insure its execution in the future;

(b) To provide for the approval of maps of the subdivision or platting of lands into streets, public places and blocks and to prohibit the filing thereof, without such approval, in the offices in which instruments affecting real property are required to be recorded.

(c) To regulate the erection of buildings and the character of buildings to be erected upon land indicated upon the official map or plan of the City as streets, although not yet opened as such;

(d) To survey, mark and establish the boundaries of the City and its several boroughs;

(e) To lay out, name, open, establish, construct, maintain, ornament, repair, permit excavations and installations in or under, alter as to location, grade or construction, discontinue, close, restrict and regulate the use of highways, streets, avenues, courtyards, parks, playgrounds, recreation piers, bridges, tunnels, viaducts, approaches to any thereof, other public places of all descriptions, and sewers and drainage canals and systems, and upon the discontinuance of any thereof to sell and convey any or all property, or interest in property, whether real or personal, which shall be deemed to be no longer required by the City;

(f) To make and perform agreements with the authorized public authorities of any other municipality, any county or other political subdivision or public corporation or body having or representing an interest in any extension of any of the foregoing outside of the City, for the construction, acquisition, discontinuance, demolition or disposition thereof or of any extension thereof outside of the City;

(g) For the purpose of more effectually securing the actual discontinuance and closing of streets and to extinguish all easements therein, to acquire the fee and any and all easements and rights in any real property in the bed of any street (or which has been actually used by the public as a street although not shown on the official map or plan) but which has been discontinued and closed as a street and to sell and convey the same in fee simple with or without restrictions.

13. **Building regulation: zoning.** (a) To make and to alter or repeal, in whole or in part, regulations and restrictions with respect to the height, number of stories and size of buildings and other structures, the percentages of the areas of lots that may be occupied, the size of yards, courts and other open spaces, the density of population, the location and use of land, buildings, and other structures for trade, industry, residence or other purposes.

(b) To divide the City into districts of such number, shape and area, as may be deemed best suited to carry out the purposes of this Subdivision; within such districts, respectively, to regulate and restrict the erection, construction, reconstruction, alteration, repair and use of buildings and other structures. All such regulations shall be made in accordance with a comprehensive plan, and regulations with respect to buildings and structures shall be uniform for each class or kind of buildings and structures throughout each district but regulations applicable in one district may differ from those applicable in any other district or districts.

(c) All regulations and restrictions shall be designed to secure safety from fire, panic and other such dangers, to promote health, to provide adequate light and air, to prevent the overcrowding of land and buildings, congestion in streets and undue concentration of population, to facilitate ample and appropriate provision of transportation, water, sewers, parks, schools and other public requirements and to promote the general welfare and shall be made with consideration for the character of each district and its peculiar suitability for particular uses and reasonable regard for conserving the value of property and encouraging the most appropriate use of land throughout the City.

14. **Organization and control of administrative agencies.** (a) To establish, consolidate, abolish and discontinue and to define the powers, duties and relations of any or all offices, boards, divisions, departments, bureaus or commissions, and branches thereof, for carrying on the public business and for administering the government of the City, the boroughs thereof and the counties therein; to transfer any of the powers or duties of any of the foregoing or of any other of the municipal or county authorities to any of the other offices, boards, divisions, departments, bureaus, commissions or other municipal or county authorities whether the office or other authority from which or to which the same may be so transferred be that of the City or of any county or of any borough therein; provided, however, that none of the following offices, boards, departments or commissions shall be abolished, nor shall any thereof or any of the chief executive officers thereof be deprived of any of the powers which are conferred upon them respectively by this Act, or by law, except such as are by the terms hereof expressly declared to be subject to the exercise by the Board of Aldermen or the Board of Estimate and Apportionment or both thereof conjointly of the power so to do, viz.: the Board of Aldermen, the Board of Estimate and Apportionment, the Police Department, the Department of Pensions, the Department of Taxes, the Board of Review, and the Municipal Civil Service Commission; courts and the judges thereof; the offices of surrogate, sheriff, county clerk, district attorney, Corporation Counsel, Chamberlain, Police Commissioner, civil service commissioner and Commissioner of Inquiry, and those of the elective officers of the City (except that any or all of the powers and duties of Borough Presidents enumerated in Section 62 may be transferred by unanimous vote of the members of the Board of Estimate and Apportionment, as provided in Subdivision 6 of Section 26).

(b) To provide for the selection and employment of counsel and expert or technical advisers in special matters;

(c) Generally, to regulate the administrative organization of the city, the borough and county governments and the manner of supervising, transacting and reporting with respect to the business of the City and the boroughs and counties therein.

15. **Control of officers and employees.** Subject to and consistently with the Constitution of the State and the Civil Service Law and this Act, but irrespective of any other law of this State, general or special, to determine and regulate the number, terms of office or employment, qualifications, methods of selection and removal, discipline of, and the security, if any, to be required from, any or all officers, members of administrative boards and bodies, and employees of the City or of any of the boroughs or counties therein, not including, however, judges, surrogates and district attorneys, but not excepting officers, appointees or attaches of courts or surrogates, nor assistants to or other subordinates of district attorneys; to fix the compensation of all such persons except judges, surrogates and district attorneys, provided that the compensation of any elective officer whatsoever shall not be changed in such manner as to decrease the compensation of an incumbent during his then unexpired term of office.

16. **Franchises and permits.** To grant franchises, for not exceeding twenty-five years, or indeterminate franchises, to be terminable by the City at such time or times but not less frequently than at the end of every twenty-five years, and upon such terms as shall be specified in the grants thereof, respectively, but upon such terms and conditions otherwise as the proper authorities of the City may prescribe, and also revocable permits to use any of the highways, streets, avenues, boulevards, concourses, driveways, parks, parkways, bridges, viaducts, waterways, docks, bulkheads, wharves, piers, and any other public grounds or waters or lands under water, belonging to or under the control of the City, but only in the manner and upon the conditions in Section 26 prescribed.

17. **Regulation of public utilities.** Subject to and consistently with the laws of the State or of the United States, whether heretofore or hereafter enacted as the same from time to time shall exist and be applicable within the City, to determine the necessity for and prescribe reasonable rules, regulations and rates of charges for services to be rendered and commodities furnished within the City of New York by any corporation or person exercising a franchise or right

under license to maintain any structures, facilities or instrumentalities, or to carry on any undertaking or business, upon, over, along, across or under the surface of any of the streets, parks, waterfront, water or public places or property of the City, but not with respect to any subject matter the regulation whereof shall have been specially provided for by any law of the State of New York or of the United States, whether heretofore or hereafter enacted, which shall be applicable within the City; to prescribe the manner and location in which any property or instrumentalities used or designed to be used in or in aid of the exercise of any such franchise or license shall be constructed, maintained or used from time to time, and, among other things, to require pipes, wires and conductors of all descriptions to be placed underground or under water.

18. **Operation of public improvements directly or under lease.** (a) To manage and operate and to enter into and direct all transactions and dealings incidental to the operation of the following improvements, works and facilities, viz.: (1) works and systems owned by the City for the supply and distribution of water for the use of the City and the public, (2) docks, piers, wharves, warehouses and other water-front improvements and facilities and bridges and tunnels, (3) markets and market facilities, (4) garbage and sewage disposal plants and systems, (5) drainage works and systems, (6) ferries operating between portions of the City or between any portion thereof and any adjacent place or places, (7) such transportation systems and facilities as the City is empowered to operate by the Rapid Transit Acts (being Chapter Four of the Laws of 1891 as amended and acts supplementary thereto) or by any other law or laws now in force or hereafter enacted, (8) telegraph, telephone and wireless systems of communication for the use of the Police, Fire and Health Departments and other municipal authorities and agencies, (9) lighting plants and systems for lighting the City streets and other public places and the bridges, tunnels, subways, buildings and other properties owned or maintained by the City, and as well to operate (10) all such, but only such, other public or municipal improvements, works and facilities which, under laws now existing or which hereafter may be enacted, the City is or shall be authorized to operate;

(b) To fix the rates or prices to be charged for, and to restrict and impose conditions upon the enjoyment or use of, any or all of the services and facilities provided by the City which by the terms of this Subdivision it is empowered to supply or afford to the public or for purposes other than its own use;

(c) To enter into contracts with individuals or corporations for the lease to and operation by any such individuals or corporations of revenue-producing improvements, other than water-works and systems, which by the provisions of this Act the City is empowered to construct, acquire or own, including among others any thereof which, by the provisions of this Subdivision, the City is empowered to operate.

19. **Incurring of debt; form of obligations; sinking funds and serial bonds; limitations upon and purposes of incurring debt; general fund bonds.** (a) To borrow money for any city or county purpose and to issue its obligations in the form of corporate stock, bonds, or short term bonds, notes or certificates; to issue interim certificates or obligations temporarily to represent any of the foregoing; to issue any of the foregoing upon such terms with respect to interest, maturity, currencies and places of repayment and otherwise, as the proper authorities of the City may determine; to pledge its faith and credit for the repayment thereof; to repay the same;

(b) To maintain existing sinking funds for the amortization and the redemption at maturity of the City's existing funded debt and to establish and maintain sinking funds for the amortization and redemption of such amounts thereof, annually during the life of any issue of corporate stock or bonds hereafter issued, as will be sufficient to effect the redemption of the entire issue at or before maturity, but no pledge of or agreement to apply specified revenues of the City to the service of any such sinking fund or funds hereafter established shall be made.

(c) No obligation of the City shall be issued for a term longer than the estimated life of any improvement which is to be financed thereby nor in any case for more than fifty years, nor for any non-revenue-producing improvement or purpose, except (1) those heretofore authorized to the extent that such authority has not been exercised; (2) for the acquisition of sites and buildings for school purposes and for colleges, museums, libraries, and art galleries and for the construction and equipment of buildings therefor; (3) assessment bonds maturing in not more than ten years in anticipation of the collection of assessments levied or to be levied for public or local improvements theretofore authorized; (4) general fund bonds; (5) bonds issued to refund maturing obligations; and (6) in the event that a consolidated pension and retirement system shall be created, as provided in Section 94, and shall have become operative, but not otherwise, bonds to such amount as shall be required to supply all then existing deficiencies in the reserves and assets of the several pension, retirement and like funds theretofore existing which shall have been fully replaced with respect to further operation by such consolidated system, all such exceptions being subject, however, to the limitations in other respects in this Subdivision contained.

(d) Money shall not be borrowed to meet the current expenses of the City or any county therein except in anticipation of the collection of taxes already levied or to be levied in the next ensuing year.

(e) Deficits arising from the operation of any public improvement, works or facility carried on, operated, or maintained by the City shall be deemed to be current expenses of the City.

(f) Prior to the authorization of the issue of corporate stock or bonds to finance any revenue-producing improvement there shall be determined, as in this Act provided, (1) the estimated life and duration of the improvement to be financed thereby and, if revenue-producing, (2) the estimated cost and the amount estimated to be required to provide for the financing of such improvement, (3) the estimated average annual earnings, and (4) the estimated average annual operating expense thereof. The term "operating expense" shall be deemed to mean and comprehend, unless the contrary be expressly stated herein, (a) all expenses of operation, (b) ordinary maintenance, (c) the amount of all other expenses and charges to which the City may be subject which upon approved accounting principles would be included in the case of a similar private enterprise, (d) the amount necessary to be paid annually in order to make provision for the amortization of the entire estimated investment in the improvement in equal annual installments during its estimated life which shall be deemed not to exceed fifty years, and (e) the amount of the average annual interest charge upon the investment, such interest being calculated thereon at not less than the rate to be borne by the corporate stock or bonds to be issued for the purpose of financing such improvement. Corporate stock or serial bonds may be issued to finance such improvement up to an amount, not exceeding the full amount estimated to be required to provide for the financing of such improvement, upon which the estimated average annual earnings thereof will suffice to provide for interest, after provision for all other such operating expense, as above defined, at the rate to be borne by the corporate stock or bonds to be issued therefor.

(g) Such provision, by way of serial maturities, shall be made at the time of the authorization of any issue of corporate bonds hereafter made, which shall not be in anticipation of the collection of taxes or shall not mature within two years from the date of issue, unless a sinking fund to provide therefor shall be established as hereinabove authorized, as will operate to retire the entire issue, in practicable annual installments, at or prior to maturity.

(h) No obligations of the City save only revenue bonds payable out of the tax-levy of the current year, shall be issued in substitution for or for the purpose of refunding (1) any debt hereafter contracted or (2) any debt heretofore contracted for any purpose for which corporate stock or bonds could not have been issued in the first instance as provided in this Act, at the date of such new issue or refunding.

(i) In the event that corporate stock or bonds shall be issued to refund any portion or portions of the funded debt of the City now existing the same shall be of a principal amount not exceeding the principal amount of the particular debt or debts refunded; such new corporate stock or bonds shall run for a term not exceeding fifty years and the provisions of this Act with respect to maturities and provision for the payment and retirement of corporate stock or bonds hereafter to be issued shall apply to and control the issue, service and payment of all such refunded obligations.

(j) Notwithstanding anything contained in this Subdivision bonds known as "General Fund bonds," to mature in 1929, may be issued annually by the Board of Estimate and Apportionment for account of the sinking fund known as "The Sinking Fund of the City of New York for the Redemption of the City Debt," to an amount equal to and in exchange for and replacement of available surplus revenues and accumulations in such sinking fund, and determined by the Board of Estimate and Apportionment, over and above the amount required to pay at maturity the bonds and stocks of the City of New York redeemable therefrom; but none of the revenues, moneys or assets of any sinking fund, whether existing or hereafter established, shall hereafter be invested in, exchanged for or transferred in replacement of General Fund bonds or any obligations of the City unless after such investment, exchange or replacement there shall remain in such sinking fund (1) money, (2) corporate stock or bonds of the issue for the amortization whereof such sinking fund is maintained or corporate stock notes representing such corporate stock or bonds, (3) revenue bonds, special revenue bonds and tax notes of the City, (4) obligations of the City payable in full prior to the date of the maturity of the issue so secured or corporate stock notes representing corporate stock or bonds to be issued and to be so payable and (5) stock and bonds of the United States and of states, counties and municipalities (other than the City or any of its counties) constituting authorized investments for savings banks under the laws of the State of New York, or some of the foregoing, sufficient in the aggregate, as computed by the Comptroller (securities other than those of the City being computed at their then fair market values), together with accumulations of interest thereon, to pay and discharge the obligations secured by such sinking fund by the time the same shall become payable. Except as last above provided, revenues and moneys belonging to any sinking fund may be invested in any obligations of the City, provided that neither the revenues nor moneys of any sinking fund other than the Sinking Fund for the Redemption of the City Debt shall be invested in, exchanged for or replaced by General Fund bonds. The proceeds of all General Fund bonds issued as aforesaid shall be credited to the "General Fund for the Reduction of Taxation," or such fund or account of like nature as may be maintained by the City, unless applied to the payment or redemption of the City's funded debt. When all of the corporate stock and bonds now redeemable from the Sinking Fund of the City of New York for the Redemption of the City Debt shall have been paid, all of the General Fund bonds then held in such sinking fund shall be cancelled.

20. **Pension fund; consolidation of existing funds.** (a) To establish and maintain a system or systems of pensions or annuities for retirement of, and of life insurance for, any or all of the officers and employees of the City and the counties contained therein and of offices, boards, bodies, commissions and corporations, maintained wholly or in part by appropriations made by the City and to provide for the payment of benefits or allowances on account of the death or disability or other withdrawal from service of any thereof; to provide, in whole or in part, and to manage and administer a fund or funds therefor;

(b) To consolidate any or all such funds now existing and any fund or funds hereafter established in a single fund, but only upon terms which shall not be violative of the then subsisting legal rights of the participants therein as defined in Section 86.

21. **Control of city money; contracts; equitable claims.** (a) To regulate the custody, handling and paying out of the moneys of the City;

(b) To prescribe and enforce conditions and regulations with respect to the making and execution, in behalf of the City, of contracts and purchases of any or all descriptions and to enforce such regulations by forfeitures, penalties and otherwise;

(c) To audit and allow claims not legally enforceable but just and equitable obligations for which the City or any county therein has received a benefit, provided that the same if they were otherwise valid would not be barred by a statute of limitations and that no power shall exist to grant extra compensation to any public officer, employee or contractor;

(d) To audit and pay the expenses of and charges upon any officer or employee of the City or of any county therein which may have been incurred by reason of or in defending himself for performing any act expressly directed by or under the express authority of any ordinance of the City;

(e) To audit and pay the reasonable expenses of any successful contestant for any office of the City or of any county therein incurred in prosecuting or defending such contest.

22. **Public offices and records.** To prescribe regulations with respect to the days and hours during which public offices of the City shall be open and with respect to access by the public to buildings, offices and structures belonging to, occupied or operated by the City or any county therein, the keeping, custody and indexing of and access to instruments affecting land in the City, the inspection of city or county records of all kinds and the fees to be paid to the City for the use thereof and for official copies thereof.

23. **General police powers.** (a) To provide for policing the City and to authorize special patrolmen for particular districts, businesses or purposes and to define their powers;

(b) To provide for the custody and care of persons accused or convicted of crime or misdemeanor and the detention of witnesses in criminal proceedings;

(c) To provide for the custody and disposition of stolen or unclaimed property and the proceeds thereof;

(d) To prevent and extinguish fires and to protect the inhabitants of the City and property within the City and as well neighboring property upon land or water without the City from loss or damage by fire or other casualty;

(e) To make rules and to compel the installation of safeguards to prevent the loss or imperiling of life or property by reason of fire or casualty;

(f) To establish and enforce a sanitary code for the City and all needful quarantine regulations and to exercise all powers requisite to prevent or abate pestilence and epidemics;

(g) To provide for the removal and disposition of dead bodies and to prohibit the location within the City, to regulate the use and to condemn and compel the discontinuance of cemeteries and interests therein;

(h) To provide for the inspection and testing of machinery, apparatus, appliances, pipes, wires and other instrumentalities, firearms and other weapons, foods and other products, commodities or articles which are or may become dangerous, deleterious or insanitary, and for the prohibition or regulation of the use, sale or retention thereof within the City and for the destruction thereof if the public interest shall so require;

(i) To provide for or require the removal of garbage, ashes and waste of all kinds and to regulate the dumping of any such materials on land or into waters and the filling in of low or waste places;

(j) To regulate the observance of Sundays and legal holidays;

(k) To prescribe rules for and to regulate pedestrian, vehicular and aerial traffic or travel and the instrumentalities thereof;

(l) To regulate, restrict or prohibit the erection, maintenance and posting of fences, hoardings, bill-boards and advertising structures and advertisements on private property which by obstructing or obscuring the view of or from highways, streets, parks or other public places may tend to endanger, obstruct or impede traffic thereon, or which by reason of instability or action of the elements may threaten to imperil or obstruct traffic or which may tend to promote or facilitate crime, vice, immorality, the occurrence of fires, or insanitary conditions or to prevent the detection thereof or shall so disfigure any such highway, street, park or other public place as to detract from the proper general enjoyment or use thereof by the public;

(m) To license and regulate businesses and occupations carried on in the City and the instrumentalities thereof;

(n) To regulate and supervise the construction, reconstruction, installation, repair and demolition of buildings and other structures and of sewers, drains, pipes, wires and connections of every description installed by private owners; to compel the remedying of conditions in buildings which are prejudical to safety or health and to prohibit the use thereof during the continuance of any such conditions, and to provide for or compel the destruction of buildings which are a menace to life or in order to prevent the spread of fire;

(o) Consistently with general laws, to provide for the licensing and solemnization of marriages within the City;

(p) To provide for the registration and reporting of births, marriages, deaths, strangers sojourning in the City, residents at hotels, tenants of buildings and the crews and passengers of vessels;

(q) To authorize the administration of oaths by designated officials of the City;

(r) To provide for offering and paying rewards;

(s) To enforce the observance of standards of weights and measures;

(t) To relieve and care for children and poor, sick, infirm, defective, insane, inebriate or invalid persons in the City, to require such of the foregoing as shall be charges upon the City and shall be reasonably capable thereof to perform labor, either with or without pay as may be just and practicable, and to provide means and facilities therefor and to dispose of the product thereof, and to enforce discipline among and to provide for the reasonable punishment of the delinquencies of all such charges;

(u) To commit, indenture, place out, discharge and transfer any minor who is a public charge and to revoke or terminate any such commitment or arrangement and to compel the support of wives, children, whether legitimate or illegitimate, and of poor persons, by those upon whom they naturally should be dependent;

(v) To provide for the burial of deceased indigent persons;

(w) To make payments to charitable, eleemosynary, correctional or reformatory institutions as per capita allowances for persons actually supported, treated, cared for or educated therein and to supervise and to require reports from any such institutions to which or to the operation whereof the City shall so contribute.

24. **Referendum as to improvements.** To require questions concerning the undertaking by the City of the construction, acquisition or operation of any improvement, works or facility, which the City shall have power to construct, acquire or operate, to be submitted to vote of the electors of the City and to provide for the time and, consistently with the Election Law, the manner of submission of any such matter and for the ballots to be employed in voting thereon.

25. **Investigations; publication of city advertisements or information.** (a) To investigate and inquire into all

matters of concern to the City or its inhabitants or any of the counties contained therein concerning which the City is hereby granted any power of legislation, determination, regulation or action, and to require and enforce by subpoena the attendance of witnesses and the production of books, papers and records at such investigations with all of the powers which the Legislature of the State of New York might exercise in the premises;

(b) To require to be published and to provide for and regulate the publication of municipal advertisements and of information of public interest or the publication whereof is required by law.

26. **General grant of power of self government.** (a) In addition to the powers herein elsewhere granted, to exercise all powers requisite or proper for the government and administration of the City and its affairs, it being intended hereby to grant to the City all rights and powers of self-government except as herein expressly limited which might be conferred thereon by the Legislature in express language.

(b) The enumeration herein of certain rights and powers shall not be construed to deny the City of New York any right or power essential or proper to the full exercise of such right of self-government.

(c) The power of legislation conferred upon the City by this Act includes the power to supersede, wholly or in part, as to and within the City of New York or to re-enact in modified form, so as to have the force of law with respect to and within the City, any law or portion of law of the State of New York, heretofore or hereafter enacted, which deals with any of the matters as to which powers are delegated to the City by this Act, save in respects as to which power is not so delegated; provided only that power shall not exist to supersede any law of the State applicable within the City hereafter enacted if such law shall expressly provide to the contrary. Such power of legislation may be exercised from time to time by original enactment, amendment or repeal.

(d) No law of this State hereafter enacted shall be deemed or construed to repeal, amend, supersede or modify any of the provisions of this Act, or to impair the power of the City thereafter to supersede or modify the provisions of such law, if and as in this Act provided, unless such law shall so expressly provide and the provisions of this Act shall be subject to and controlled by only (1) such laws, whatsoever their nature, as shall be passed hereafter and shall by their express terms or by unmistakable indication of such intent be made applicable to the City of New York and (2) laws or parts of laws heretofore passed to which by the express terms of this Act or its plain intendment the same is made subject and then only with respect to subjects as to which such provision is so made. Nothing herein nor any ordinance passed in pursuance of the powers hereby conferred, shall diminish the tax-rate for State purposes fixed by act of the Legislature.

Distribution of Powers Conferred Upon the City

SECTION 5. Each of the officers, boards, departments, bureaus and commissions of the City, except the Board of Aldermen, shall possess only the powers granted to him or it by this Act or otherwise under its authority, and each officer of any of the counties comprised in the City, except county officers whose powers are not made subject to control by the City in Subdivision 14 of Section 4, shall possess only the powers now conferred upon them by law of which they shall not have been deprived as authorized by this Act and the powers conferred upon them by the City under the authority hereof. All of the powers conferred upon the City by this Act which are not granted by this Act to, or conferred under its authority upon, some other board or boards or upon specified officers, departments, bureaus or commissions of the City shall be exercised in its discretion by the Board of Aldermen or, as it may deem necessary for the performance of administrative duties or ministerial acts, by officers, boards, departments, commissions or other authorities of the City or any county therein under delegation and as authorized by it. As between the Board of Aldermen and every other authority of the City, said Board shall be deemed entitled to exercise all of the powers conferred upon the City which by this Act are not, or under its authority shall not be, granted in express terms or by clear intendment to one or more of the other authorities of the City or of a county therein.

ARTICLE II

Elective Officers

Titles

SECTION 6. The Mayor, Comptroller, President of the Board of Aldermen, the Presidents of the several boroughs, and the members of the Board of Aldermen, who in the first instance shall be * * * in number, shall be the elective officers of the City. Each of the Presidents of boroughs shall be known as "Borough President" of his borough and members of the Board of Aldermen shall be known as "Aldermen."

Board of Estimate

SECTION 7. The Mayor, Comptroller, President of the Board of Aldermen and the five Borough Presidents when sitting as a body, shall constitute the Board of Estimate and Apportionment of the City.

Manner of Election and Terms of Officers

SECTION 8. The Mayor, the Comptroller and the President of the Board of Aldermen shall be elected by the electors of the City at large by plurality votes. Each Borough President shall be elected by like vote of the electors of his borough. At the general election in the year 1925 and every four years thereafter each of said officers shall be elected for a term of four years to commence on the first day of January following such election.

Aldermanic Districts

SECTION 9. The City shall be divided into * * * * Aldermanic districts as follows:

[Here insert descriptions of Aldermanic Districts.]

Number of Aldermen to be Elected in Each District

SECTION 10. [Here specify the number of members to be elected in each Aldermanic District.]

Manner of Election and Terms of Aldermen

SECTION 11. Candidates for Aldermen shall be nominated and voted for, the votes cast for candidates shall be counted and Aldermen shall be elected by and in such manner as may be provided in the Election Laws or otherwise as may be provided by the City pursuant to legislative authority. Aldermen shall be elected at the general election in the year 1925 and every two years thereafter for a term of two years to commence on the first day of January following such election.

Elections

SECTION 12. The Board of Aldermen may make, by ordinance, needful rules and regulations, not inconsistent with this Act or with the Election Law, for the conduct of elections of city and county officers, the prevention and punishment of fraud in connection therewith and the recount of ballots in cases of doubt or apparent fraud.

Change of Districts or Apportionment of Aldermen

SECTION 13. The Board of Aldermen may once, but not more than once, after the return of each enumeration of inhabitants in any State or Federal Census, which shall provide the data necessary for so doing, beginning with the Federal Census to be taken in the year 1930, increase or decrease the number of Aldermanic districts, the total number of Aldermen to be elected and the number thereof to be elected by the Aldermanic districts respectively and may alter the boundaries of such districts. Every Aldermanic district shall be of as compact form as practicable and shall consist of contiguous territory and no borough shall be divided in the formation of Aldermanic districts except to form two or more districts wholly within such borough.

Removal

SECTION 14. 1. Any of said elective officers, except Aldermen, may be removed by the Board of Aldermen upon charges of misconduct in office or of incapacity preferred by the Board of Estimate and Apportionment by means of a resolution adopted by not less than ten votes, provided two-thirds of all of the qualified members of the Board of Aldermen shall vote in favor of his removal; but only after trial of such charges, at which the Vice-President of the Board of Aldermen shall preside over said Board, and full opportunity to make defense.

2. Any of said elective officers, except Aldermen, may be removed from office by the Governor in the same manner as sheriffs, except that the Governor, in his discretion, may direct the inquiry required by law to be conducted by the Attorney-General, and after charges have been received by the Governor, he may, pending the investigation, suspend such officer for a period not exceeding thirty days.

3. Any Alderman may be removed from office by resolution of the Board of Aldermen adopted by not less than a two-thirds vote of all of the qualified members of said Board.

Vacancies

SECTION 15. 1. In case of a vacancy in the office of Mayor, the President of the Board of Aldermen shall be Mayor during the unexpired term.

2. In case of a vacancy in the office of Comptroller, the Mayor shall appoint a person to be Comptroller who shall hold office until the first day of January following the election of a person to hold office for the remainder of the unexpired term. Such person shall be elected at the next general election at which municipal officers shall be elected, occurring more than 30 days after the occurrence of the vacancy.

3. Any vacancy in the office of President of the Board of Aldermen shall be filled by election by the Board of Aldermen.

4. Any vacancy in the office of Borough President or Alderman shall be filled by election by the Aldermen representing districts in the borough in which or in any district of which the vacancy occurs, except that in boroughs having less than three Aldermen, such vacancies shall be filled by election by the Board of Aldermen. Any person so elected shall hold office during the unexpired term of his predecessor.

Salaries

SECTION 16. Until otherwise provided by joint action of the Board of Aldermen and the Board of Estimate and Apportionment as authorized by Subdivision 6 of Section 33, the annual salaries of said elective officers shall be the following:

Mayor, $36,000; Comptroller, $30,000; President of the Board of Aldermen, $18,000; Borough President, $15,000; Aldermen, $6,000.

ARTICLE III

Board of Aldermen

Powers as Legislative Body

SECTION 17. The Board of Aldermen shall have all of the powers of a legislative body for the purpose of determining the qualifications of its members, its rules and methods of procedure and for all other purposes within the scope of its powers.

President of the Board

SECTION 18. The President of the Board of Aldermen, when present, shall preside over the sessions of said Board when acting as such, except as provided in Section 14, and shall have such powers with respect to the appointment of committees and employees of and the proceedings of said Board and of any of its committees and the direction of its employees as may be conferred upon him by the rules or resolutions of said Board. He shall not be entitled to a vote as a member of said Board, but, as the presiding officer thereof, he or in his absence the Vice-President thereof or other presiding officer, shall be entitled to a casting vote in the event that the votes of Aldermen upon any ordinance, resolution, motion or other proposition shall be equally divided. The Vice-President or such other presiding officer shall also be entitled to his vote as a member of the Board.

Vice-President of the Board

SECTION 19. The Board of Aldermen shall elect from their own number a Vice-President who shall possess the powers and perform the duties of the President of the Board of Aldermen when the latter is absent, incapacitated, under suspension or acting as Mayor or when a vacancy exists in the office of President of the Board of Aldermen, and who, at such times, shall be a member of every committee, board and body, of which the President of the Board of Aldermen is a member by virtue of his office.

Officers; Publicity of Proceedings

SECTION 20. The Board shall choose a clerk and such other officers as it may deem necessary and shall keep and publish a journal of its proceedings, and its proceedings shall be public except when by a two-third vote of all of its qualified members it shall declare that the public welfare requires secrecy.

Meetings, Quorum

SECTION 21. The first meeting of the Board of Aldermen in each year shall be held, unless sooner convened by the Mayor, on the first Tuesday of January at noon, and thereafter as the Board may for itself determine, but at least once in each month, except July and August. A majority of the Board of Aldermen shall constitute a quorum, and no measure having the effect of law shall be passed by vote of less than a majority of all the members of the Board.

Record of Vote

SECTION 22. The ayes and noes shall be called and recorded upon the final passage of any ordinance or of any resolution, which, if adopted, may have the force of law, and, at the request of any two members, upon the final adoption of any other proposition.

Delay Before Vote

SECTION 23. Unless the Mayor shall certify that an emergency requiring immediate action exists no ordinance or resolution, which if enacted would have the force of law, shall be passed unless it shall have been printed and upon the desks of the members, in its final form, at least one week prior to its final passage.

Action by Mayor, Action of Board After Veto

SECTION 24. Every ordinance or resolution of the Board of Aldermen, except such resolutions as concern only its own organization, rules, committees and procedure, shall be presented to the Mayor, after its passage and before it takes effect; if he approve he shall sign it; if not, he shall return it to the Clerk of the Board of Aldermen within ten days (Sundays excepted) after its presentation to him with his objections, which shall be entered at large on the journal of said Board, and the Board, within fifteen days after such return of the ordinance or resolution or at its next meeting, if held subsequently to the expiration of such period of fifteen days, shall proceed to reconsider it. If after such reconsideration it shall again be passed by a vote of two-thirds of all of the Aldermen voting for or against the same, those voting for the same being at least a majority of all of the members of the Board, it shall take effect notwithstanding the objections of the Mayor. If, upon the first vote upon such reconsideration, the ordinance or resolution shall fail to receive such number of affirmative votes, such ordinance or resolution shall be deemed to be finally lost. In all cases of votes upon such reconsideration of any ordinance or resolution, the vote shall be taken by yeas and nays and the names of the members voting and their votes respectively shall be entered in the journal of the Board. If any ordinance or resolution shall not be approved or returned by the Mayor as above provided within ten days (Sundays excepted), after it shall have been presented to him, the same shall take effect in like manner as if he had approved it. In case an ordinance or resolution shall embrace more than one distinct subject and the several subjects shall be separately treated therein, the Mayor may approve the provisions relating to one or more subjects and disapprove the others. In such case, those which he shall approve shall become effective but the remainder of the ordinance or resolution shall be dealt with in the same manner and with the same effect as if it constituted an entire ordinance or resolution which the Mayor had failed to approve.

Elective Officers, Right to Attend Board Meetings

SECTION 25. The Mayor, the Comptroller and each of the Borough Presidents may attend any of the meetings of the Board of Aldermen and may participate in the deliberations, except during the trial or proceeding in respect to trials of an elective officer, but none of them shall be entitled to vote upon any proposition which may be the subject of action by the Board.

ARTICLE IV

Board of Estimate and Apportionment

Powers

SECTION 26. The Board of Estimate and Apportionment shall have, and is hereby vested with authority to exercise or provide for the exercise of all or any of the powers hereinafter in this Article specified and to determine the necessity or the desirability and propriety of, and to authorize, the exercise by any officer, board, department, bureau, commission or other authority, which it shall designate, of the City or of any borough or county therein of any of said powers in this Article specified which are administrative or ministerial in their nature or appropriate to carry into execution the action of the Board; and whenever it shall have determined that any particular power or powers shall be exercised by any such officer, board, department, bureau, commission or other authority to fix the conditions upon which, and the manner in which, the same shall be exercised or in its discretion to delegate the authority to fix such conditions and manner of exercise to the same or some other officer, board, department, bureau, commission or other authority; provided, however, that any of the powers which by the terms of this Article the Board of Estimate and Apportionment is empowered to exercise but which by reason of delegation as aforesaid or other-

wise some other officer, board, department, bureau or commission is also authorized to exercise, but subject to the power of the Board of Estimate and Apportionment conferred by Subdivision 6 of this Section, shall not be exercised by the Board of Estimate and Apportionment unless or until the same shall have been withdrawn from such other officer, board, department, bureau or commission and assumed exclusively by the Board of Estimate and Apportionment by resolution thereof as permitted by Subdivision 6 of this Section.

Said powers of the Board of Estimate and Apportionment are the following:

1. **Powers in subdivisions 11, 12, 17 of section 4.** All and several the powers enumerated in Subdivisions 11, 12 and 17 of Section 4.

2. **Improvements not over $500,000 and streets; improvement defined.** The power to authorize any public or local improvement and, when required, proceedings to acquire title to property therefor, but only if the estimated aggregate cost of the improvement in question in any particular instance when ascertained as hereinbelow provided shall not exceed the sum of $500,000. The word improvement as used in this Article comprehends every form of improvement, works, facility and structure referred to in Subdivisions 8, 9, 10 and 12 of Section 4, provided that the estimated aggregate cost of any improvement in question shall not exceed the sum of $500,000; provided, however, that said limitation of cost shall not apply to the acquisition of title to land for, or the opening, grading, paving or repaving, curbing or otherwise constructing or making ready for use of highways, streets, avenues or bridges, tunnels or viaducts forming parts of highways, streets or avenues and not crossing over or under navigable waters, the approaches to such bridges, tunnels or viaducts, or sewers or drainage systems.

3. **Excess condemnation.** In connection with the acquisition of land by the City for any park, highway, street or other public place, the power to authorize the acquisition of or to cause to be acquired in fee simple, as part of the same transaction or proceeding, by purchase, condemnation or otherwise, lands additional to those required for such purpose but suitable for building sites to abut upon such park,

highway, street or other public place or upon already existing directly intervening streets upon which any such park or other public place also shall abut, and land in the bed of any discontinued street which intersects or abuts upon such park, highway, street or other public place.

4. **Apportionment of cost of improvement.** (a) With respect to any public or local improvement which the Board of Estimate and Apportionment is empowered to authorize without concurrence of the Board of Aldermen, the power to determine whether any and, if so, how much of the cost of the improvement in question shall be borne by the City as a whole, and if the whole thereof is not to be so borne to apportion the cost thereof as it shall deem just and reasonable among the boroughs of the City, or to allocate the same in whole or in part to any particular borough or boroughs or any part or parts of any thereof; to determine, consistently with the provisions of Subdivision 3 of Section 4, whether all or any part thereof, and if so what part, shall be provided for by the assessment of property deemed to be benefited thereby.

(b) With respect to any and every public or local improvement whatever which shall have been duly authorized by said Board or otherwise, the following powers so far as the exercise of the same shall be requisite or as it may deem the exercise thereof advisable in the premises: (1) the powers vested in it by Article XXIV or by Article XXV; (2) any of the powers of the City enumerated in Subdivision 3 of Section 4 which by the terms of Article V are not vested in said Board and the Board of Aldermen, conjointly, or which by the terms of Article XXIV or of Article XXV are not required to be exercised by some other authority; (3) when the cost of any improvement is to be met by the assessment of property, the power to determine the area or areas of assessment for benefit, or any division thereof into zones or sub-areas of benefit and the proportion in percentages of the cost and expense of the proceedings which shall be made a charge upon and shall be distributed over and between such zones or sub-areas of benefit in proportion to the benefit received; and to revise and alter any such area, sub-area or zone, or any such proportion of such cost and expense which it may theretofore have determined upon.

5. **Zoning; building regulations; public hearings.** The powers enumerated in Subdivision 13 of Section 4, provided that the Board, in the exercise of any such power, at any time hereafter, shall not adopt any resolution to establish or change any district, or establish, change or supplement any limitation, regulation or restriction, until after a public hearing in relation thereto, at which parties in interest and citizens shall have an opportunity to be heard.

In case of a protest against the enactment or change of any such regulation or restriction signed by the owners of twenty per cent. or more of the area of the lots affected thereby or of those immediately adjacent in the rear thereof extending one hundred (100) feet therefrom, or of those directly opposite thereto extending one hundred (100) feet from the street frontage of such opposite lots, such enactment or change shall not be made except by the unanimous vote of the Board. Otherwise the same may be made by a majority vote thereof. The Board of Appeals or other authority exercising substantially the same functions may determine and vary the application of any or all of the regulations and restrictions established as above provided, in harmony with their general purpose and intent and in accordance with general or specific rules prescribed by the Board of Estimate and Apportionment.

The districts established and existing at the date when this Act shall come into force and the regulations, limitations and restrictions then in force shall continue until altered by the Board of Estimate and Apportionment as hereinabove provided.

6. **Organization and control of administrative agencies.** The powers enumerated in Subdivision 14 of Section 4, provided (a) that any action taken in the exercise of any of said powers shall receive the affirmative vote of the Mayor, (b) that any action whereby powers of Borough Presidents shall be transferred shall be taken by unanimous vote of the Board of Estimate and Apportionment and not otherwise, and (c) that the Police Department, the Department of Pensions, the Department of Taxes and the Municipal Civil Service Commission shall always remain separate and distinct departments, with such chief executive officer and with such powers as provided in this Act.

Nothing in the foregoing provisions of this Subdivision shall be deemed to prohibit the Board of Estimate and Apportionment from exercising with respect to any of said specified departments any of the powers enumerated in Subdivision 14 of Section 4 save only the power to abolish any such department or to consolidate it with another or to deprive such department or its chief executive officer of any of the powers conferred upon it or him by this Act, except such as are by the terms hereof made subject to the action of this Board.

The Board of Estimate and Apportionment in its discretion may abolish the Board of Water Supply of the City of New York and in that event provide for the exercise of its powers and functions and the discharge of its duties by such department of the City as shall be charged with the duty of providing and distributing water in the City or that any of such powers and functions shall be exercised by a separate department of the City, the establishment, organization, powers and duties whereof may be provided for by it.

In the event that any office, board, department, bureau or commission or the Board of Water Supply of the City of New York shall be abolished or any of the powers of any thereof shall be transferred to any other office, board, department, bureau or commission, by action of the Board of Estimate and Apportionment as authorized hereby, no action or proceeding, whether initiated by or for the benefit of or against the City or any county therein or by or against any officer, board or commission of the City or any county therein or said Board of Water Supply of the City of New York, pending under or as authorized by any of the provisions of any law or laws, nor any action or proceeding with respect to any action taken or attempted under any such law or laws by any such authority of the City or any such county or by said Board of Water Supply of the City of New York or with respect to matters arising from or in the course of the execution of any public or local improvement or of any project initiated or attempted to be initiated by said Board of Water Supply of the City of New York, shall abate or be stayed by reason of any such action of the Board of Estimate and Apportionment, but the same shall be continued by or against the City or county, or the city or county officer, board or commission to which the powers in question shall have been transferred or in which they shall be vested, but without nominal change of parties, as if such action of the Board of Estimate and Apportionment had not been taken; and the City in such event in every respect shall possess all of the rights and remain subject to all of the obligations which it would have possessed or to which it would have been subject had such action of the Board of Estimate and Apportionment not been taken, and any officer, board, department, bureau or commission to which powers of any other authority of the City or any county or of the Board of Water Supply of the City of New York shall be transferred or in which the same may be vested shall possess and be entitled to enjoy and exercise all of the rights, benefits, privileges, powers and authority theretofore enjoyed or exercised by the officer, board, department, bureau or commission theretofore entitled to exercise the same or of said Board of Water Supply of the City of New York, as the case may be, to the same extent (except as such powers may be limited by action of the Board of Estimate and Apportionment) as if it had been named in the laws or ordinances conferring such powers instead of the officer, board, department, bureau or commission named therein or said Board of Water Supply of the City of New York, as the case may be, and shall be authorized to control the prosecution or defense of any and every such action or proceeding to the same extent as the original grantee of such powers would have been entitled to control the same but for such action of the Board of Estimate and Apportionment.

7. **Franchises and permits.** The powers set forth in Subdivision 16 of Section 4, provided that no franchise shall be granted unless the resolution granting such franchise shall be passed by at least twelve votes.

8. **Audit and allowance of certain claims.** The power to audit and allow any claim certified by the Comptroller to be not legally enforceable but in his opinion a just and equitable obligation for which the City or any county therein has received a commensurate benefit, provided that the same, if it were otherwise valid, would not be barred by a statute of limitations and that the allowance of any such claim shall be by unanimous vote of the Board; to audit and cause to be paid the expenses of and charges upon any officer or employee of the City or of any county therein

which may have been incurred by reason of or in defending himself for performing any act expressly directed by or under the express authority of any ordinance of the City; to audit and cause to be paid the reasonable expenses of any successful contestant for any office of the City or of any county therein incurred in prosecuting or defending such contest.

9. **Transfer of budget appropriations.** The power to transfer budgetary appropriations exceeding the requirements of the purpose or purposes specified in the budget to another purpose or other purposes provided for in the same budget if the appropriation therefor is determined by the Board to be inadequate, provided that the action of the Board shall be by at least twelve votes.

10. **Issue of stock or bonds.** The power to authorize the issue of corporate stock or bonds to the extent permitted by Subdivision 19 of Section 4, for any purpose and amount authorized by this Act, other than such bonds as the Comptroller is authorized to issue by the terms of Article VII, provided that in the case of any issue designed to provide for the financing of any revenue-producing improvement (a) the aggregate amount required to accomplish the purpose which such issue is intended to finance shall not exceed the sum of $50,000,000 and (b) the cost of any such improvement and its net earning capacity shall have been determined in the manner in Section 27 provided.

11. **Refunding debt; fixing conditions of stock or bonds; sinking funds; general fund bonds.** The power to authorize the refunding of any debt of the City which by the terms of Subdivision 19 of Section 4 the City is authorized to refund; to fix the rate of interest to be borne by all corporate stock, serial bonds, general fund bonds and assessment bonds to be issued by the City and to determine whether the same severally shall be payable in gold or in legal currency of the United States and whether the same shall be payable, in any foreign coin or the currency of any foreign country, the place or places of payment and the rate or rates of exchange, if any, to be employed; to invest the income and all moneys belonging to any sinking fund as the Board may deem best, subject, however, to the provisions of Subdivision 19 of Section 4; to collect all amounts due upon

and to sell securities held in any sinking fund or to exchange the same for other securities; to apply any of the income or assets of any sinking fund to the redemption, retirement or extinguishment by cancellation of obligations of any issue the payment whereof is secured by such sinking fund; but all obligations, while held in any sinking fund, shall be kept alive and interest thereon collected until the same shall be disposed of, applied or cancelled as authorized in this Act; to determine the amount of moneys in the Sinking Fund of the City of New York for the Redemption of the City Debt, which, as provided in said Subdivision 19 of Section 4, may be paid out against the receipt of general fund bonds, and the amount of such bonds to be issued for said sinking fund from time to time as authorized by said Subdivision 19; to apply the proceeds of general fund bonds to the extinguishment of any of the City's debt or to direct the same to be carried into the General Fund for the Reduction of Taxation or such other fund or account of like nature as may be maintained; except as otherwise provided in Article V, to exercise all other powers heretofore vested in the Board of Commissioners of the Sinking Fund, which Board is abolished.

12. **Payment and compromise of taxes.** The power to provide for and supervise the collection and the enforcement of the payment, or, when it may deem such course to be just and expedient, the release or compromise of claims for taxes or assessments for public or local improvements that shall be in default and in any such case for the reduction, release or discharge of liens for taxes or assessments.

13. **Actions at law; compromises.** The power to cause actions or proceedings in any court to be instituted, maintained, defended, appealed or discontinued and to authorize controversies to be compromised or settled upon terms to be prescribed or approved by it; to authorize the employment of counsel and expert or technical advisers in special matters.

14. **City Record.** The power to provide for and supervise the publication and management of the *City Record* and to authorize or require information of public interest to be published therein.

15. **Other powers.** The Board of Estimate and Apportionment also shall exercise such other powers as are expressly conferred upon it by other provisions of this Act or are requisite to the performance of the duties imposed upon it hereby.

Estimates in Respect to Revenue-producing Improvements

SECTION 27. For the purpose of any action to be taken by the Board of Estimate and Apportionment with respect to the issue of corporate stock or bonds for the purpose of financing revenue-producing improvements, the estimated life and cost, the amount estimated to be required to provide for the financing of any improvement proposed to be acquired or constructed and the estimated average annual earning capacity and operating expense thereof (as defined in Subdivision 19 of Section 4), shall be ascertained and reported to the Board by the Chief Engineer, if any, of the Board or by any engineer or engineers or other expert adviser or advisers, whether individual or incorporated, whom the Board shall appoint for the particular purpose. The cost of any property, improvement or facility already owned by the City shall be reported to the Board in writing by the Comptroller.

Public Hearings Required in Certain Cases

SECTION 28. None of the following powers shall be exercised by the Board of Estimate and Apportionment except at or after a public hearing of said Board of which public notice shall be given by publication in ten consecutive issues of the *City Record* not less than seven nor more than thirty days before such public hearing:

(a) To change the map or plan of the City.

(b) To authorize the acquisition of land by condemnation the cost of which is to be borne in whole or in part by the owners of property deemed to be benefited thereby.

(c) To determine how the cost of any public or local improvement shall be apportioned among the boroughs of the City; if such cost is to be met by assessments upon property deemed to be benefited, to determine the area or areas of assessment for benefit or any division thereof into zones or sub-areas of benefit and the proportion in percentages of the cost and expense of the proceedings which shall be made a charge upon and shall be distributed over and between such zones or sub-areas of benefit; to revise and alter any such area, sub-area or zone or any such proportion of such cost and expense which it may theretofore have fixed.

(d) To authorize the acquisition of real estate for the supply or distribution of water.

(e) To establish or change any district or establish, change or supplement any limitation, regulation or restriction in exercising the powers enumerated in Subdivision 13 of Section 4.

(f) To grant any franchise.

(g) To authorize the construction of, or the acquisition of real estate for, or the operation by the City of, any revenue-producing improvement.

The foregoing requirement of public hearings and notices thereof is in addition to any and every requirement of a public hearing elsewhere contained in this Act with respect to any particular matter or matters and shall not be deemed to dispense with any of such special requirements.

Action by Board; Quorum

SECTION 29. Except as otherwise specifically provided in this Act, every act of the Board of Estimate and Apportionment shall be by a majority of the whole number of votes authorized by this section to be cast by the members of said Board, six votes of which majority must be the votes of members authorized to cast three votes each. The Mayor, Comptroller and the President of the Board of Aldermen shall each be entitled to cast three votes; the presidents of the boroughs of Manhattan and Brooklyn shall each be entitled to cast two votes; and the presidents of the boroughs of The Bronx, Queens and Richmond shall each be entitled to cast one vote. A quorum of said Board shall consist of members thereof authorized to cast at least nine votes, at least two of whom shall be members hereby authorized to cast three votes each. No resolution or amendment of any resolution shall be passed at the same meeting at which it is originally presented unless twelve votes shall be cast for its adoption.

Mayor to Preside

SECTION 30. The Mayor shall preside over every meeting of the Board of Estimate and Apportionment at which he shall be present.

To Appoint Commissioner of the Budget

SECTION 31. The Board of Estimate and Apportionment shall appoint and, at its pleasure may remove, a Commissioner of the Budget, whose office shall be a bureau of the Board. The Commissioner of the Budget shall be charged with the duty of preparing the proposed annual budget, which as provided in Article XXI, he is required to submit to the Board of Estimate and Apportionment, and for that purpose every board, department and commission of the City and of each of the counties therein and every officer not subject to any board, department or commission, and also the Board of Education, from time to time as the Commissioner of the Budget may require, shall furnish to the Commissioner all such reports, statements and estimates as to actual and estimated expenditures and revenue of its or his office, board, department or commission and all other information pertinent to the actual or probable requirements of appropriations therefor as the Commissioner may request.

Rules; Delegation of Powers; Secretary

SECTION 32. The Board of Estimate and Apportionment may make rules for the conduct of its proceedings, all whereof shall be open, and may delegate administrative and ministerial powers to its committees and officers. It shall choose a secretary who shall keep records of its proceedings, and cause the same promptly to be published in the *City Record*, and it may choose its other officers and subordinates and may establish such offices and bureaus to assist in the performance of its duties as it shall deem needful. The position of Secretary of the Board of Estimate and Apportionment and the office of Commissioner of the Budget, if the Board so determine, may be held by the same person.

ARTICLE V

Conjoint Jurisdiction of the Board of Aldermen and the Board of Estimate and Apportionment

Powers of Boards Acting Conjointly

SECTION 33. The Board of Aldermen and the Board of Estimate and Apportionment shall have and are hereby vested with authority, when acting conjointly as in this Article V provided, (a) to exercise or provide for the exercise of all or any of the powers hereinafter in this Article specified or (b) to determine the necessity or the desirability and propriety of and to authorize the exercise by any officer, board, department, bureau, commission or other authority which they shall designate of the City or of any borough or county therein of all or any of said powers which are administrative or ministerial in their nature, and (c) whenever said two Boards shall so have determined that any particular power or powers shall be exercised by any such officer, board, department, bureau, commission or other authority to fix the conditions upon which and the manner in which the same shall be exercised or in their discretion to delegate the authority to fix such conditions and manner of exercise thereof to the same or some other officer, board, department, bureau, commission or authority.

The said powers are the following:

1. **Authorization of improvements not under power of board of estimate and apportionment; improvement defined.** The power to determine the necessity for and to authorize public or local improvements, and the acquisition of title to property therefor, other than such improvements as the Board of Estimate and Apportionment is empowered to authorize by the provisions of Subdivision 2 of Section 26. The word improvement as used in this Article comprehends every form of improvement, works, facility and structure referred to in Subdivisions 8, 9 and 10 of Section 4 and also bridges and tunnels over or under navigable waters, and the approaches thereto, provided that the estimated aggregate cost of any improvement in question shall exceed the sum of $500,000.

2. **Carrying out and assessing cost of such improvements.** In connection with and for the purposes of such improvement, the power to determine the nature and location thereof, the method, whether by purchase or condemnation or otherwise, by which property therefor shall be acquired, whether and how much of the cost thereof shall be borne by the City, any borough or boroughs or any part or parts of any thereof, and consistently with the provisions of Subdivision 3 of Section 4, whether all or any part thereof, and if so what part, shall be assessed and levied upon property benefited thereby; but the construction of such improvement, the acquisition of property and proceedings therefor, proceedings for the making of assessments and awards and determinations, except as aforesaid, preliminary thereto and all other action looking to the execution of such determinations of said Board of Aldermen and Board of Estimate and Apportionment, acting conjointly, shall be provided for, taken or carried out by the authorities and in the manner elsewhere in this Act specified in such cases or in the absence of such specification by or under authority of the Board of Estimate and Apportionment.

3. **Local improvement districts and boards; powers.** The power to subdivide the City into local improvement districts; to create, provide for the membership and define the powers and functions of local improvement boards; and to empower such local improvement boards to authorize any local improvement (and assessments therefor upon the property benefited), involving a cost not exceeding three thousand dollars.

4. **Reserve funds and accounts.** The power to establish, maintain and provide against the depletion of street and park opening, improvement, administrative and reserve funds and accounts.

5. **Cession of property to State or United States.** The power to cede to the State of New York or the United States of America any property of the City or any interests or rights in or with respect to any thereof.

6. **Control of officers and employees.** The powers conferred upon the City by Subdivision 15 of Section 4, and any action taken in the exercise of any of said powers shall be effective and binding notwithstanding any law of contrary

or different effect in existence at the time of the taking of such action.

7. **Financing improvements over $50,000,000.** The power to authorize the issue of corporate stock and bonds to finance a revenue-producing improvement, when the estimated amount required for financing the same shall exceed the sum of $50,000,000. Such power shall be exercised upon the same conditions and subject to the same limitations otherwise as are provided in Article IV hereof with respect to the exercise of like power by the Board of Estimate and Apportionment in connection with improvements requiring for their financing not to exceed $50,000,000.

8. **Authorization of revenue-producing improvements; estimate of cost and, if over $50,000,000 unless for water supply, court determination of probable gross annual earnings and operating costs.** The power to provide that, and to prescribe the conditions upon which, the City shall engage in the operation of any revenue-producing improvement, including works or facilities comprised therein, the operation whereof by the City is authorized by Subdivision 18 of Section 4, provided that the estimated life and cost of constructing or acquiring the plant, equipment and other property of any revenue-producing improvement and the amount estimated to be required for the financing of such improvement shall first have been ascertained as provided in Section 27 and that if the same, including the cost of property already owned by the City to be comprised therein, shall exceed the sum of $50,000,000 such power shall not be exercised with respect to any improvement other than for the supply of water, except upon and after compliance with the following conditions, as well as all other conditions, not inconsistent with the provisions hereof, prescribed by any law or laws other than this Act then in force and applicable in such case:

(a) The Board of Estimate and Apportionment shall prepare or cause its Chief Engineer or any engineer or engineers designated by it, to prepare, pursuant to its directions, plans and specifications of the improvement, including all plant, works, facilities and equipment required therefor and a statement of project, which shall comprise a description of the nature of the undertaking and of the proposed method of conducting the same and a statement of the rates or prices proposed to be charged for the service to be furnished thereby and of authorized readjustments, if any, of such rates and prices. An estimate of the cost of the improvement, if or to the extent that the same already shall be owned by the City, shall be prepared by the Comptroller, and furnished to the Board of Estimate and Apportionment. Thereupon the probable cost of the improvement including such property as already may be owned, and such as shall be required to be acquired or constructed by the City, and the probable gross annual earnings and the probable gross annual operating expense of such improvement, as defined by Subdivision 19 of Section 4, shall be determined as follows:

The Board of Estimate and Apportionment, provided said Board and the Board of Aldermen shall by joint resolution authorize such action, shall submit said plans and specifications and statement of project and the statement, if any, prepared by the Comptroller, to the Appellate Division of the Supreme Court, First Department, by petition reciting such joint resolution and praying for a judicial determination of the probable cost of such plant and equipment and the probable gross annual earnings and probable gross annual operating expense of such improvement, as defined in Subdivision 19 of Section 4, which thereupon shall be determined as follows: Said Court shall appoint a Commission consisting of three members, all of whom shall be residents of the City and none of whom shall be an officer of or a person holding any position or exercising any employment under the City or any county therein. The Court shall refer to such Commission said plans, specifications, statement of project and statement, if any, of the Comptroller for its consideration and for report to be made by it of the estimated life of such improvement (which shall be assumed not to exceed fifty years), the estimated cost of such improvement, the estimated gross annual earnings and the gross annual operating expense of such proposed improvement and the Court in its discretion may in its order of reference, or from time to time by subsequent order, regulate the method of procedure of such Commission. The Commission shall investigate the matters so referred to it and shall have and may exercise, among others, all or any of the powers which would be possessed by referees appointed by the Supreme Court to try, and report findings upon specific questions of fact. It may obtain data and other information by means of the personal investigations of its members, as well as by means of testimony and other evidence. It shall permit the introduction of relevant and material evidence by the City or by civic bodies or citizens of the City. Within such period as may be prescribed in the Court's order of reference or in any order supplementary thereto, the Commission shall report to the Court its conclusions, the grounds therefor, the detailed estimates adopted and the data employed by it in reaching the same, and all evidence, if any, that it shall have taken. The Commission, in reporting upon the subjects submitted to it, shall not make any finding or determination with respect to any matter other than the probable cost of such plant and equipment, the probable gross annual earnings and the probable gross annual operating expense of the proposed improvement, as the same is defined in Subdivision 19 of Section 4, and matters the determination of which is involved in the determination of the matters last aforesaid. The Commission shall act by majority vote of its members but explanatory reports may be filed by individual members. The Commission shall have power to employ experts and other assistants and to fix their compensation, and such compensation and the other reasonable expenses of the Commission, when approved by the Court, shall be paid by the City. The members of the Commission shall be entitled to receive from the City reasonable compensation for their services, which shall be fixed by order of said Court.

Immediately upon the filing of said report, said Court shall by order set down for hearing the matter of the confirmation of said report and shall cause a copy of such order and of the report or reports of such Commission and of its members, severally, if any, to be transmitted to the Mayor of the City, who shall cause the same forthwith to be published in the *City Record*. At such hearing, the Mayor, the Board of Estimate and Apportionment and the Board of Aldermen shall be entitled to be represented by such attorneys as they may designate, respectively, and the Court shall permit to be represented at such hearing such civic bodies and individual citizens as in its opinion it shall be desirable to hear in order that divergent views, if any, of citizens of the City as to the correctness of the facts and the validity of the conclusions stated in the report of the Commission may be presented to it.

After such hearing, if the Court shall be of the opinion that the conclusions of the Commission are justified by the evidence and data submitted therewith and the reasons adduced therefor, it shall by order confirm said report; otherwise, it shall by order disapprove the same. In either event, a certified copy of its order and of the report of the Commission shall be remitted by the Clerk of said Court to the Board of Estimate and Apportionment and to the Board of Aldermen, severally.

(b) In the event that it shall appear by the report of said Commission, if confirmed by order of said Court as above-provided, that the estimated average gross annual earnings of such improvement during the estimated life thereof, which in every case shall be assumed to be not exceeding fifty years, at least equal the estimated average gross annual operating expense thereof, as in Subdivision 19 of Section 4 defined, it shall be lawful for the Board of Aldermen and the Board of Estimate and Apportionment, by joint resolution, to provide that the City shall engage therein and for the establishment thereof, or that the City shall engage therein provided that such joint resolution be approved by the electors of the City, either at the next general election held in an odd numbered year or at a special city election, which may be called for the purpose by the Board of Aldermen. In event that any such proposition shall be submitted to the Electors of the City, the action of the Board of Aldermen and the Board of Estimate and Apportionment taken as aforesaid shall not come into force or possess any virtue as an authorization of action thereunder unless it shall be confirmed by the affirmative votes of a majority of all of the electors voting in favor of or against the confirmation thereof.

9. **Lease of revenue-producing improvements; conditions of contract or lease.** The power to make contracts for the lease to and operation by any individual or individuals or any corporation or corporations of public works or facilities constituting or to constitute the plant or equipment, or

both, of any revenue-producing improvement with respect to which the City shall be empowered to make such contract as provided in Subdivision 18 of Section 4, upon such terms and subject to such conditions in each instance as may be prescribed in such contract, provided (a) that every such contract shall reserve rental, and provide security for the payment thereof, which shall be sufficient (first) to reimburse the City for interest upon its investment in said improvement at a rate not less than the rate or the average rate payable upon obligations of the City issued to finance the same, or, if there be no such obligations, a rate at least equal to the average quoted interest-yield upon the most lately issued stock and serial bonds of the City of an aggregate amount equal to such investment, as such average quoted interest-yield shall be computed by the Comptroller, and (second) to provide for the amortization of such investment in annual installments within the estimated life of such improvement and in any event within fifty years, (b) that any such contract shall effectually reserve to the City the right to terminate the same and to retake possession and control of the property so leased in the event of any failure of the lessee to make payments of rental and amortization installments as and at the times required by such contract or within specified periods of grace thereafter which in no case shall exceed one year or of any failure substantially to perform any other material covenant or promise of such contract and (c) that every such contract shall be made upon such conditions and shall contain such provisions, not inconsistent with the provisions hereof, otherwise, as shall be provided for in any law or laws other than this Act then in force and applicable thereto.

10. **Powers as to pension funds.** The powers enumerated in Subdivision 20 of Section 4, subject to and consistent with the provisions of Article XV of this Act.

11. **Appropriations; making and adoption of budget.** The power to make and revoke appropriations of moneys to any city or county purpose and to make and adopt the Annual Budget of the City as and in the manner provided in Article XXI hereof.

Revenue-producing Improvements to be Self-supporting if Practicable; Gross Expenses Defined; Tax-payers' Suit; Section Not to Apply to Improvements Now Operated

SECTION 34. It shall be the duty of the Board of Estimate and Apportionment, to the fullest extent which in the exercise of a reasonable discretion it shall determine to be practicable, so to operate any and every revenue-producing improvement which the City shall operate and so to fix and adjust the rate or rates, price or prices, collected by the City for the service furnished thereby that the realizable gross earnings of such enterprise during each fiscal year thereof shall be at least equal to the gross expenses and charges thereof for the same period; and the right and power is hereby conferred upon the Board of Estimate and Apportionment from time to time to readjust any or all of such rates or prices, notwithstanding any law, ordinance, joint resolution or contract to the contrary or otherwise providing.

Any tax-payer of the City and any owner of corporate stock or bonds issued by the City in order to finance any such revenue-producing improvement shall be entitled to maintain in any court of competent jurisdiction proceedings for an order of mandamus or for an injunction to enforce the duty of the Board of Estimate and Apportionment, in this Section or in Subdivision 8 or Subdivision 9 of Section 33 declared, or to restrain any violation thereof, and power and jurisdiction are hereby conferred upon the Supreme Court sitting in any county comprised within the City to enforce the performance or restrain the violation of such duty and, if in the judgment of the Court it shall be necessary so to do in order to give complete relief in the premises, by its order or judgment to determine and to enforce the adoption of rates or prices fixed by it which in its opinion shall comply with the requirements hereof.

The term "gross expenses and charges", or any equivalent phrase, used in this Section with regard to the operation of any such revenue-producing improvement during a calendar year, shall be deemed to mean and comprehend: (a) all expenses of operating and conducting such enterprise during such calendar year, (b) ordinary maintenance thereof for such year, (c) and all other expenses and charges to which the City may be subject which upon approved accounting principles should be deemed to be or attributed as an expense of such improvement for such year, (d) a proper contribution to a reserve fund, which shall be created and maintained in such manner and amount as the Board of Estimate and Apportionment shall determine, by and solely for the benefit of such improvement, the annual contributions whereto shall be adequate, as nearly as can be estimated, to provide for any deficit that may occur in the gross annual earnings of such improvement, as compared with its gross annual expenses and charges, during the period for which any such deficit may be deemed liable to exist notwithstanding the provisions of this Section for the readjustment of rates or prices, (e) the amount necessary to be paid during or with respect to such year in order to amortize the entire investment in such improvement in equal annual installments during the estimated life of such investment, which shall be deemed not to exceed fifty years, and (f) the entire amount of interest accruing during such year upon all obligations of the City issued in order to finance such improvement which shall then be outstanding less the amount of any fund which shall exist in cash or marketable securities, other than obligations of the City, which shall be available and applicable solely and shall be irrevocably pledged to the redemption of such outstanding obligations.

Neither the provisions of this Section nor the limitations and conditions prescribed in Subdivision 8 of Section 33 upon the exercise of powers of the City conferred in Subdivision 18 of Section 4 shall apply to the continued operation of specific improvements which are now operated by the City but all thereof shall apply, according to their terms, to proposals to engage in and to the operation of all revenue-producing improvements, other than for the supply of water, hereafter undertaken or proposed to be undertaken whether or not the property thereof or required therefor be now owned by the City in whole or in part.

Conjoint Action by Joint Resolution

SECTION 35. Every act of the Board of Aldermen and the Board of Estimate and Apportionment with respect to which conjoint action of said two Boards is required shall be by joint resolution except as otherwise expressly provided in this Act. Such resolutions, except as provided in Article XXI with respect to the Annual Budget, may originate in either body and may be concurred in, rejected and, subject to concurrence by the coordinate body, amended by the other.

Veto of Mayor; Passage Over Veto

SECTION 36. Every joint resolution adopted by the Board of Aldermen and the Board of Estimate and Apportionment shall be presented to the Mayor and by him signed or returned with his objections or retained without signature and, in case it is returned with objections to the same in whole or in part, reconsidered by the two Boards, except as next herein below provided, all in like manner, within the periods of time and in every respect with the effect provided in Section 24 of this Act with respect to ordinances and resolutions of the Board of Aldermen. In the event that a joint resolution is returned by the Mayor with objections it shall be so returned to the Board with which it originated and if after reconsideration by said Board it shall again be passed by it by not less than a two-thirds vote, it shall be sent with the Mayor's objections to the other Board and if upon reconsideration by that Board it shall also be passed by not less than a two-thirds vote, it shall take effect notwithstanding the objections of the Mayor. This Section, however, shall not apply to proceedings for the adoption of the Annual Budget which shall be as prescribed in Article XXI.

ARTICLE VI

The Mayor

Chief Executive Officer

SECTION 37. The Mayor shall be the chief executive officer of the City.

Powers of Mayor

SECTION 38. The Mayor shall have power and it shall be his duty:

1. **Appointment and removal.** At his pleasure to appoint and to remove, except as otherwise specifically provided in this Act, all officers (except elective officers and

their subordinate officers), all heads of departments, and any or all of the members of permanent boards and commissions of the City, whether established by this Act or under its authority, and neither certiorari nor other proceeding for judicial review of his action in so doing shall lie or be entertained; provided (a) that subject to the exercise by the Board of Estimate and Apportionment of the power conferred by Subdivision 6 of Section 26, all officers and employees subordinate to any Borough President shall be appointed and may be removed by such Borough President at pleasure but subject to and consistently with the Civil Service Law whenever applicable, and (b) that officers and heads of departments and members of boards or commissions concerning whose terms of office or removal express provisions are contained in this Act may be removed only in the manner and upon the conditions expressly provided herein with respect thereto; to fill all vacancies in offices which he is empowered to fill by appointment in the first instance.

2. **Supervision of city government.** To observe the operations of all of the officers and departments of the City government, and of the boroughs and counties within the City, and to supervise generally the operations of all offices, departments, boards and commissions the heads whereof he is empowered by this Act to appoint or remove.

3. **Enforcement of law and ordinances.** To be vigilant in causing the ordinances of the City and the laws of the State to be executed and to be enforced within the City.

4. **Call of special meetings of boards.** At his pleasure to convene special meetings of the Board of Aldermen and of the Board of Estimate and Apportionment and to determine the character and length of notice required therefor. He shall call a special meeting of the Board of Aldermen upon written request of ten Aldermen and he shall call a special meeting of the Board of Estimate and Apportionment upon written request of members thereof authorized to cast six votes in said Board.

5. **Making recommendations to boards.** To recommend to the Board of Aldermen and, with respect to matters as to which the Board of Aldermen and the Board of Estimate and Apportionment are required to act conjointly, to the Board of

Estimate and Apportionment, all such measures as he shall deem expedient.

6. **Annual statement to board of aldermen.** To communicate to the Board of Aldermen at least once in each year a general statement of the condition of the government and finances and the public works, improvements and property of the City.

Mayor a Magistrate

SECTION 39. The Mayor is a magistrate and at his pleasure may exercise within the City all of the powers conferred upon magistrates by law.

ARTICLE VII

The Comptroller

Financial Officer

SECTION 40. The Comptroller shall be the chief financial officer of the City.

Control of City Money

SECTION 41. Consistently with the other provisions of this Act, the Comptroller shall prescribe the manner and form in which all revenues and other moneys of the City or of the counties therein shall be collected, deposited, evidenced, transmitted, disbursed and accounted for, and shall designate the banks and trust companies in which moneys of the City may be deposited and the limits of the deposits to be made in the same severally, and may make the payment of a specified rate or specified rates of interest upon deposits by depositaries a condition of the designation of such depositaries respectively.

Prescribing Accounting Methods

SECTION 42. The Comptroller shall prescribe the form and methods of accounting to be used by all offices, boards, departments, commissions, by the executive staffs of revenue-producing improvements and by corporations maintained wholly or in part by appropriations made by the City, and, for such purpose, may conduct such inquiries and require such information as he may deem necessary..

Accounts, Operations of Revenue-producing Improvements

SECTION 43. 1. **Audit of accounts.** The Comptroller shall cause each and all of the receipts, disbursements, financial transactions and accounts of every officer, board, department, bureau and commission of the City, or of any of the counties therein, of every corporation maintained in whole or in part by means of appropriations made by the City, and of every other person or body who shall hold, receive, disburse or be responsible for any of the revenues or moneys of the City or any of its financial transactions, to be regularly examined and audited.

2. **Publication of result of operation of revenue-producing improvements.** At least once in each calendar year prior to the first day of July the Comptroller shall cause to be prepared and published in the *City Record* a statement setting forth the true results of the operation during the preceding calendar year of each revenue-producing improvement operated by or under contract with the City, including an income account of the character which in accordance with approved accounting methods would be prepared by private corporations operating properties of like character, and a statement of the true financial condition of such improvement, which shall in every case accurately exhibit the cost of the improvement or properly attributable thereto and of the indebtedness of the City contracted for the purpose of financing the same or properly attributable thereto and which shall include a general balance-sheet, together with a proper profit and loss account, and shall set forth in detail all items of expense, if any, which are carried in any suspense account or otherwise held in suspense or abeyance for distribution over subsequent years or for any other purpose. Each such statement shall be prepared in such manner that a person without knowledge of technical accounting may ascertain therefrom the true condition of such improvement and the actual results of the operation thereof by the City. The provisions of this Section shall apply with respect to all revenue-producing improvements now operated or carried on by the City as well as to all such as hereafter may be established.

Payment of Public Money

SECTION 44. No payment or disbursement of public moneys shall be made except upon a warrant drawn and signed by or for the Comptroller and countersigned by or for the Mayor; and no warrant for any disbursement or payment by the City for any city, county or other purpose shall ever be signed except for a purpose and in an amount theretofore duly authorized, nor unless the Comptroller or an auditor of accounts shall have certified that the charges therefor are just and reasonable or have been duly fixed by judicial proceedings to which the City or the Comptroller was a party or by public letting or that the same have been settled and adjusted by the Comptroller.

Audit of Contracts

SECTION 45. All contracts with the City or any public officer acting in behalf thereof, or for any of the counties therein, or with any board, commission or corporation maintained wholly from appropriations made by the City shall be subject to audit by and the approval of the Comptroller.

Certificate of Sufficient Unexpended Balance Necessary for Contracts Unless Payable by Assessment on Property

SECTION 46. No contract, the expense of the execution whereof is not to be paid by assessments on property benefited, shall be of any force unless the Comptroller shall endorse thereon his certificate that there remains unexpended and unapplied a balance of the appropriation or fund applicable thereto sufficient to pay the estimated expense of executing such contract, as certified by the officer making the same; provided, however, that in the case of any contract for the purchase of materials or supplies not to be delivered in their entirety within the current year, it shall be sufficient compliance herewith if the Comptroller shall endorse thereon his certificate that there remains unexpended and unapplied a balance of the appropriation or fund applicable thereto sufficient to pay the estimated expense of executing such contract during the then current year and from time to time thereafter a certificate as to the portion of such contract then unexecuted and any such contract shall be of force to the extent that the execution thereof shall be covered by such certificate.

Adjustment of Claims

SECTION 47. The Comptroller shall adjust all claims in favor of and against the City or any of the counties therein or any officer, board, department, commission or corporation maintained wholly by appropriations made by the City.

Examination of Claimants

SECTION 48. The Comptroller may require any person presenting a claim or demand for any cause whatever to submit to examination under oath, and may by subpoena require the attendance of witnesses, and the production of books, papers and records, and wilful false swearing in any such inquiry shall be perjury and shall be punishable as such.

Audit as to Amount of Claim in Suit; When Conclusive

SECTION 49. If in any action to recover upon any claim, the amount claimed by the plaintiff exceeds that audited and settled by the Comptroller, no testimony shall be admitted to show a promise or agreement by any officer or employee of the City or of any of the counties contained therein or by any board, commission or corporation maintained wholly from appropriations made by the City, unless empowered by or under authority of this Act to make such promise or agreement, to pay any larger sum than the amount so audited and allowed by the Comptroller.

Claim on Comptroller Before Action to Enforce Money Liability; One Year Limitation Upon Bringing Certain Actions

SECTION 50. No action or special proceeding to enforce any money liability shall be prosecuted or maintained against the City or any of the counties therein or any officer, board, department, commission or corporation maintained wholly from appropriations made by the City, unless it shall appear by and as an allegation in the complaint or necessary moving papers that at least thirty days have elapsed since the demand or claim upon which such action or special proceeding is founded was presented to the Comptroller for adjustment and that he has disallowed the same in whole or in part or has neglected or refused to make an adjustment or direct payment thereof; and, in the case of claims against the City or any of the counties therein or any officer, board, commission or corporation maintained wholly from appropriations made by the City, accruing after the passage of this Act, for damages for injuries to personal property or for the destruction thereof, no action thereon shall be maintained, unless commenced within one year after the cause of action therefor shall have accrued nor unless notice of intention to commence such action and of the time when and placè where the damages were incurred or sustained, together with a verified statement showing in detail the property alleged to have been damaged or destroyed and the value thereof, shall have been filed with the Comptroller within six months after such cause of action shall have accrued.

Custody of Securities

SECTION 51. The Comptroller shall be the custodian of all securities, bonds, agreements of indemnity or assurance, contracts for the payment of money and other evidences of indebtedness belonging to the City or any county therein and of all agreements containing or evidencing obligations to any of the same and of duplicate originals and copies of all agreements and other evidence of obligations of the City or any of said counties.

Consent to Purchase of Real Estate

SECTION 52. The assent of the Comptroller shall be necessary to all agreements hereafter entered into for the acquisition by purchase of any real estate or interest therein when such an agreement involves an obligation to pay or an expenditure of any money of, or appropriated or to be raised by, the City.

Approval of Confession of Judgment Against City

SECTION 53. No offer, consent to, or confession of judgment or final order or decree in favor of or against the City or any officer, board, commission or corporation maintained wholly by appropriations made by the City shall be of any force or effect, except as provided in Section 71, unless previously approved in writing by the Comptroller.

Form, Time of Payment and Sale of Obligations of City

SECTION 54. The Comptroller shall prescribe the forms of all corporate stock, bonds, bills, notes and other like obligations, if any, of the City. He shall fix the times at which the same shall be payable severally and shall sign the same. He shall be charged with the duty of selling such obligations as the City shall issue and, except corporate stock, serial bonds, general fund bonds or assessment bonds which may be purchased for investment by the Board of Estimate and Apportionment for any sinking fund or by the Board of Pension Fund Trustees, all such stock and bonds shall be sold by him to the highest bidder or bidders after advertisement for not less than ten days inviting proposals therefor. The Comptroller may reject any or all bids and may thereupon advertise for new proposals for any stock or bonds not sold, or may, after the rejection of any such bid, sell the whole or any part thereof at private sale for any price in excess of the price bid therefor in any proposal so rejected, but no sale of any corporate stock or bonds shall be made for less than par value and accrued interest.

Short Term Obligations

SECTION 55. The Comptroller may issue on behalf of the City and sell from time to time short term obligations of the City to be known as "revenue bonds," "revenue bills," "special revenue bonds," (particular issues whereof may be denominated "tax notes"), and "corporate stock notes," in such form as may be prescribed by the Comptroller as follows:

1. **In anticipation of taxes.** Revenue bonds and revenue bills in anticipation of the collection of taxes for the then current year, but the aggregate amount of which issued in any such year at any time hereafter outstanding shall not exceed the amount of the unpaid taxes provided for or to be provided for in the tax levy for such year, nor such an amount as may be necessary to meet expenditures, as they are

required to be made under appropriations for the then current year, which bonds and bills shall be redeemed out of the proceeds of taxes in anticipation of the collection of which they are issued.

2. **Special revenue bonds.** Special revenue bonds (a) to meet expenditures duly authorized by the Board of Aldermen and the Board of Estimate and Apportionment acting conjointly, other than those provided for in the budget for the current year, and (b) to pay judgments, awards, and other liquidated liabilities of the City or of any of the counties therein, which shall be presently payable, made or established pursuant to law and not provided for in appropriations for the current year, all of which special revenue bonds shall be provided for in and redeemed out of the tax levy for the year next succeeding the year of their issue.

3. **Corporate stock notes.** Corporate stock notes to provide for expenditures for public improvements to be financed out of the proceeds of corporate stock or serial bonds, the issue whereof shall have been authorized by the Board of Estimate and Apportionment or by the Board of Aldermen and the Board of Estimate and Apportionment, acting conjointly, as in such case may be required, which notes shall mature in one year or less, and upon maturity may be renewed until redeemed but shall be redeemed out of the proceeds of the sale of the corporate stock or serial bonds in anticipation of the sale of which the notes shall have been issued.

Report to Board of Aldermen

SECTION 56. The Comptroller shall report to the Board of Aldermen within two months after the close of each calendar year upon the receipts and expenditures of public moneys during the preceding year, the different sources of receipts and the purposes of disbursements, the money borrowed on the credit of the City and the payments made on account of the City's obligations and generally upon the condition of the finances of the City.

Appointment of Deputies

SECTION 57. The Comptroller may appoint, and at pleasure remove, as many deputies and assistant deputies as may be authorized in the Annual Budget, and may authorize any or all of them to exercise such powers and perform such duties of the Comptroller as he may specify in written designations to be filed in the office of the Comptroller, the Mayor and the Chamberlain.

ARTICLE VIII

President of the Board of Aldermen

Presiding Officer of Board

SECTION 58. The President of the Board of Aldermen shall be the presiding officer of the Board of Aldermen.

Acting Mayor

SECTION 59. Whenever there shall be a vacancy in the office of Mayor, or whenever by reason of disability or absence from the city the Mayor shall be prevented from attending to the duties of his office, the President of the Board of Aldermen shall act as Mayor and possess all of the powers and rights of the Mayor during such vacancy, disability or absence, except that the power of appointment to or removal from office shall not be exercised by him during the disability or absence of the Mayor, unless such disability or absence shall have continued for thirty days, nor the power of veto unless such disability or absence shall have continued for nine days.

ARTICLE IX

Borough Presidents

Office in Borough

SECTION 60. Each Borough President shall have an office in such public building of his borough as may be designated for such purpose by the Board of Estimate and Apportionment.

Appointment of Commissioner of Public Works; Powers of Commissioner

SECTION 61. He shall appoint and at pleasure may remove a Commissioner of Public Works of his borough who may exercise all of the powers of Borough President conferred by Section 62, and who shall in case of the disability or absence from the City of the Borough President discharge all of the duties of the Borough President, and who in case of a vacancy in the office of Borough President shall discharge all such duties until the election of a successor Borough President, as elsewhere in this Act provided.

Powers Within the Borough

SECTION 62. Subject to and pending the exercise by the Board of Estimate and Apportionment of the powers enumerated in Subdivision 6 of Section 26, each Borough President shall have cognizance and control within the borough for which he shall have been elected:

1. **Street work.** Of the work of grading, curbing, flagging, paving, repaving, resurfacing, repairing, guttering and otherwise constructing or altering streets and public roads, and the laying of sidewalks and cross walks and the relaying of all pavements removed or opened for any cause.

2. **Street clearing.** Of the removal of encumbrances from streets and roads of his borough.

3. **Street signs.** Of the placing of all signs indicating the names of streets and other public places.

4. **Surface railway tracks.** Of the laying and relaying of surface railway tracks in any public street or road, of the form of rail to be used, the character of the roadbed or substructure and the method of construction of such surface railway and the restoration of the pavement or surface.

5. **Permits affecting streets.** Of the issue of all permits for the temporary use or opening the surface of streets and for the construction of vaults under sidewalks.

6. **Bridges, viaducts and tunnels.** Of the construction and maintenance of all bridges, viaducts and tunnels within his borough which form portions of highways thereof, except such bridges, viaducts and tunnels as cross over or under navigable waters.

7. **Drainage and sewers.** Of the making of plans for the drainage of the borough, the construction of sewers, when duly authorized as in this Act provided, and the management, care and maintenance of the sewer and drainage system of the borough and the licensing of cisterns and cesspools.

8. **Public buildings.** Of the construction, repair, maintenance and cleaning of public buildings in his borough except school houses and fire station houses and such other buildings with respect whereto special provision shall be made by the Board of Estimate and Apportionment.

9. **Other establishments.** Of the location, establishment, erection, maintenance and care of public baths, day nurseries, comfort stations and other authorized establishments in his borough devoted exclusively to the comfort, entertainment or recreation of the public, except such thereof as may be otherwise provided for by the Board of Estimate and Apportionment.

10. **Fencing, filling, digging down lots.** Of the filling of sunken lots, the fencing of vacant lots and the digging down of lots.

ARTICLE X

Departments, Officers and Employees

Permanent Departments

SECTION 63. The following are established as administrative departments of the City, and shall not be abolished but shall be maintained as separate departments, subject only to the provisions of Subdivision 14 of Section 4:

Police Department;
Department of Pensions;
Department of Taxes;
Municipal Civil Service Commission.

Each of said departments except the Municipal Civil Service Commission and every other department and every office not subject to any department that may be established by or as permitted by this Act, whether of the City or any borough or county therein, shall have its own chief executive officer who shall be appointed and may be removed and, until he shall die, resign or be removed or his office shall become vacant otherwise, shall be charged with duties and possess powers and functions, if any, as in this Act provided and such powers and functions, consistent with the provisions of this Act, as the Board of Estimate and Apportionment may prescribe.

Chief Executive Officers

SECTION 64. The chief executive officers of the following departments shall be, respectively:

Of the Police Department, the Police Commissioner;
Of the Department of Pensions, the Commissioner of Pension Funds;
Of the Department of Taxes, the Commissioner of Taxes.

Permanent Offices

SECTION 65. The Mayor shall appoint and at pleasure may remove the following officers whose positions shall not be abolished:

The Corporation Counsel;
The Chamberlain;
The Commissioner of Inquiry.

Power of Appointment and Removal by Chief Executive Officers

SECTION 66. 1. **First deputy.** Each chief executive officer of a department shall appoint and at pleasure may remove at least one deputy or assistant (who if there be more than one shall be known as the "First" Deputy or Assistant), who during the absence from the City or the disability of such chief executive officer or of a vacancy in his office shall exercise his powers and functions until the Mayor shall appoint his successor or an acting successor, but in any case of vacancy the Mayor shall appoint a permanent chief executive officer within sixty days from the occurrence of such vacancy except as otherwise provided in this Act.

2. **Other deputies, assistants and employees.** Each chief executive officer shall have and, subject to the provisions of the Civil Service Law, may appoint, such deputies or assistants and employees as may be authorized by the Board of Aldermen and the Board of Estimate and Apportionment, acting conjointly, and, except as otherwise provided in this Act, may at his pleasure remove any or all of the same; provided that no person holding a position in the classified municipal civil service subject to competitive examination shall be removed except upon charges nor until he

has been given an opportunity to make defence thereto personally or in writing. The true grounds of removal of any such person in every case shall be entered forthwith upon the records of the department, office, board or commission of which he may be a subordinate and a copy of the charges and of his defense and of such record shall be filed with the Municipal Civil Service Commission with all possible expedition. Except as otherwise provided in this Act and in the Civil Service Law, no person so removed shall be entitled to a judicial review of the proceedings for his removal by mandamus, certiorari or in any form of action or proceeding.

Officers and Employees Other Than First Deputy Only Those Provided for in Budget

SECTION 67. Except as above provided with respect to first deputies or assistants, the number of officers (including deputies and assistants) and of employees of every office, board, department, bureau and commission shall always be such and such only as shall be provided for in the Budget for the current year.

Reports to Mayor

SECTION 68. Each of the Borough Presidents and the chief executive officer of each department and of each office which is not subordinate to a department including offices of counties within the City and the chief executive of every revenue-producing improvement operated by the City shall, once in each calendar half-year, in every case prior to the first day of March or the first day of September, as the case may be, and at such other times as the Mayor may direct, make to him a report which shall exhibit fully and clearly the results of all of the operations of such department, office, or improvement, which, immediately upon the receipt thereof by the Mayor, shall be published in the *City Record*. All such officers shall when required by the Mayor furnish to him such additional information as he may require and in such form as he may prescribe and within such reasonable time as he may direct.

Records to Be Public and Published in City Record

SECTION 69. In every office, board, department, bureau or commission, there shall be kept a record of all of its transactions, which shall be accessible to the public, and once a week a brief abstract, omitting formal language, shall be prepared of all transactions entered into and of all contracts of every description awarded or entered into for work or material, which abstracts shall set forth the names and residences, by streets and numbers, of the parties thereto and of their sureties, if any. A copy of such abstract in every case shall be transmitted forthwith to and published in the *City Record*. Notice of all appointments and removals from office, and of all changes of salaries, shall in like manner, within one week after they are made, respectively, be transmitted to and published in the *City Record*.

ARTICLE XI

The Corporation Counsel

Legal Adviser of City and Its Officials

SECTION 70. The Mayor shall appoint and at pleasure may remove a Corporation Counsel who shall be the attorney, counsel and legal adviser of the City, the Board of Aldermen, the Board of Estimate and Apportionment, and every officer, board, department, bureau, commission and agency of the City and of each of the boroughs and counties therein, except the office of sheriff or of district attorney; and no officer, board, department, commission, or employee of the City, or of any borough or county therein, except the Corporation Counsel, shall employ any attorney or counsel, except at his own expense and for the prosecution or defense of his individual claims or rights, in any action or special proceeding, or in connection with any legal matter with which the City or any such county is concerned, or in which it is a party in interest. The Corporation Counsel, when authorized, so to do by the Board of Estimate and Apportionment, may, and, if directed by said Board, shall, employ special counsel to assist him in, or, if the Board of Estimate and Apportionment shall so direct, to take exclusive control of, any action, proceeding or legal matter.

Trial of Cases, Compromises

SECTION 71. The Corporation Counsel, in his discretion, may institute, prosecute and defend actions and proceedings and appeals which involve the right of the City to property, revenues or money belonging to or claimed by it, or any action or proceeding the purpose of which is to enforce city ordinances or laws of the State in the enforcement of which the City has a direct or special interest, and shall so do with respect to such actions, proceedings and appeals as the Board of Estimate and Apportionment may direct. In the preparation and trial of any action or proceeding, or upon any appeal under his charge, he shall have and may exercise the authority and discretion ordinarily exercised by attorneys or counsel in such cases; provided, however, that he shall not compromise or settle any action or proceeding, nor confess or suffer or accept any confession of judgment against or in favor of the City, without the approval of the Comptroller, except in the case of actions for penalties where the penalty sued for does not exceed two hundred and fifty dollars.

ARTICLE XII

The Chamberlain

Treasurer of City and Its Officials; Receiver and Custodian of City Money; Payment of Warrants

SECTION 72. The Chamberlain shall be the treasurer of the City and of each of the counties therein and of every office, board, commission and corporation, exercising under authority of law any public powers or functions in territory coincident with the City or any territorial subdivision or subdivisions thereof and entitled by law to receive or disburse public revenues or moneys of the same. All taxes and other revenues and moneys, which the City shall be entitled to collect or receive shall be paid to the Chamberlain and every officer or employee of the City or any county therein receiving any moneys belonging to the City or any fees or emoluments under sanction of any law shall forthwith pay the same to the Chamberlain and account therefor to the Chamberlain and to the Comptroller. The Chamberlain at all times shall be custodian of all moneys belonging to the City, but, except as he may be permitted to retain the same in his own custody by order of the Board of Estimate and Apportionment, shall deposit them in such banks and trust companies as may be designated by the Comptroller. He

shall pay all warrants drawn upon the City Treasury as provided in Section 44. He shall observe all such requirements and directions of the Comptroller as may be made or given as authorized by said Article VII.

Bureaus Established by Chamberlain

SECTION 73. Subject to the exercise of the power conferred upon the Board of Estimate and Apportionment by Subdivision 6 of Section 26, the Chamberlain shall establish and maintain the following bureaus, each of which shall have its own chief executive officer, and shall maintain an office in each of the boroughs of the City:

1. **Taxes.** The Bureau of Taxes, which shall be charged with the collection of all taxes payable into the City Treasury, other than arrears of taxes, the chief executive officer whereof shall be and be called the "Receiver of Taxes";

2. **Assessments and arrears.** The Bureau of Assessments and Arrears, which shall be charged with the collection of assessments for improvements and of arrears of taxes, assessments, and arrearages of water rents and of other ordinary city revenue, the chief executive officer whereof shall be called the "Collector of Assessments and Arrears";

3. **City revenue.** The Bureau of City Revenue, which shall be charged with the collection of the interest, rents and other payments for the use of property, revenues derived from the sale of City property and from public markets, water rents, periodical payments, which the City is entitled to receive under contract, and all other revenues periodically payable to the City, except such as are provided for in Subdivisions 2 and 4 of this Section, to which the City may be entitled, the chief executive officer whereof shall be called the "Collector of City Revenues";

4. **License collection.** **The Bureau of License Collections, which shall be charged with the duty of receiving and receipting for license fees and payments of every description payable to the City as a condition of the issuance of or under any license which may be granted by the City or by any officer, board,**

department or other authority thereof, the chief executive officer whereof shall be and be called the "Collector of License Fees."

Subject to the exercise of the power of the Board of Estimate and Apportionment in that regard, the Chamberlain is empowered to define the powers and functions to be exercised by said bureaus, respectively.

ARTICLE XIII

The Commissioner of Inquiry

Appointment of Deputies; Designation of Deputy as Acting Commissioner by Mayor

SECTION 74. The Commissioner of Inquiry shall appoint and may remove at pleasure two persons who shall be deputy commissioners of inquiry, who shall perform such duties as the Commissioner shall direct. When so designated by the Commissioner, any such deputy may preside at any investigation authorized by this Article. Such designation may be general in terms but shall be in writing and filed in the office of the Commissioner of Inquiry, and may be revoked at any time by the written order of the Commissioner filed in his office. Any such deputy commissioner, in the event of sickness, disability or absence from the City of the Commissioner, or in case there be a vacancy in the office of the Commissioner, may be designated by the Mayor with full power and authority to act in place of such Commissioner. Such designation may be general in terms but shall be in writing and filed in the office of the Mayor and of the Commissioner of Inquiry, and may be revoked at any time by the written order of the Mayor filed in said offices.

Examinations to be Made by Commissioner; Reports

SECTION 75. 1. **Financial condition of city every three months.** It shall be the duty of the Commissioner of Inquiry, once in three months, to make an examination of the offices of the Comptroller and Chamberlain and, to the extent necessary in connection with such examination, of the offices of officers and departments making returns thereto, and to report to the Mayor a detailed and classified statement of the financial condition of the City as shown by such examinations.

2. **Operation and organization of all parts of administration and revenue-producing improvements.** He shall also make periodical examinations, of the organization, accounts, financial or other transactions, methods of operation and conduct, of all and every of the officers, boards, departments, bureaus and commissions of the City and of the boroughs and counties therein and of every revenue-producing improvement which the City may have been engaged in operating during the period for which such examination shall be made. He shall also make such special examinations as the Mayor may deem advisable in the interest of the City and direct by written order.

3. **Reports to mayor and board of aldermen.** He shall report to the Mayor and to the Board of Aldermen the result of every examination made by him and shall report with respect to every such office, board, department, bureau, commission and improvement his conclusions as to the wisdom and efficiency of its operations and methods and his recommendations, if any, looking to greater economy and efficiency in the conduct of the public business.

4. **Limits of examination of certain officers.** He shall not have the power, nor shall the Mayor have power to direct him, to make examinations with respect to District Attorneys, Surrogates and judicial officers, except with respect to the receipt and disbursement of money and accountability for property.

5. **Power to compel testimony.** For the purpose of ascertaining facts in connection with any examination, the Commissioner or a deputy commissioner designated as aforesaid shall have full power to issue subpoenas to compel the attendance of witnesses, to administer oaths and to examine such persons as he may deem necessary. False swearing in the course of any such examination shall be perjury and punishable as such.

ARTICLE XIV

Police Department

Police Commissioner; Removal by Mayor or Governor

SECTION 76. The Police Commissioner shall be a citizen of the United States. He shall, unless sooner removed, hold office until his successor shall be appointed and shall have qualified. Whenever in the judgment of the Mayor or Governor the public interest shall so require, he may be removed from office by either, and shall be ineligible for reappointment thereto during the term of the Mayor then in office. Within ten days after any vacancy shall occur in the office of the Police Commissioner, the Mayor shall appoint a successor.

Power of Police Commissioner

SECTION 77. The Police Commissioner always shall have direct control of the administration of the Police Department, and of the organization, disposition, direction and discipline of the police force; he shall be chargeable with and responsible for the discipline and efficiency of the force; he shall have power:

1. **General.** (a) To appoint such deputy or assistant commissioners as may be authorized by or under authority of this Act; to remove any of such deputies or assistants at his pleasure; to define their duties; to delegate to them or any of them any of his powers except the power of making appointments, and to designate one of them to act, during the absence or disability of the Commissioner, as the Acting Commissioner; but an Acting Commissioner shall not have the power to make appointments.

(b) To assign one of the inspectors or captains (or person holding equivalent rank under some other title) to act as Chief Inspector, and at pleasure to revoke such assignment; to invest the Chief Inspector with power to exercise actual command of the entire police force, and to delegate to him any of the powers of the Commissioner except the power of making appointments.

(c) To assign from the captains (or persons holding equivalent rank under some other title) such number as may be authorized by the Board of Aldermen and the Board of Estimate and Apportionment, acting conjointly, to act as inspectors, and at his pleasure to revoke each such assignment.

(d) To detail as many members of the police force as may be determined by him to be necessary to serve as detectives in such bureau or bureaus as he may establish, or maintain, and to revoke each such detail.

(e) To make, revoke and change other assignments and details to duty, but, except as authorized by this Act or expressly required by law or by ordinance, no assignment or detail to any duty whatsoever shall be made or continued except in the proper interest of the police service; to grant and revoke leaves of absence.

(f) To distribute the powers and functions of the Department among his subordinates; to make, alter and enforce rules and orders for the conduct and discipline of the police force and the management of the Department; to limit and define the duties of the members of the police force and by rule or order to regulate the exercise of any of the powers vested in him or in any of his subordinates.

2. **Subject to powers of boards of estimate and apportionment and aldermen.** Subject to the exercise by the Board of Aldermen, the Board of Estimate and Apportionment or by said two Boards acting conjointly, of the powers herein conferred upon them respectively, the Commissioner also shall have power:

(a) To appoint, remove and to suspend from pay or duty, or both, and to recommend for retirement members of the police force.

No person shall be appointed to or shall be a member of said force who shall not be a citizen of the United States or shall have been convicted of a felony, but persons of especial skill and experience who are not citizens of the United States may be appointed solely for duty as detectives. No person under twenty-six or over twenty-nine years of age shall hereafter be appointed a member of the police force; nor shall any permanent appointment be made unless the appointee shall have served a probationary period of at least three months in the police force under provisional appointment. No person shall continue to be a member of the force after attaining the age of sixty-five years. Any person of unsound mind may be removed from the force by the Commissioner or retired. No person who has been lawfully dismissed from the police force shall be reappointed to any position therein or in the Police Department.

(b) To establish ranks and grades in the police force, assign titles and designations thereto and to make promotions of and award honors to members of the force.

(c) To prescribe the uniforms, shields, insignia and weapons of the police force and the wearing, display and use thereof.

(d) To appoint and at pleasure remove special patrolmen for any purpose authorized by law or ordinance and to make rules regulating the performance of their duties. Nothing contained in this Act shall be deemed to prevent the establishment by ordinance of a separate park police force or such other special police force as may be created by ordinance to serve the peculiar requirements of some department of the City government.

(e) To establish, maintain and discontinue stationhouses, central stations and police headquarters, fix the boundaries of precincts, establish, maintain and abolish marine, mounted and automobile patrols and provide such stations, headquarters and patrols with equipment.

(f) To offer rewards out of any unexpended appropriation therefor for information leading to the detection, arrest or conviction of persons guilty of felonies and to pay such rewards to persons entitled thereto.

(g) To direct, control, restrict and regulate aerial traffic and movements over the City and pedestrian, animal and vehicular traffic of every kind in streets, parks and other public places and, subject to the exercise of the powers of the Board of Estimate and Apportionment, to make and publish regulations with respect thereto; to issue permits for street parades and processions and for the carrying of firearms in the City.

(h) To exercise supervision over, to inspect and to require reports from pawnbrokers, street-venders, dealers in and custodians of junk and all forms of second-hand articles and merchandise, intelligence offices, places of public amusement or exhibition and persons or places having or required by law or ordinance to have licenses or permits.

(i) To make such inquiries as may be necessary to the proper performance of his duties or the duties of the Police Department or force and for that purpose the Commissioner and any deputy or assistant commissioner or officer of the police force designated by him, by written delegation filed in the office of the Mayor and in his own office, shall have power to call and examine witnesses and to issue subpoenas which shall be attested in the name of the Commissioner. The Commissioner, each deputy or assistant commissioner, the chief-clerk of the Police Department, if any, and such other clerks and officials of the Department and members of the police force as may be authorized by ordinance shall have power to administer oaths and affirmations in matters pertaining to the duties of the Department or necessary in connection therewith.

Special Detail Not to Affect Promotions

SECTION 78. Any member of the force, while assigned or detailed pursuant to Subdivisions 1 (b), 1 (c), 1(d) or 1 (e) of Section 77, shall retain his rank or grade in the force and shall be eligible to promotion as if serving in the uniformed force, and the time during which he may serve on any such assignment or detail shall count for all purposes as if he had so served in his rank or grade in the uniformed force.

Duty of Inspector or Captain

SECTION 79. Each inspector or captain (or person holding equivalent rank under some other title) shall be chargeable with and responsible for the efficiency and discipline of the force under his command.

Duties of Members of Department

SECTION 80. The Commissioner, every deputy or assistant commissioner and all officers and members of the police force shall enforce all laws and ordinances with respect to felonies and misdemeanors, preserve the public peace and order, suppress riots, mobs and insurrections, disperse unlawful and dangerous assemblages and assemblages which obstruct the free use or passage of streets, parks and other public places, prevent crime, detect and arrest offenders, protect personal and property rights, suppress nuisances, mendicancy, begging and vice, co-operate with the Fire Department and the health authorities of the City in enforcing regulations with respect to fires and for safe-guarding the public health, protect, advise and assist immigrants, strangers and street-passengers, repress all disorderly conduct and practices, and generally perform, as the rules of the Department or the orders of the Commissioner may require or authorize, the duties of the Commissioner and such duties as may be prescribed by ordinance.

Powers of Members of Force

SECTION 81. Members of the police force may arrest without warrant any person who shall commit, or attempt or threaten to commit in the presence or within view of such member any breach of peace, any offense or act prohibited by law or ordinance or shall resist or obstruct the lawful enforcement of any law or ordinance or of any regulation or order made under authority thereof. They shall possess throughout the State all of the common-law and statutory powers of constables, except with respect to service of civil process, and any warrant for search or arrest issued by any magistrate within the State may be executed anywhere within the State by any member of the police force. No person other than a member of the police force shall serve any criminal process within the City under authority of this Act or of any authority conferred by the City.

Absence from Duty; Resignations

SECTION 82. No member of the police force shall be absent from duty, resign or withdraw from the force except by authority of the Commissioner and any attempt so to resign or withdraw shall be without effect.

Board of Aldermen to Specify Causes for Discipline; Trial; Court Review Limited

SECTION 83. The Board of Aldermen shall by ordinance specify the causes for which discipline and punishment of members of the police force may be imposed and provide regulations with respect to the preferring of charges, the places of trials and the official or officials before whom trials shall take place, and shall define the powers and duties of the Commissioner and his subordinates with respect to suspensions of members of the police force from pay or duty, or both, and the effect thereof, the making of rules regulating the investigation of offenses, the procedure at trials and the imposition of punishment and the degree of punishment to be imposed for particular offenses or classes of offenses and shall prescribe the proceedings, if any, that may be taken for the review by authorities of the City of orders imposing punishment. No proceedings shall be entertained by any court by writ of certiorari or otherwise to review any order or decision made pursuant to the provisions of any ordinance authorized hereby except only orders of dismissal from the force or orders suspending the pay of members of the force for more than thirty days.

Present Force and Rules Continued

SECTION 84. The police force as now constituted and the rules now governing the same, including rules with respect to all or any of the matters mentioned in Section 83, are continued subject to the provisions of this Act and of ordinances adopted under authority hereof and consistent herewith.

Exemption from Military or Jury Duty or Arrest

SECTION 85. No officer or employee of the Police Department and no member of the police force shall be liable to military or jury duty or, while on duty, to arrest on civil process or to subpoena in any civil action or proceeding.

ARTICLE XV

Department of Pensions

Definitions

SECTION 86. The word "Commissioner" wherever used in this Article signifies the Commissioner of Pension Funds. The word "Board" signifies the Board of Pension Fund Trustees. The term "Advisory Committee" or the word

"Committee" signifies the Pension Fund Advisory Committee. The word "participant" signifies a person who is a member or beneficiary of or who is actually entitled, by provision of any law, ordinance or contract or as the successor or representative of any other person to share, presently or upon the happening of some contingency or the making of some election or otherwise, in any of the benefits of any of the pension, retirement, relief or life insurance systems or funds over which the Board of Pension Fund Trustees is conferred jurisdiction by this Article. The word "fund" signifies any such system or fund so subject to the jurisdiction of the Board. The word "Actuary" signifies the Actuary of Pension Funds.

Powers of Commissioner

SECTION 87. The Commissioner of Pension Funds shall be the chief executive officer of the Department of Pensions and as such, subject to the rules which may be adopted by the Board of Pension Fund Trustees, shall have direct control of the disposition, work and discipline of the employees of the Department. He shall supervise and direct the keeping of the accounts and the making of the computations and reports required to be made by law, ordinance, or the orders of the Board, in discharge of the duties of the Department. He shall have the custody of the property used by the Department and shall be charged with the care thereof. He shall be a member and Chairman of the Board, may call meetings thereof, of the Advisory Committee and of participants in any fund or funds, in the manner prescribed in the rules of the Board and as required by the provisions of this Article. Communications of and to the Board and decisions and orders of the Board shall be made through him.

Members of Board; Rules; Powers

SECTION 88. A Board of Pension Fund Trustees is hereby created to consist of seven members as follows, viz.: the Commissioner, the Mayor, the Comptroller, the Corporation Counsel, the Police Commissioner, the Fire Commissioner and the President or other chief officer of the Board of Education or such board or corporation as shall discharge the same or like functions. All of the members of the Board of Pension

Fund Trustees shall serve without compensation as such trustees.

The Board of Pension Fund Trustees shall be known by that name, shall adopt rules for its own procedure and government and shall prescribe the organization and the distribution of powers and duties among the officers and employees of the Department. Every action of the Board, other than such as shall concern its own organization and procedure, shall be taken by the affirmative vote of at least five members of the Board.

The Commissioner shall call the first meeting of the Board for some date not later than the fifteenth day of January, 1926.

Board to Manage Pension and Retirement Funds

SECTION 89. The Board of Pension Fund Trustees shall from and after January 1, 1926, be the trustees and managers of the Police Department Pension Fund, the Fire Department Relief Fund, the Fire Department Life Insurance Fund, the City of New York Employees Retirement Fund, the Teachers' Retirement System of the City of New York, the Board of Education Retirement System, the College of the City of New York Retirement Fund, the Hunter College Retirement System of the City of New York, the Department of Street Cleaning Relief and Pension Fund, the Health Department Pension Fund, the New York City Employees Retirement System, the Supreme Court, First Department, Retirement Fund, the Court of General Sessions, New York County, Retirement Fund, the County Court, Kings County, Retirement Fund, and of each and every other pension, retirement or relief or life-insurance fund or system existing or which hereafter may be established for the maintenance whereof the City is responsible in whole or in part or to which it is under obligation, actually or contingently, to contribute. All moneys, properties, bonds, securities, investments of any kind, revenues and incomes of any of said funds, in whosever hands the same may be, shall be paid or turned over to the Commissioner on or before January 2, 1926, to be held and disposed of as directed by the Board, except that all moneys, save such as by law are authorized to be held on deposit in any bank or trust-company to the credit of any fund, forthwith shall be paid over to the Chamberlain. Except as expressly provided otherwise in this Act, the Board from and after said date shall possess with respect to each such fund all and every of the powers, rights, estates and interests and shall be charged with the duties theretofore possessed by or imposed upon the trustee or trustees or upon the treasurer or other custodian of such fund, except that the power and duty of the Board of Estimate and Apportionment to include in the city Budget and of said board or the Board of Aldermen to make appropriations for the service of any such fund shall devolve upon the Board of Aldermen and the Board of Estimate and Apportionment, acting conjointly, as in this Act provided with respect to the Budget and appropriations generally.

Pension Funds to be Kept Separate Until Consolidated Fund Established

SECTION 90. Subject to the exercise of the power of the Board of Aldermen and the Board of Estimate and Apportionment, acting conjointly, to establish a consolidated pension and retirement system, each of said funds shall remain and be kept separate and distinct and the participants therein shall continue to have the same interests in and rights with respect to the benefits thereof as heretofore. Each such fund shall consist when turned over of the then existing capital and the accumulated income then belonging thereto and shall remain entitled to the same additions, deductions from pay and contributions and payments by the City to which the fund theretofore was entitled by law or ordinance and also to receive any forfeitures and penalties imposed upon or derived from members of the department or departments or other body or bodies for the benefit whereof the fund is established and to all gifts, as now provided by law; provided, however, that any contributions or payments which any such fund was entitled to receive or have paid into it out of particular revenues or receipts of the City or any county, borough or other subdivision shall no longer be paid specifically to or into the fund but the City shall retain the same and shall pay into such fund, out of its general revenues including the proceeds of taxes, such amounts as shall be the equivalent of the amounts so retained, and there shall be included in the Annual Budget for the service of each such fund not only the amounts which by existing law the City is under obligation to provide through the medium of tax levies, but also additional amounts equal to the amounts retained by the City as in this Section provided which otherwise would have been paid into or paid over to or for the use of such fund.

Power of Board

SECTION 91. The Board of Pension Fund Trustees shall have the exclusive power from and after January 1st, 1926:

1. **Make investments and manage funds.** Subject to the limitations and conditions then imposed by the laws governing the investment of said funds, respectively, to invest each and all of said funds, to hold, purchase, sell, assign, transfer or otherwise realize upon or deal with any of the securities or other property in which any such fund may be invested and to invest and reinvest the proceeds of any such investments and the income and other moneys belonging to such fund; and generally to manage each and all of said funds and to perform such functions as may be appropriate to the transaction of the business of any such fund.

2. **Appoint actuary.** To appoint an Actuary of Pension Funds, who shall be the principal technical adviser of the Board.

3. **Fix payments into funds.** Having regard to the advice of the Actuary, the Board shall (a) adopt for any fund for which the same may be required mortality, service and other tables, (b) certify the rates of deduction from compensation computed to be necessary for the service of any fund as to which rates of deduction are not fixed by law and (c) certify the contributions which the City shall be under obligation to make to any such fund.

Duty of Actuary

SECTION 92. The Actuary shall: (a) periodically, as required by the Board, and at least once in each five-year period elapsing after December 31, 1925, make an actuarial investigation into the mortality, service and compensation experience of all participants in each fund and a valuation of the assets and liabilities thereof and report to the Board with respect thereto; (b) perform such other duties as the Board shall prescribe; (c) and make an annual valuation of the assets and liabilities of each of the funds in each calendar year, as of such date in each year for each such fund as the Board shall direct or approve.

Publication of Statement of Funds

SECTION 93. Annually not later than June first, the Board shall publish in the *City Record* a statement certified by the Actuary of the valuation of the assets and liabilities of each of the funds in its charge for the preceding calendar year, which shall contain a list of the investments of such fund, a statement of the amount of money on hand in or to the credit of the fund, the amount, if any, which the City shall be under obligation presently to pay into such fund and the present value of the amount, which, as computed on the basis of the mortality and service tables adopted by the Board, will be required to meet all deficiencies of reserves or assets which will be occasioned by the satisfaction of the obligations of the fund arising or to arise from commitments already undertaken by the fund.

Board to Prepare Plan for Consolidated Pension Fund; to Protect Participants in Existing Funds

SECTION 94. It shall be the duty of the Board, with all practicable expedition, and in any event prior to July first, 1927, to prepare and report to the Board of Aldermen and to the Board of Estimate and Apportionment the text of a proposed joint resolution, which shall provide for a single pension and retirement system, to operate on a reserve basis in accordance with sound actuarial principles, to which from the date of the establishment of such system the City and all of the officers and employees of the City and of every county therein and of every office, board, commission or corporation maintained in whole or in part out of appropriations made by the City shall contribute through the medium of appropriations, equitable deductions from pay and other payments, if any, and in the benefits of which, to accrue from and after said date, all of such officers and employees who shall comply with the requirements of such system shall share. Such proposed joint resolution shall not deprive any participant in any existing fund of any part of the accrued value of any benefit therefrom to which such participant shall be entitled actually or contingently at the date of the establishment of such consolidated system nor, in case it shall provide for the merging of the funds heretofore established in such consolidated system, shall it deprive any such participant of any part of the then existing security for the payment of such accrued benefits unless fully equivalent and equally realizable security therefor shall be provided, but such proposed joint resolution may restrict the rights of all participants and of all officers and employees of the City and of any county therein and of every office, board, commission or corporation maintained in whole or in part out of appropriations made by the City, with respect to any pension, annuity, allowance, privilege or other benefit or any option with respect to any thereof which shall accrue after the consolidated system shall become operative, to such rights as shall be provided for in such proposed joint resolution and by the fund established thereby. Said proposed joint resolution shall not have any force or effect unless adopted by the Board of Aldermen and the Board of Estimate and Apportionment, conjointly, but, if and when the same shall be so adopted and shall come into force, it shall have the same force in all respects as an act of the Legislature in the same terms would possess. Any consolidated system the establishment of which hereafter may be provided for by the Board of Aldermen and the Board of Estimate and Apportionment, conjointly, shall be consistent with the foregoing provisions hereof with respect to such proposed joint resolution and shall provide for contributions from both the City and officers and employees made in such manner that all benefits to accrue during the active service of an officer or employee who becomes a participant, without credit for previous service, shall be liquidated by level or uniform payments to the fund or by payments computed to bear a constant ratio to the compensation of the officer or employee during his active service; and that all benefits accrued or to accrue on account of any participant, entitled to credit for service rendered prior to the establishment of the consolidated system, which are not covered by contributions already made therefor, shall be liquidated by level or uniform payments to the fund or by payments computed to bear a constant ratio to the compensation of all participants in active service; provided that such payments shall be calculated to liquidate such accrued liability within the period of thirty years immediately following the establishment of the consolidated system and to liquidate such liability thereafter to accrue, within a period of thirty years or within the period of active service for any participant who shall remain in service for a period in excess of thirty years. Pending the establishment by the Board of Aldermen and the Board of Estimate and Apportionment, conjointly, of a consolidated pension and retirement system no further pension or retirement fund or systems shall be established by the City or by any authority thereof, nor shall the scope of an existing system be extended or the benefits thereof increased.

Audit by Comptroller

SECTION 95. All of the accounts, other than actuarial computations, of the Board and of each fund, including all receipts and disbursements of the Department and of each fund shall be audited by the Comptroller.

Chamberlain Custodian of Funds

SECTION 96. The Chamberlain shall be the custodian of the several funds and shall deposit the moneys thereof in authorized City depositaries. He shall hold and disburse the same as directed by the Board and the same shall not be used for any purpose except such as shall be authorized by the Board. The City shall allow and pay over to each such fund all interest which it shall receive upon such deposits of its moneys.

Pension Fund Advisory Committee

SECTION 97. Prior to April 1, 1926, the Board shall adopt rules for the election not later than May 1, 1926, and every four years thereafter, by the participants in the existing funds of seven representatives upon and to be members of a Pension Fund Advisory Committee. The Board shall also adopt rules for the filling of vacancies in said Committee, the organization and procedure of said Committee and the calling of meetings of the participants in the various funds under the jurisdiction of the Board and shall cause the first elections of members of the Committee to be held not later than May 1, 1926, and the first meeting of the Committee to be convened not later than June 1, 1926. In the event of the establishment of a consolidated pension and retirement system as contemplated by Section 94, the joint resolution providing for the establishment thereof, shall provide for an Advisory Committee, elected by the participants in such consolidated system, which shall possess powers and functions with respect to such consolidated system substantially of the same nature as those in this Article provided to be possessed and exercised by the Advisory Committee.

Powers of Advisory Committee

SECTION 98. 1. **Designate member of committee to attend board meetings.** The Advisory Committee from time to time may designate one of its members who, until the designation of a successor by the Committee, shall have the right to be notified of and to attend all meetings of the Board and to participate in its proceedings, but not to vote. Such designation may be changed at the pleasure of the Committee.

2. **Examine books and records.** The Committee at all reasonable times, to be determined by the Commissioner in the exercise of a reasonable discretion, may, through any subcommittee or subcommittees of its members appointed by it, examine the records of meetings and investments, the accounts and actuarial computations and tables of the Board, either as a whole or with respect to a particular fund or funds, and report to the Board its recommendation of any corrections or changes which in the opinion of the Advisory Committee should be made in any thereof.

3. **Make independent audit.** It shall also have the right, if it so elect, but not more often than once in two years, to cause to be made by accountants or actuaries to be designated by it, but at such time or times as the Commissioner may determine in the exercise of a reason-

able discretion, an independent audit and examination of the accounts and investments and valuation of the assets and liabilities of any particular fund or funds and the Board of Estimate and Apportionment, in its discretion, may order the expense of any such audit and valuation to be paid out of any appropriation available or which it may make available for the expenses of the Department of Pensions and in such case, upon its request so to do, the Comptroller shall sell an amount of special revenue bonds sufficient to, and from the proceeds thereof shall, reimburse such appropriation. Whenever any such independent audit or valuation shall have been made a written report in triplicate of the result thereof shall be made with all practicable expedition and the Advisory Committee shall cause one original thereof forthwith to be filed with the Comptroller and another to be delivered to the Commissioner.

4. **Meeting of participants.** At the request of the Advisory Committee, made by resolution adopted by the affirmative vote of at least five of its members, the Commissioner shall call a meeting, in the manner provided by the rules of the Board, of all participants in any specified fund or funds in order that the Committee may make to such meeting any communication which it may deem advisable.

5. **Advice to board.** The Board may in its discretion request the Advisory Committee to consider and advise the Board with respect to any specified subject or subjects concerning which the Board may contemplate the possibility of action by it and in such case the Committee with all practicable expedition shall consider the same and report to the Board its conclusions with respect thereto.

Board to Have Sole Right to Retire Officers and Employees

SECTION 99. Nothwithstanding anything to the contrary contained in any law or in any ordinance or resolution of the City heretofore or which hereafter may be passed, no chief executive officer of any office, board, department, commission or other officer or authority save only the Board of Pension Fund Trustees shall have power to retire any officer or employee of the City or of any county therein or of any board, commission or corporation who upon or in consequence of retirement shall or may be entitled to any pension, annuity, retirement allowance or other benefit from any fund heretofore or hereafter established; provided, however, that the chief executive officer of any such office, board, department, commission or corporation or any member of the Board of Estimate and Apportionment may recommend to the Board the retirement of any such officer or employee and if under any law or valid ordinance applicable to the case, such officer or employee shall be entitled to be retired and shall have applied for retirement or such retirement is obligatory, the Board shall order such retirement and in any case in which under any law or any valid ordinance the retirement of any such officer or employee shall be discretionary with the Board or with any other officer, board, department, commission or other authority, the Board shall have power, in its discretion, to order such retirement.

ARTICLE XVI

Department of Taxes

Commissioner of Taxes; Duties

SECTION 100. 1. **Control of officers and employees.** The Commissioner of Taxes shall be the chief executive officer of the Department of Taxes and as such, consistently with the provisions of this Act, shall prescribe the duties of the First Assistant Commissioner and of the other assistant commissioners, if any, and control the organization, assignments to duty and discipline of the officers and employees of the Department and the operations thereof.

2. **Duties of deputies; records and maps.** Subject to the exercise of the powers of the Board of Aldermen conferred by Section 165, the Commissioner (a) may prescribe the duties of deputy tax-commissioners and the forms of records of assessed valuations and of assessment-rolls, of the tax-roll and the entries thereon, of the forms of advertisements required to be published in connection with the assessment and levy of taxes and all other details of procedure in the assessment and levy of taxes which are administrative or ministerial in their nature; (b) shall maintain, complete and continue block and other maps as provided, and which

shall be disposed of as prescribed by Chapter 491 of the Laws of 1916 of the State of New York, and the Commissioner shall have power to employ and appoint such engineers and assistants as may be required for the prompt performance of said work.

3. **Office in each borough.** The Commissioner shall maintain the principal office of the Department of Taxes in the Borough of Manhattan and an office of the Department in each of the other boroughs of the City.

Enter Upon Real Property and Examine Buildings; Compel Testimony

SECTION 101. The Commissioner or any assistant commissioner or deputy tax-commissioner or other representative of the Commissioner who shall be authorized in writing by him, shall have power to enter upon real property and into buildings and structures thereon at all reasonable times, in order to make such examination as is necessary to ascertain the value thereof or of the contents thereof for purposes of taxation; and the Commissioner, any assistant commissioner and any deputy tax-commissioner shall have power by subpoena to compel the attendance of witnesses upon any examinations in respect of the correction or cancellation of assessments and to administer oaths or affirmations for that purpose. False swearing under any such oath or affirmation in any such examination shall be perjury and punishable as such.

Commissioner to Appoint Deputies

SECTION 102. The Commissioner shall appoint eighty deputy tax-commissioners or such other number thereof as shall be authorized and provided for in the Annual Budget.

Commissioner to Appoint Boards for the Correction of Tax Assessments

SECTION 103. Prior to the first day of October in each year, commencing with the year 1926, the Commissioner shall appoint at least one board for the correction of tax assessments (hereinafter called "tax-board") for each borough and such additional number of tax-boards for any particular borough as he shall deem necessary for the prompt hearing and determination of applications for the correction of tax-assessments, as in this Article provided. Each such tax-board shall consist of three persons. The Commissioner may designate himself as a member of any one or more of such tax-boards, and the other members of each board shall be designated by him from among the assistant commissioners and deputy tax-commissioners. The Commissioner shall designate the chairman of each board. The Commissioner at his pleasure may change the membership of any such board. All appointments to membership in any board shall be in writing and filed with the records of the Department.

Duties of Department

SECTION 104. The Commissioner, any assistant commissioner, the deputy tax-commissioners and the employees of the Department of Taxes shall perform the duties and discharge the functions prescribed in Article XXII of this Act. The Commissioner may authorize and direct any assistant commissioner to discharge any of the functions and to exercise any of the powers of a deputy tax-commissioner and in such event such assistant commissioner shall be empowered so to do.

ARTICLE XVII

Municipal Civil Service Commission

Mayor to Appoint and Remove on Charges

SECTION 105. The Mayor shall appoint a Municipal Civil Service Commission as prescribed in the Civil Service Law. The Mayor may remove any Municipal Civil Service commissioner for incompetency, inefficiency, neglect of duty or violation of the provisions of this Act or of the Civil Service Law, or the rules and regulations in force thereunder, specifying in writing the particulars of the incompetency, inefficiency, neglect of duty or violation charged, first giving such commissioner an opportunity to make a personal explanation in self-defense. The Mayor shall within thirty days after the removal of any commissioner cause to be published in the *City Record* such charges and any answer thereto. The Mayor shall fill vacancies in the membership of the Commission promptly as they occur. Any person appointed to fill a vacancy shall hold office during the unexpired portion of the term of his predecessor.

Organization and Action of Commission

SECTION 106. The Commission shall elect its own chairman and appoint a Secretary, prescribe rules for its own procedure and may appoint such examiners as may be necessary to the discharge of the duties of the Commission prescribed by law and provisions shall be made in the Annual Budget of the City for the necessary expenses of the Commission occasioned by the discharge of duties prescribed by law or ordinance. The determinations and orders of the Commission, except as otherwise provided by law, shall be made by the affirmative votes of not less than two of its members and only at meetings of the Commission duly called and held or at which all of the members of the Commission are present and consent to act.

Power of Commission

SECTION 107. (a) The Commission shall be charged with the duty and shall have power, to be exercised in the manner and upon the conditions prescribed by the Civil Service Law of the State and in all respects subject to and consistently with the provisions thereof, to adopt, amend, repeal and enforce rules for the classification of offices, positions and employments in the public service of the City and for appointments and promotions therein and examinations therefor and for the registration and selection of laborers for employment therein and generally to cause the Civil Service Law and the valid rules and regulations thereunder to be observed and enforced; (b) notwithstanding anything whatsoever elsewhere contained in this Act, all appointments, and changes of status of persons in the public service of the City, except as otherwise provided in this Act, shall be made in the manner prescribed by the Civil Service Law; and (c) no officer of the City shall draw, sign or authorize the drawing, signing or issuing of any warrant for the payment of any salary or compensation to any person whose appointment or retention in the service of the City has not been and shall not be in accordance with the Civil Service Law and the valid rules and regulations in force thereunder.

ARTICLE XVIII

Board of Standards and Appeals and Board of Appeals

Organization of Board

SECTION 108. 1. **Members.** The Board of Standards and Appeals is hereby established. The word "Board" when used in this article refers to said board. It shall consist of the executive head of the Fire Department, the chief of the uniformed force of the Fire Department, the principal official in each borough charged with the duty of issuing building permits and six other members to be appointed by the Mayor who are hereinafter referred to as the appointed members. Of the appointed members first appointed by the Mayor, two shall be appointed for terms of one year, two for terms of two years and two for terms of three years, each such term to commence in the first instance on or as of the first day of January, 1926, and annually thereafter the Mayor shall appoint two members for terms of three years each.

2. **Qualifications of appointed members; compensation.** At all times there shall be among the appointed members of the Board persons, other than the Chairman, qualified as follows: one shall have had not less than ten years' experience as an architect; one shall have had not less than ten years' experience as a structural engineer; one shall have had not less than ten years' practical experience as a builder. The appointed members of the Board other than the Chairman shall receive such compensation for attendance at meetings of either board as may be fixed by joint resolution of the Board of Aldermen and the Board of Estimate and Apportionment.

3. **Chairman and secretary.** The Mayor shall designate one of the appointed members of the Board as Chairman and shall also appoint a Secretary of the Board. The Chairman of the Board shall be an architect or structural engineer of at least fifteen years' experience, shall be a salaried officer of the City, shall act as Chairman of the Board and of the Board of Appeals, hereinbelow provided for, and shall not be engaged in any other occupation or employment.

4. **Compel testimony.** The Chairman, or in his absence the Acting Chairman, may administer oaths and, by sub-

poena issued and attested by him, may compel the attendance of and examine witnesses. All meetings of either board shall be open to the public.

5. **Board of appeals.** The term "Board of Appeals" when used in this article refers to, and comprehends only, the appointed members of the Board of Standards and Appeals and the chief of the uniformed force of the Fire Department, when acting under the powers conferred by this Article.

6. **Official members.** Whenever in this Article reference is made to the Fire Department, the Fire Commissioner, the Chief of the uniformed force of the Fire Department, the Superintendent of Buildings, the Department of Labor of the State, the Industrial Commission or the Tenement House Commissioner, or any other board, body or official, such reference shall be deemed to be to, and to comprehend also, every board, department, bureau, commission, officer or other body or person hereafter discharging functions of substantially the same description as those herein referred to, heretofore discharged by the board, department, commission, officer or other body or official herein mentioned.

Powers of Board

SECTION 109. The Board shall:

1. **Test materials; make investigations.** Have power to test materials to be used in accordance with law and to make investigations concerning all matters relating to the enforcement and effect of the provisions of this Article, the building code, and the rules and regulations made by the Board.

2. **Rules and regulations generally.** Make, amend and repeal rules and regulations for carrying into effect the provisions of the laws and ordinances in respect of any subject or matter, jurisdiction whereof is conferred upon the Board by this Act, or conferred by any legislative enactment or ordinance upon a superintendent of buildings or upon the Fire Commissioner in relation to the prevention of fires, and to include in such rules and regulations provisions applying to specific conditions and prescribing means and methods

of practice to effectuate such provisions and for carrying into effect the powers of the Board. Such rules and regulations shall supersede any rules or regulations made by a president of a borough, a superintendent of buildings or the Fire Commissioner to the extent that they shall conflict with or cover the same subject matter as any of such last-mentioned rules or regulations.

3. **Rules and regulations in respect to certain buildings.** Make, amend and repeal rules and regulations regarding the enforcement of those provisions of the Labor Law and other laws which relate to the construction, alteration, structural changes in, plumbing and drainage of, elevators in, fire escapes on, adequacy and means of exit from and fire alarm systems for, buildings, except tenement houses, within the City.

All such rules and regulations made by the Board shall supersede any provisions of the industrial code and any rules or regulations of the Labor Department conflicting therewith or covering the same subject-matter.

4. **Certain powers over buildings.** Exercise, exclusively, with respect to buildings situated in the City of New York, the same powers as are conferred upon the Industrial Commission by Chapter 719 of the Laws of 1915.

Action on Rules or Regulations; Publication

Section 110. A least eight affirmative votes shall be necessary to the adoption, repeal or amendment by the Board of any rule or regulation. At least ten days' notice of intention to consider the adoption, amendment or repeal of any rule or regulation shall be given by publication in the *City Record,* and a public hearing shall be given before any action is taken thereon. The rules and regulations and amendments and changes thereof adopted by the Board shall take effect not less than twenty days after adoption and the publication thereof in the *City Record.*

Action of Board; Public Record; Publication in Bulletin

Section 111. Every rule, regulation, every amendment or repeal thereof, and every order, requirement, decision or determination of the Board and of the Board of Appeals shall immediately be filed in the office of the Board and shall be a public record. The Board shall print and publish monthly or oftener at its option, a bulletin in which it shall publish every rule, regulation, every amendment or repeal thereof made by the Board, and every order, requirement, decision and determination of the Board of Appeals, and the reasons therefor, if it be practicable so to do, and such other matters, including indices and digests, as the Board may deem it advisable to publish.

Inspection

SECTION 112. Each member of the Board and the Secretary shall have all of the powers to enter, inspect and examine buildings and structures, which shall be possessed by a superintendent of buildings or by the Fire Commissioner.

Existing Rules Continue in Force Until Changed

SECTION 113. All rules and regulations heretofore lawfully adopted by a president of a borough, a superintendent of buildings, the Fire Commissioner or by any other officer, department, board or bureau of the City or by the Labor Department of the State or the Industrial Commission thereof relating to any matter within the jurisdiction of the Board, shall continue in force until amended, repealed or superseded and shall be enforced as rules and regulations of the Board of Standards and Appeals.

Powers of Board of Appeals

SECTION 114. 1. **Appeals and reviews.** The Board of Appeals shall hear and decide appeals from and review any rule, regulation, amendment or repeal thereof, order, requirement, decision or determination of a superintendent of buildings or the Fire Commissioner made under the authority of any legislative enactment, including the Labor Law, or of any ordinance.

2. **Matters referred by Board of Estimate; buildings in streets.** They shall also hear and decide all matters referred to them or upon which they are required to pass under any resolution of the Board of Estimate and Apportionment adopted pursuant to the provisions of this Act, and applications for permits for buildings in streets laid out on the offi-

cial map or plan of the city. If land within a street shown on the official city map is not yielding a fair return to the owner, the Board of Appeals shall, on application of the owner, in a specific case, grant a permit for a building of a temporary character to be specified by it and calculated to yield a fair return, and such Board in the interests of the City or the public may impose reasonable requirements as a condition for granting such permit.

3. **Member disqualified on certain questions.** No member of the Board of Appeals shall pass upon any question in which he or any corporation in which he as a stockholder or security holder is interested.

Number of Votes Necessary for Reversal

SECTION 115. The concurring vote of five members of the Board of Appeals shall be necessary to reverse any lawful order, requirement, decision or determination of any administrative official, or to effect any variation from the general provisions of any ordinance.

Actions from Which Appeal May Be Taken; Who May Appeal

SECTION 116. An appeal may be taken to the Board of Appeals from any order, requirement, decision or determination made under the authority of a legislative enactment or any ordinance by any superintendent of buildings (except an order requiring an unsafe building, staging or structure to be made safe, and except an order punishing, removing or dismissing an employee, inspector or other subordinate), or by the Fire Commissioner in relation to the prevention of fires, and from any order, rule, regulation, amendment or repeal thereof made by any administrative official relating to the construction, alteration, structural changes in, equipment, occupancy or use of any building or structure, or vaults and sidewalks appurtenant thereto. Such appeal may be taken by any person aggrieved or by any officer, department, board or bureau of the City.

Time of Taking Appeal

SECTION 117. Such appeal shall be taken within such time as shall be prescribed by the Board of Appeals by general rule, by the filing with the officer from whom the appeal is taken and with the Board of Appeals of a notice of appeal, specifying the grounds thereof. The officer from whom the appeal is taken shall forthwith transmit to the Board all of the papers constituting the record upon which the action appealed from was taken.

Appeal to Act as Stay

SECTION 118. An appeal shall stay all proceedings in furtherance of the action appealed from, unless the officer from whom the appeal is taken certifies to the Board of Appeals, after the notice of appeal shall have been filed with him, that by reason of facts stated in the certificate, a stay would, in his opinion, cause imminent peril to life or property, in which case proceedings shall not be stayed otherwise than by a restraining order which may be granted by the Board of Appeals or by the Supreme Court, on application, after notice to the officer from whom the appeal is taken and on due cause shown.

Hearing; Action on Appeals

SECTION 119. The Board of Appeals shall fix a reasonable time for the hearing of the appeal and give due notice thereof to the parties, and decide the same with all practicable expedition. Upon the hearing, any party may appear in person or by agent or by attorney. The Board of Appeals may reverse or affirm, wholly or partly, or may modify the order, requirement, decision or determination appealed from and may make such order, requirement, decision or determination as in its opinion ought to be made in the premises and to that end shall have all the powers of the officer from whom the appeal is taken. Where there are practical difficulties or unnecessary hardship in the way of carrying out the strict letter of the law, the Board of Appeals shall have power in passing upon appeals, to vary or modify any rule or regulation or the provisions of any existing law or ordinance relating to the construction, use, structural changes in, equipment, alteration or removal of buildings or structures, or vaults and sidewalks appurtenant thereto, in such manner that the purpose of the law shall be observed, public safety secured and substantial justice done. The decision shall be in writing and shall be filed in the office of the Board and promptly published in the bulletin of the Board. Each decision shall so far as is practicable be in the form of a general statement or resolution which shall be applicable to cases similar to or falling within the principles announced in such decision. The Board of Appeals shall not vary or modify the Tenement House Law nor any rule, regulation or ruling of the Tenement House Commissioner.

Review on Motion of Member of Board of Appeals

SECTION 120. Any rule, regulation, amendment or repeal thereof and any order, requirement, decision or determination from which an appeal may be taken to the Board of Appeals under the provisions of this Article, may be reviewed by the Board of Appeals at its own instance, upon motion of any member thereof, but no such review of a decision upon an appeal shall prejudice the rights of any person who has in good faith acted thereon before it is reversed or modified. The provisions of this Article relating to appeals to the Board of Appeals shall be applicable to such review.

Petition to Supreme Court for Review

SECTION 121. Any person or persons, jointly or severally aggrieved by any order, determination or decision of the Board of Appeals made upon any such appeal, or upon any application made as provided in Section 114, or any officer, department, board or bureau of the City, or the Industrial Commission or the Labor Department of the State, may present to the Supreme Court a petition, duly verified, setting forth that such decision is illegal, in whole or in part, specifying the grounds of the illegality. Such petition must be presented to a Justice of the Supreme Court or at a special term of the Supreme Court within thirty days after the filing of the decision in the office of the Board of Appeals and its publication in the bulletin.

Certiorari; Restraining Order

SECTION 122. Upon the presentation of such petition, the Justice or Court may allow a writ of certiorari directed to the Board of Appeals to review such decision of the Board of Appeals and shall prescribe therein the time within which a return thereto must be made and served upon the relator's attorney, which shall not be less than ten days but may be extended by the Court or a Justice thereof. Such writ shall be returnable to a special term of the Supreme Court of the judicial district in which the property affected, or a substantial portion thereof, is situated. The allowance of the writ shall not stay proceedings upon the decision appealed from, but the Court may, on application, after notice to the Board of Appeals and on due cause shown, grant a restraining order.

Return of Copies of Papers Sufficient

SECTION 123. The Board of Appeals shall not be required to return the original papers acted upon by it, but it shall be sufficient to return certified or sworn copies thereof or of such portions thereof as may be called for by such writ. The return must concisely set forth such other facts as may be pertinent and material to show the grounds of the decision appealed from and must be verified.

Preference; Action of Court

SECTION 124. All issues in any such proceeding shall have preference in trial or hearing over all other civil actions and proceedings except election cases. If, upon the hearing, it shall appear to the Court that testimony is necessary for the proper disposition of the matter, it may take evidence or appoint a referee to take such evidence as it may direct and report the same to the Court with his findings of fact and conclusions of law, which shall constitute a part of the proceedings upon which the determination of the Court shall be made. The Court may reverse or affirm, wholly or partly, or may modify the decision brought up for review.

Costs

SECTION 125. Costs shall not be allowed against the Board, unless it shall appear to the Court that it acted with gross negligence or in bad faith or with malice in making the decision appealed from but in the discretion of the Court costs may be allowed against the City.

ARTICLE XIX

The Public School System

City a School District; Administered Separate from Concerns of City

SECTION 126. The City of New York is hereby declared to be a state school district and as such to constitute a political subdivision of the State for school purposes. The School District of the City of New York shall be administered and maintained separate and apart from the concerns of the City and if and whenever a city officer, board or other municipal authority is required or authorized by this Act or otherwise to perform any act with respect to the educational system or affairs of such school district, such officer, board or authority shall be deemed with respect to such matter to be an agency of the State for the purpose of public school administration.

Schools Administered by Board of Education

SECTION 127. The public school system of said School District, which, however, shall not be deemed to include the College of the City of New York or Hunter College of the City of New York, shall continue to be administered by the Board of Education (said term, wherever used in this Act, being deemed to include also such successor board or authority, if any, discharging substantially the same functions, as may be provided for hereafter by law). The Board of Education derives and shall continue to derive its existence and powers from, and has and shall continue to have its functions and duties defined by the Education Law and other acts of the Legislature, if any, affecting it and the public school system which is or shall be under its control.

School Appropriation in Control of Board of Education; Funds of Board Not City Money

SECTION 128. The expenditure of moneys appropriated as provided in this Act for the purposes of the public school system of said School District shall be unconditionally controlled by the Board of Education, except that moneys appropriated for new school sites and buildings and the equipment thereof, for new educational service or to meet emergencies or defray extraordinary items of expense shall be expended by it for the purposes and within the terms of the appropriations with respect thereto, but no appropriation for such new sites, buildings, equipment or service or to meet emergencies or extraordinary expense shall be conditioned upon any particular use of moneys appropriated for other purposes. The Chamberlain of the City shall be custodian of the funds of the Board of Education but payments thereof shall be made upon requisition of the Board of Education, upon warrants executed as in the case of warrants for the payment of city moneys. Moneys included in the tax-levy for educational service under control of the Board of Education, revenues, if any, of the Board of Education and contributions by the State to the funds of the Board of Education shall not be deemed or treated as city revenues or moneys.

City College and Hunter College

SECTION 129. The College of the City of New York and Hunter College of the City of New York are hereby continued as distinct bodies corporate with the powers, organization, functions, obligations and limitations respectively, prescribed or provided for in the laws in force relative to said Colleges, respectively, at the time when this Act shall come into force. The trustees and officers of each of said Colleges shall be appointed in the manner and for the terms and shall possess the powers and be subject to the duties in such laws provided; but no obligation shall rest upon the City to appropriate for the support of either of them any sum in excess of such amount as the Board of Aldermen and the Board of Estimate and Apportionment shall determine to include for the purpose in any Annual Budget.

ARTICLE XX

Interim Provisions for the Administrative Organization of City and County Governments

Board of Estimate and Apportionment to Provide for Initial Administration Under Act

SECTION 130. The Board of Estimate and Apportionment of the City of New York, as the same shall be constituted after the thirty-first day of December, 1923, hereafter in this Article called the "Present Board" is hereby authorized and directed to provide by resolution or resolutions, to be adopted as provided in this Article, prior to the first day of January, 1925, for the establishment on and after the first day of January, 1926, of such officers, boards, departments, bureaus and commissions of the City and of the several counties therein, other than officers, boards, departments, bureaus or commissions expressly provided for in this Act, as the Board of Estimate and Apportionment of the City is permitted by Subdivision 14 of Section 4 and Section 26 to establish on or after the first day of January, 1926, and as the present Board acting under authority of this Article may determine to establish. Consistently with the provisions of this Act, the present Board may define the powers and relations of all officers, boards, departments, bureaus and commissions of the City or any county therein, including among others the officers, boards, departments, bureaus, and commissions established by this Act, as and to the extent that the Board of Estimate and Apportionment is authorized by this Act to define the same on or after the first day of January, 1926, and may make such transfers of powers to take effect on the first day of January, 1926, from any officer, board, department, bureau or commission which the present Board may so determine to continue or establish as the Board of Estimate and Apportionment of the City is authorized by this Act to make and to the extent that it is authorized to make the same on or after the first day of January, 1926; and the present Board, acting under authority of this Article, may add to, otherwise, or discontinue any of the powers or functions of any officer or of any board, department, bureau or commission, to be exercised on and after the first day of January, 1926, in the same manner and to the same extent as the Board of Estimate and Apportionment of the City is authorized by this Act to do on or after the first day of January, 1926, and may make such other provision, to take effect on or after the first day of January, 1926, with respect to the administrative organization of the city and county governments and the supervision, transacting and reporting of the business and affairs of the City and the counties therein as the Board of Estimate and Apportionment of the City is authorized to make on or after the first day of January, 1926.

Schedule of Laws to be Repealed

SECTION 131. On or prior to the fifteenth day of January, 1925, the present Board shall transmit to the Legislature of the State of New York certified copies of all resolutions which it shall have adopted under authority of this Article and therewith a schedule of all laws and parts of laws which in its opinion should be repealed specifically to the end that the Charter and all laws affecting the City shall be simplified and the purpose of this Act to secure self-government to the City shall be accomplished.

Comptroller to Prescribe Rules

SECTION 132. The Comptroller of the City of New York after the thirtieth day of June, 1925, and prior to the first day of December, 1925, is likewise authorized and directed to prescribe such rules and regulations and to issue such instructions with respect to the form and method of accounting and all matters as to which the Comptroller by this Act is authorized to prescribe rules or regulations or to give instructions on or after the first day of January, 1926, as the Comptroller shall determine to be requisite for the administration of the government and affairs of the City and of the counties therein on and after the first day of January, 1926.

Effect of Action by Board of Estimate and Apportionment and Comptroller

SECTION 133. Subject always to the exercise, on or after the first day of January, 1926, of the powers of the Board of Estimate and Apportionment and of the Comptroller of the City, any and every action that may be taken prior to the first day of January, 1926, as authorized and directed by this Article, either by the present Board or by the Comptroller shall have the same force and effect on and after the first day of January, 1926, that the same action would have had if it had been taken by the Board of Estimate and Apportionment or the Comptroller of the City forthwith upon the taking effect of this Act on the first day of January, 1926;

provided, however, that such schedule of specific repeals shall not be effective unless or except to the extent that the same shall be enacted by the Legislature.

Establishment of Health Department

SECTION 134. Notwithstanding anything contained elsewhere in this Act, the present Board, in the performance of the duties above in this Article provided to be performed by it, shall provide for the establishment on, or the continued existence after, January 1, 1926, of, a single officer, board or department which shall possess substantially the powers which at the time this Act shall take effect shall be possessed by the Department of Health, the Board of Health and the Commissioner of Health with respect to (a) the protection and promotion of health, (b) the exclusion and removal from the City and the care and control of persons affected by contagious, pestilential or infectious diseases and the maintenance and management of hospitals for the treatment thereof, (c) measures that may be taken in times of imminent peril to guard against the introduction or spread of pestilence or epidemic, (d) the exclusion, removal, destruction and the regulation of the handling, storage and disposition of substances and the regulation or prohibition of businesses or occupations which may be deemed likely to introduce or spread disease, produce insanitary or unhealthful conditions or to be or become offensive, (e) the inspection and regulation of the sale, custody and use of drugs, poisons, medicines, foods and like substances, (f) the abatement, and the prosecution of actions and proceedings for the abatement, of nuisances which injuriously affect or are deemed calculated so to affect life or health, including the making of orders and regulations and the prosecution of actions and proceedings to compel the vacation, repair, alteration or destruction of buildings and other structures deemed to be injurious to health or to endanger life or to restrict or regulate the use thereof or of any part of any thereof, (g) the investigation of the causes of disease and death and of preventive remedies and measures and the dissemination and publication of such information and of vital statistics, (h) the registration of births, marriages and deaths, and as well, (i) the powers of the Department of Health, the Board of

Health and the Commissioner of Health with respect to the enforcement of regulations and orders as to any or all of the matters aforesaid and as to the making of reports and the giving of information germane thereto and with respect to the defence of actions and proceedings which involve the validity of the exercise of any such powers or the carrying into effect or the observance of any such orders or regulations; and no action by the present Board pursuant to authority conferred by this Act or otherwise shall be deemed effective to repeal or supersede any of the provisions of Titles 1 to 7, inclusive, of Chapter XIX of the Greater New York Charter or of any law with respect to any of the above-mentioned subjects or matters applicable generally throughout the State or specially to or within the City, except (1) that, subject to the foregoing provisions of this Section, any of the powers or functions vested in or required to be discharged by the Department of Health, the Board of Health or the Commissioner of Health, if the present Board shall so determine, may be continued in or transferred from said Department, Board or Commissioner and may be vested in one or more of the other officers, boards or departments of the City, and (2) that nothing contained in this Section shall be deemed to impair or limit any of the powers of the City conferred by this Act or any of the powers of the Board of Estimate and Apportionment set forth in Subdivision 6 of Section 26, provided that such powers be exercised after the first day of January, 1926.

Ten Votes of Board of Estimate Necessary

SECTION 135. Any action by the present Board as authorized by this Article shall be by not less than ten votes but shall not require the affirmative vote of the Mayor for its validity.

ARTICLE XXI

The Budget

Board of Estimate and Apportionment to Make Annual City and Educational Budgets

SECTION 136. The Board of Estimate and Apportionment shall annually, between the thirtieth day of September and the first day of November, make (a) a budget of the amounts estimated to be required for expenditure by the City during the next ensuing calendar year and the estimated revenues available therefor from each and every source whatsoever during such year other than taxes to be levied, which shall be known as the "City Budget," and, also, (b) a budget to be known as the "Educational Budget" of the amounts estimated to be required for expenditure by the Board of Education during such year and of the estimated revenues, if any, of, and of all State contributions to, funds subject to be expended by the Board of Education.

Transmission of Estimates of Expenditures and Receipts

SECTION 137. Each of the officers and heads of offices, boards, departments, bureaus and commissions of the City (including, among others, all officers who are members of the Board of Estimate and Apportionment) and of each of the counties therein, and of every corporation and institution maintained wholly or in part by appropriations made by the City, and also the Board of Education, shall annually, not later than the first day of September, transmit to the Commissioner of the Budget and shall lodge with the Comptroller a written estimate, in each case in duplicate, of the probable amount of expenditures and of receipts of revenue of or arising from the operations of its or his office, board, department, bureau, commission, corporation or institution for the ensuing calendar year, specifying in detail the objects and sources thereof.

Comptroller's Estimates

SECTION 138. On or prior to the fifteenth day of September, the Comptroller shall transmit to the Commissioner of the Budget, in duplicate, a printed statement which shall set forth in such detail as he shall deem practicable:

1. **Tax limit.** A computation of the amount which, in conformity with the provisions of the State Constitution and of this Act, the City shall then be empowered to raise by taxation for the ensuing year and such estimate, as he may be able to make, of the amount it will be empowered to raise as of the third day of March of the ensuing year, in each case, distinguishing between the amount which must

be comprised in the constitutional limitation of a percentage of the assessed valuation of real and personal estate and amounts which may be raised in excess thereof.

2. **Debt-incurring power within debt limit.** An estimate, as of the third day of March of the ensuing year, of the amount, if any, for which the City consistently with the provisions of the Constitution and of this Act, may incur further indebtedness, otherwise than by the issue of revenue and special revenue bonds and tax notes, which shall include a statement of the City's power in this respect as of the last date for which accurate or approximately accurate figures are available.

3. **Revenues.** An estimate of the revenues of the City for the ensuing year, from any and every source whatsoever and of every office, department, commission or other body and of every fund under its control or to a beneficial interest in which the City is entitled, other than revenue from taxes, including the estimated receipts of the General Fund for the Reduction of Taxation or such fund or account of like nature as shall be maintained and including also the estimated receipts of the several sinking funds. In his statement the Comptroller shall set forth in parallel columns (a) the items of accrued and estimated revenue of the current year and (b) the items of estimated revenue of the ensuing year.

4. **Expenditures.** An itemized computation of the known and estimated amounts which the City will be required to expend during the ensuing year for all and every of the purposes enumerated in Subdivisions 1, 2, 7 and 8 of Section 141 and of all other amounts which it will be required so to expend by reason of any law, contract, the judgment of any court or, in reasonable probability, under like compulsion. In such computation, allowance shall be made for any amounts of maturing indebtedness, the refunding of which the Comptroller may recommend, the items whereof shall be specified.

Preparation and Form of City Budget

SECTION 139. The Commissioner of the Budget, under the supervision of the Budget Committee, if there be any, of the Board of Estimate and Apportionment, shall prepare and, prior to the first day of October, shall report to the Board of Estimate and Apportionment a proposed City Budget, including, in such detail as the Board of Estimate and Apportionment shall have directed or otherwise as the Commissioner may deem practicable, the items of all proposed appropriations, including appropriations for The College of the City of New York and Hunter College of the City of New York but not including appropriations for educational service under the control of the Board of Education. The proposed Budget shall be printed and shall exhibit in parallel columns (a) the items and amounts appropriated by the Budget for the current year, (b) the departmental estimates for the ensuing year and (c) the items and amounts of the proposed appropriations for the ensuing year. The proposed Budget shall also exhibit in parallel columns: (a) all items of accrued and estimated revenues of the current year, to the control or benefit of which the City may be entitled, (b) the items of revenues as estimated by him for the ensuing year, and (c) the departmental estimates of revenues for the ensuing year. With such proposed Budget, the Commissioner of the Budget shall transmit one original of each of the departmental estimates and one original of the Comptroller's statement above provided for.

Preparation and Form of Educational Budget

SECTION 140. The Board of Education, annually and prior to the first day of October, shall prepare and propose to the Board of Estimate and Apportionment an Educational Budget, which shall be printed and shall exhibit in parallel columns (a) all items and amounts appropriated for educational service under the control of the Board of Education for the current year and (b) the items and amounts of proposed appropriations for the ensuing year, and also in parallel columns (a) the items and amounts of the accrued and estimated revenue, if any, and of all State funds subject to expenditure by the Board of Education for the current year and (b) the items and amounts of estimated revenue, if any, and an estimate of all State contributions to such funds for the ensuing year.

Provisions in City Budget

SECTION 141. The City Budget shall make provision for:

1. **City debt.** The interest upon the City debt to accrue during the next ensuing calendar year, and (a) such amounts of the principal of the funded debt of the City as are to fall due during said year and may not be refunded consistently with the provisions of this Act, provided that available provision for the payment of any such debt does not exist in the sinking fund, if any, out of which the same is payable; (b) all amounts which by law or contract are required during the ensuing year to be raised or collected for or paid into sinking funds which the City is under obligation to maintain; provided, however, that no revenues or moneys of the City which have been derived from taxes shall be appropriated, by means of the Budget or otherwise, for the amortization of the City's debt through any sinking fund or for the payment of interest upon obligations of the City held in any sinking fund, in excess of such amount, to be computed by the Comptroller as may be necessary, in addition to special revenues received by or available for the use of such sinking fund, (1) to maintain the reserves required for the complete amortization by maturity of each issue of corporate stock or bonds the payment whereof is secured by such sinking fund and (2) to pay the interest upon obligations of the City comprised in such necessary reserves; (c) all revenue bonds, if any, issued during the current calendar year which, as estimated by the Comptroller, the taxes collected and collectable prior to the end of such year will not suffice to redeem; (d) all special revenue bonds and tax notes issued during the current calendar year; (e) all revenue bonds, special revenue bonds and tax notes, issued during any preceding calendar year and subsequently to the taking effect of this Act, which shall not have been redeemed out of appropriations theretofore made therefor; and (f) such further amounts, if any, of the principal of the City debt as the City shall have the right and the Board of Estimate and Apportionment may determine to pay during the ensuing year.

2. **State taxes.** The quota of state taxes chargeable upon the City and the counties therein.

3. **Compensation of officers and employees.** The compensation of all officers and employees of the City; the compensation (including supplementary compensation) of officers and employees of counties within the City, justices of the Supreme Court, county judges, surrogates, judges of General Sessions and of the City Court, justices of Special Sessions and of Municipal Courts, magistrates and boards and commissions, if any, the compensation whereof is required to be paid by the City.

4. **Administration and maintenance.** The cost of the administration, maintenance and equipment of all the offices, boards, departments, bureaus and commissions of the City and of the counties therein, including, among other things, deficits arising in the operation of revenue-producing improvements and the rent of buildings or offices not owned by the City, and the expenses of or instant to the administration of justice in and of maintaining the courts here within the City, the libraries thereof and the offices of the justices and judges thereof, distinguishing between City expenses and expenses chargeable to said counties or any thereof.

5. **Elections.** The expenses of or incident to elections to be held in the City during the ensuing year, including among other things the registration of voters.

6. **Registry of voters.** The cost of preparing and publishing the registry of voters and the records of assessed valuation of real estate and personal property and of all advertising required by law or ordinance and the cost of publishing the *City Record.*

7. **Unpaid assessments.** All unpaid assessments for benefits to property of the City confirmed during the preceding calendar year.

8. **Uncollected taxes and assessments.** The amount of all taxes and assessments for public or local improvements levied or made prior to the then current calendar year and subsequently to the taking effect of this Act which shall be deemed by the Board to be uncollectable, so far as the same shall not have been provided for in prior tax levies. All taxes and assessments which shall have been in default for more than four years after the same shall be due and payable shall be for the purposes of this provision be deemed uncollectable.

9. **Judgments payable.** All amounts which pursuant to the judgment of any court or other tribunal of competent jurisdiction shall be presently payable.

10. **Other purposes; contingent fund for emergencies.** Other appropriations which the Board shall determine to make for City or county purposes, which may include an appropriation of not exceeding two million dollars, to be subject to subsequent allotment by the Board of Estimate and Apportionment, for the purpose of providing for emergencies for which provision is not made otherwise in the Budget or for purposes not foreseen at the time of the adoption of the Budget.

Provisions in Educational Budget

SECTION 142. The Educational Budget shall make provision for:

1. **Operation and maintenance of schools.** Such amounts as, having been included in the Educational Budget submitted to the Board by the Board of Education, shall be required for the proper and adequate operation and maintenance during the ensuing year of the public schools and other educational activities which at the time shall be lawfully operated and maintained by the Board of Education.

2. **Sites and buildings.** The acquisition of sites for and the construction and equipment of such new school buildings as, upon recommendation of the Board of Education, the Board shall deem requisite to supply the needs of the School District of the City of New York, other than such as shall be provided for by issues of bonds made or to be made as authorized in this Act.

3. **New educational service; emergencies.** Such additional amounts, included in such Educational Budget submitted by the Board of Education as the Board, in its discretion, may determine to appropriate for new educational service in said school district or to meet emergencies or defray extraordinary expenses thereof.

Procedure on Budget

SECTION 143. The City Budget and the Educational Budget shall at all times be kept separate and distinct and shall be separately adopted. The procedure with respect to each thereof shall be as follows and wherever in this Section, or in Section 144 or in Section 145, the word "Budget" occurs, it shall be deemed to refer to each of said budgets, but severally and not collectively:

1. **Completion after hearings; transmittal to Board of Aldermen.** After the Budget shall have been received by it, the Board of Estimate and Apportionment shall fix a time or times for hearing any residents or tax-payers of the City who may desire to be heard in regard thereto, and shall give notice of the date or dates so fixed by advertisement in the *City Record* and the Board shall afford to residents and tax-payers an opportunity to be heard. Thereafter the Budget shall be completed by the Board of Estimate and Apportionment. Not later than October 30th, the Budget shall be transmitted to the Board of Aldermen, together with one set of the departmental estimates provided for in Section 137 and of the Comptroller's statement provided for in Section 138; provided, however, that after October twenty-sixth no item in the Budget shall be increased by the Board of Estimate and Apportionment except as hereinafter expressly provided.

2. **Publication, consideration and adoption by Board of Aldermen.** Simultaneously with the transmission to the Board of Aldermen of the Budget as approved by the Board of Estimate and Apportionment, it shall be published in the *City Record* and simultaneously the Mayor shall call a special meeting of the Board of Aldermen forthwith to receive and consider it, which shall continue from day to day until final action shall be taken thereon. Except with respect to obligations imposed by law or contract or the judgment of a court of competent jurisdiction, the Board of Aldermen may reject or reduce any of the items of the Budget and its action in so doing shall be final subject to the veto of the Mayor as hereinafter provided. It also may increase any item or vary the conditions of its expenditure or insert any new item or items, but its action in so doing shall not be effective for any purpose unless accepted by the Board of Estimate and Apportionment. The Board of Aldermen shall finish its consideration of the Budget and take final action thereon not later than the thirtieth day of November. If it

shall not have taken such action on or prior to said date, it shall be deemed to have adopted the Budget transmitted to it by the Board of Estimate and Apportionment, as modified by such reductions and rejections and (but subject to concurrence by the Board of Estimate and Apportionment) by such increases, insertions and changes in conditions of expenditure as then shall have been made by it. If the Board of Aldermen shall not have made any such increase, insertion or change in the Budget as so transmitted to it, the Budget, as modified by such reductions and rejections, if any, as it shall have made, shall be deemed to have been adopted by both of said Boards, subject to veto by the Mayor as hereinafter provided.

3. **Consideration by board of estimate and apportionment if changed.** Immediately upon the adoption of the Budget by the Board of Aldermen or the settlement thereof as provided in Subdivision 2 of this Section, if the Board of Aldermen shall have increased any item or items of the Budget or inserted any new item or items or shall have changed the conditions of any of the expenditures, the Budget as so modified shall be transmitted to the Board of Estimate and Apportionment, and a special meeting thereof forthwith to receive and to consider the same simultaneously shall be called by the Mayor. Said Board may agree to or reject any or all of such increases, insertions or changes, but any thereof to which it shall not have agreed on or prior to the fifteenth day of December shall be deemed to have been rejected by it. At midnight of said last mentioned day the Budget, as agreed to by both said Boards or settled in accordance with the provisions of this Article, shall be deemed to have been adopted by said Boards subject to veto by the Mayor as next hereinafter provided.

4. **Mayor's veto of changes.** Each and every reduction, rejection, increase and change in the conditions of expenditure of any of the items and every new item contained in the Budget as so agreed to or settled, as compared with the Budget transmitted to the Board of Aldermen by the Board of Estimate and Apportionment, shall be subject to the veto of the Mayor, to be exercised on or before December twentieth by a communication transmitted to the Board of Aldermen, a special meeting whereof he simultaneously shall call to

receive and consider the same forthwith. Such veto may be over-ridden as to any particular item or items by not less than a three-fourths vote of the Board of Aldermen only, provided that such vote shall be taken on or prior to December twenty-fourth, and in that event the item or items as to which it is so over-ridden shall remain as they stood in the Budget as agreed to or settled as provided in Subdivisions 2 or 3 of this Section.

5. **Filing in comptroller's office.** On or prior to December thirtieth the Budget as finally adopted or settled shall be certified by the Mayor and the President of the Board of Aldermen, and on or prior to said day shall be filed in the office of the Comptroller and thereupon the sums specified therein shall be deemed to be and shall be appropriated to the several objects and purposes therein set forth.

6. **Publication as adopted.** On or prior to December thirty-first the Budget as so finally adopted or settled shall be published in the *City Record.*

No Appropriation of Specific Revenues Except to the Debt

SECTION 144. In no manner or event shall any specific revenue of the City be appropriated to a particular purpose or as such to any purpose, except the redemption or amortization of the city debt, but all revenues and moneys of the City available for appropriations by it, as well as taxes, shall, for all other purposes of budgetary or other appropriations, be deemed to constitute one general fund, from which, but not from any particular part or parts of which, all appropriations shall be made.

In the event that specific revenues of the City shall be appropriated to the redemption or amortization of the city debt or such revenues shall be applied thereto under other authorization, the amount of all such revenues and the fact of such appropriation or application thereof shall be shown in the Budget, so that the Budget shall clearly set forth in full the estimated revenues of the City for the ensuing year and all of the proposed expenditures by the City.

Budget to Exhibit Changes

SECTION 145. In every case the Budget, as first submitted to the Board of Estimate and Apportionment, shall exhibit, by items and amounts, in parallel columns:

(a) The several appropriations contained in the Budget of the preceding year;

(b) The departmental estimates for the ensuing year; and

(c) The appropriations proposed for the ensuing year.

Whenever the Board of Estimate and Apportionment or the Board of Aldermen or the Mayor shall have completed consideration of the Budget in any stage of the formulation thereof, there shall be added another parallel column showing by items and amounts, corresponding as closely as practicable with those already appearing therein, the appropriations or proposed appropriations included or remaining in the Budget as the result of the action of either of said Boards or of the Mayor, so that the Budget, as finally adopted or settled, shall exhibit in such parallel columns, in detail, the results, severally, of the successive considerations thereof and actions thereon as well as the appropriations finally made through the medium thereof.

ARTICLE XXII

Assessment and Levy of Taxes

Deputy Tax Commissioners to make Assessments

SECTION 146. 1. **Assessment generally.** Commencing on the first day of April in the year 1926 and in each year thereafter, it shall be the duty of the deputy tax-commissioners to ascertain and assess, under the supervision of the Commissioner of Taxes (in this Article elsewhere called the Commissioner) all taxable property of the class and in the districts assigned to them severally by the Commissioner.

2. **Real estate.** With all practicable expedition and not later than such day as may be prescribed by the Commissioner, each deputy tax-commissioner assigned to assess real estate shall make a return verified by his oath to the Commissioner containing a description of every separate parcel of taxable real estate embraced in his district, giving the street, lot, ward, town and map number together with the name, if ascertainable, of the owner thereof and of the sum for which in his judgment the same as it exists would sell in ordinary circumstances and also if improved of the sum for which it would so sell if wholly unimproved.

3. **Personal property.** Each deputy tax-commissioner assigned to assess personal property shall likewise make a return of all personal property ascertained by him to be taxable and the name of the owner thereof and the sum for which in his judgment the same would sell and of such other information relative to such personal property as shall be prescribed by ordinance.

4. **Details of returns.** Each deputy tax-commissioner shall return such further details with respect to either real estate or personal property or the extent or nature of the examination made by him as the Commissioner may prescribe.

5. **Classes of property.** In the event that the Board of Aldermen shall have provided by ordinance for differing bases of assessment for different classes of property, real or personal or both, the deputy tax-commissioners shall assess and return the values of property included in such classes, respectively, upon and in accordance with the bases of assessment so provided.

Taxable Status; Fixed on October 1

SECTION 147. The taxable status of all persons and property assessable for taxation in the City shall become fixed, each year, on the first day of October of the year preceding the year in which taxes shall be levied thereon.

Tax Board to Fix Valuations

SECTION 148. Before the records of assessed valuation shall be opened for public inspection, a tax-board of which the Commissioner shall be a member and Chairman, having regard to the returns of the deputy tax-commissioners, shall fix the valuations of property in each borough and throughout the City and, if deemed necessary, may so adjust the same that in its judgment a just and proportionately equal relation between the valuations of the several classes of property as between the boroughs and throughout the City as a whole will be established. The assessed valuations of property in each borough in the City returned by the deputy tax-commissioners for such borough and so adjusted, if such adjustment be deemed necessary, shall be entered under the direction of the Commissioner in "Records of Assessed Valuations," for real estate and personal property, severally, in such boroughs which shall be completed prior to October first.

Record Open to Public

SECTION 149. The Record of Assessed Valuations of real estate shall be open to public inspection during business hours from the first day of October until the fifteenth day of November, inclusive, and the record of assessed valuations of personal property shall be open from the first day of October until the first day of December, inclusive, except in each case upon Sundays and holidays. Notice of the fact that such records are and will be so open for inspection shall be published in the *City Record,* and also in such newspapers of general circulation published in the City as, subject to action of the Board of Estimate and Apportionment, the Commissioner may designate, at least once in each calendar week or fraction of calendar week between October first and November fifteenth inclusive.

Application for Revision or Cancellation of Assessments

SECTION 150. The Commissioner from the whole number of deputy tax-commissioners shall designate for each borough one or more deputy tax-commissioners who, between the first day of October in each year and the 15th day of November following as to real estate, and the first day of December following as to personal property, (a) shall receive applications for the revision or cancellation of assessments entered in the records of assessed valuation in such borough, (b) take evidence on each such application and reduce the same to writing, and (c) within ten days after taking such evidence return such application and evidence with his recommendation to the Commissioner, who shall thereupon refer the same to a tax-board for the borough in which the real property in question is situated or the owner of the personal property resides, as the case may require. Such deputy tax-commissioners are authorized to administer oaths for the purpose of taking evidence upon applications for revision or cancellation of assessments. A tax-board or more than one such board may be designated by the Commissioner, to hear all applications of corporations for revision or cancellation of assessments, which applications shall be made to the Commissioner at the main office of the Department in the Borough of Manhattan. As to all other applications, the Commissioner shall prescribe the time and place of hearing thereof in the several boroughs, and give public notice of such hearing in the *City Record*. Every applicant for the revision or cancellation of any assessment shall be heard by and may introduce evidence before the tax-board to which his application shall have been referred. All evidence taken by any tax-board upon any such application shall be reduced to writing and such evidence and all evidence taken thereon by any deputy tax-commissioner, as hereinabove provided, shall constitute part of the record of the assessment with respect to which the same shall have been taken. The decision of the proper tax-board upon any application for revision or cancellation of any assessment shall be made by a majority of the members of such board and shall be rendered before the first day of February of the year in which the tax, in anticipation whereof such assessment has been made, shall be levied.

Alteration of Assessment; Addition of Omitted Property

Section 151. 1. The Commissioner, at any time while the record of assessed valuation, either of real estate or of personal property, remains open for public inspection, after giving at least ten days previous notice to each party in interest, may increase the assessed valuation of any taxable property entered therein as in his judgment may be just or as may be necessary to comply with law or any valid ordinance and may add any real estate or the name of the owner of any personal property which may have been omitted from either such record when the same was opened and the assessed valuation of either as the case may require or may apportion the assessment of any real estate assessed in gross as between several interests therein.

2. The appropriate tax-board may, at any time before the first day of February of the year in which the tax, in anticipation whereof such assessment has been made, shall be levied, decrease the assessed valuation of any property real or personal as in its judgment may be just or as may be necessary to comply with any such law or ordinance; but

valuations shall not be increased or added after such records are open for public inspection except upon notice as aforesaid given to the individual or corporation affected by such increase or addition on or before the fifteenth day of December. The individual or corporation so notified may apply for correction of any such increase or addition on or before the fifteenth day of January in the ensuing year with the same force and effect as if such application were made on or before the fifteenth day of November as to real property, or on or before the thirtieth day of November as to personal property.

Preparation of Assessment Rolls

SECTION 152. 1. **Real estate; payment of first installment of tax.** Beginning with the first day in October in each year, commencing with the year 1926, the Commissioner shall cause to be prepared from the Record of Assessed Valuation of Real Estate in the several boroughs tax assessment rolls, on which rolls the Commissioner shall cause to be set down opposite the several sums therein entered as the assessed valuations of real estate the sums in dollars and cents, rejecting fractions of a cent, which shall respectively equal in amount one per cent. of said assessed valuations of real estate, and said sums shall be payable on the second day of January next ensuing as a first installment of the tax upon the parcels of real estate, respectively. The Commissioner shall, as soon as said rolls are completed, annex to each thereof a certificate that the same is correct in accordance with the entries in said several records, and deliver the same on or before the fifteenth day of November to the Receiver of Taxes, at the same time notifying the Comptroller of the amount of such first installments of taxes appearing in each of said rolls in order that he may cause the proper sum to be charged to the Receiver of Taxes for collection. The Receiver of Taxes upon receiving said assessment rolls shall immediately cause the assessment rolls for each borough to be filed in his office in such borough, and shall thereupon give public notice for at least five days in the manner prescribed in Section 150 for the publication of notices of hearings, that said assessment rolls have been delivered to him and that the first installment of the tax on real estate, amounting to one per cent. of the assessed value thereof as the same appears in said assessment rolls, will be due and payable at his office in such borough on the second day of January.

2. **Excess payments.** If an assessment appearing on any such rolls, on which the first installment of taxes shall have been so paid, thereafter shall be reduced or cancelled, the excess of such payment over one per cent. of the corrected assessment, together with interest upon such excess at the rate of six per cent. per annum from the date of payment of such installment to the first day of the month succeeding the day when the second installment becomes due and payable, as hereinafter provided, shall be credited as a payment upon the second installment of the tax payable upon the real estate in question or, in the event that such excess together with such interest shall exceed the amount payable as the second installment of tax as finally assessed, the amount by which the former exceeds the latter shall be refunded by the Chamberlain and warrants therefor shall be prepared and delivered with all possible expedition.

3. **Rolls returned to commissioner.** On the fifteenth day of February said original assessment rolls of real estate shall be returned by the Receiver of Taxes to the Commissioner to enable the Commissioner to note therein such corrections of assessments therein as shall have been made as in this Article provided.

4. **Personal property.** Beginning with the first day of December in each year the Commissioner shall cause to be prepared from the Records of Assessed Valuations of Personal Estate in the several boroughs, assessment rolls of personal property for each of said several boroughs.

5. **Correction of errors.** On return to the Commissioner by the Receiver of Taxes of the assessment rolls of real estate on the fifteenth day of February, the Commissioner shall cause to be entered in such assessment rolls of real estate such corrections of assessments as shall have been made and shall, as soon as the rolls of real estate and personal property are completed, annex to each of said rolls his certificate that the same is correct in accordance with the final entries in said several records.

6. **Delivery of rolls to Board of Aldermen.** The rolls so certified must on the first day in March, which is not a Saturday, Sunday or legal holiday, and in any event not later than the third day of March, be delivered by the Commissioner to the Board of Aldermen.

Assessment Rolls; Form and Result of Errors

SECTION 153. 1. **In general.** The assessment rolls for real estate and personal estate so classified and so arranged with respect to columns and containing such entries as the Commissioner shall prescribe shall be sufficient to identify the property and persons assessed and to show each total assessed valuation.

2. **Real estate.** Real Estate shall be described on the assessment rolls by the numbers by which such property is designated on the tax maps and in the annual record of assessed valuations and such numbers shall import into the assessment roll of real estate any necessary identifying description shown by the tax maps. To the assessment of improved land there shall be added a statement of the value of the land, appraised as if unimproved. An omission of the name of the owner of real property or an error in the statement of his name shall not affect the validity of the assessment. No assessment of real property shall be deemed to be erroneous or illegal because of any division of title or ownership of the property assessed.

3. **Personal property.** The entry of an assessment of personal property upon the assessment roll shall contain at least: (a) the name of the owner; (b) a statement of the amount of the assessment. Names of owners shall be arranged alphabetically. Only a substantial error in the name of the owner shall render an assessment invalid.

Comptroller's Statement of Amount of Tax, Levy of Taxes

SECTION 154. At least as early as the twenty-first day of February in each year, the Comptroller shall submit to the Board of Aldermen a statement setting forth (a) the amounts required to be provided during the then current year for City purposes and for the proper purposes of each county included within the City and for educational service under control of the Board of Education, (b) the amounts required by law, contract or necessitated by the judgment of any court to be raised by tax in such year, (c) an estimate of all of the probable receipts of the City during the then current year from sources other than the tax levy thereupon to be made, with the assumed sources thereof and (d) the amounts included therein, if any, which are not applicable to the reduction of taxation.

Board of Aldermen to Levy Tax

SECTION 155. The Board of Aldermen shall order and cause to be raised by tax in such year a sum not less than the difference between (a) the amount which is required to be provided for city and county purposes and for educational service under control of the Board of Education, including in each instance all amounts required by law or contract or necessitated by the judgment of any court to be raised by tax, and (b) the amount of such estimated receipts available for the reduction of taxation. The amount so to be raised for city and county purposes other than educational service under control of the Board of Education and the amount to be raised for such educational service shall be separately determined and stated.

County Taxes May Be Levied on Counties

SECTION 156. The Board of Aldermen, in its discretion, may levy and order to be collected the sums to be raised for the purpose of defraying county salaries, expenses and charges, or any thereof, upon and out of the taxable property within said counties, severally, in such manner that each thereof shall bear the amounts incurred for its own proper county purposes, but the rate fixed by said Board to be levied upon any given class of property shall be uniform throughout the county to which it applies.

Action of Board of Aldermen in Fixing Rates and Completing Assessment Rolls

SECTION 157. The Board of Aldermen must meet each year, at noon on the first day in March which is not a Saturday, Sunday or legal holiday, and in any event not later than the third day of March, at its usual place of meeting in the Borough of Manhattan to receive the assessment rolls of real and personal property and to fix the annual tax rates. In determining such rates, said Board shall fix each rate in cents and hundredths of a cent upon each dollar of assessed valuation.

Entry of Tax on Assessment Rolls

SECTION 158. The Board of Aldermen must cause (a) the assessment rolls to be completed by setting down thereon (1) opposite the valuations of the several items of real and personal property, the respective sums, in dollars and cents, rejecting fractions of a cent, to be paid as taxes upon the same, the amounts to be paid (first) for city and county purposes and (second) for educational service, including the service of the debt incurred for such service, to be entered separately but also totaled with respect to each such item, and (2) the aggregates of the assessed valuations of real property and personal property, severally in each borough, (b) a certificate setting forth such aggregate valuations, severally, to be transmitted forthwith to the Comptroller of the State.

Delivery of Rolls to Receiver of Taxes

SECTION 159. The assessment rolls of each borough corrected and finally completed as required by this Act or fair copies thereof shall be delivered to the Receiver of Taxes on or before the twenty-eighth day of March, with warrants annexed requiring him to collect so much of the several sums entered in said rolls as taxes to be paid as shall not already have been paid in accordance with the provisions of Section 152.

Taxes Enforced as a Unit

SECTION 160. The aggregate of all taxes levied upon any particular item of real or personal property, whether for city and county purposes or for educational service under the control of the Board of Education or otherwise, shall be collected and enforced by sale, lien or in any other manner as a single integral tax but in the preparation of tax bills and tax receipts the amount of the tax for such educational service shall in every case be separately set forth upon the face of such tax bill or tax receipt so that the amount of the tax therefor included in the total of such tax bill or tax receipt shall plainly appear.

Payment of Taxes

SECTION 161. 1. **Public notice by receiver of due date.** The Receiver of Taxes, immediately after he shall have received the assessment rolls so corrected and finally completed, shall give public notice for at least five days by publication, in the manner provided in Section 150, that said assessment rolls have been delivered to him, and that all taxes will be due and payable at his office in said respective boroughs as below in this Section provided, which in said notice shall be specified:

All taxes upon personal property and upon special franchises shall be due and payable on the ensuing first day of May, and so much of the taxes upon real estate as shall in any case constitute the balance of such tax over the first installment of one per cent. of assessed value due and payable on the second day of January shall also be due and payable on the first day of May.

2. **Penalty for delay.** In the event that the installment of the tax levied upon any particular parcel or item of taxable property payable as in this Article provided on the second day of January or on the first day of May shall not be paid during the month of January or the month of May, as the case may be, the Receiver of Taxes shall add thereto and there shall be collected and paid, with the amount of tax so levied on such installment, interest at the rate of half of one per cent. for each month and for each fraction of a month that shall have elapsed from and after the first day of May or of January, as the case may be, upon which such tax or installment became payable until the day of payment thereof, provided that the same be paid within four months from the date upon which such installment became due and payable; but in the event that the same shall not be paid until after the expiration of such period of four months, the Receiver of Taxes shall add thereto and there shall be collected and paid with the amount of such tax or installment, in addition to such interest at the

rate of half of one per cent. per month for such period of four months, interest to the date of payment of such tax or installment at the rate of three-quarters of one per cent. for each month and for each fraction of a month which shall have elapsed after the expiration of said period of four months. If any tax or installment of tax on real estate or any tax on personal property shall remain unpaid on the first day of January following the date upon which the same shall have become due and payable it shall be the duty of the Receiver of Taxes to charge and collect upon such tax or installment so unpaid, in addition to interest as provided in this Section, a penalty of one per cent. of the amount of the taxes levied.

Receiver to Pay Over Taxes to Chamberlain

SECTION 162. The Receiver of Taxes shall, from day to day as the same are collected, pay over all taxes, interest and penalties collected by him to the Chamberlain.

Apportionment of Tax Among Parties in Interest

SECTION 163. If a sum in gross shall have been taxed upon any parcel of real estate and any person or corporation shall claim a divided part thereof or an undivided interest therein, the Commissioner of Taxes upon application of such person or corporation, may apportion the assessment of such parcel between the several interests shown to exist therein and in writing certify such apportionment to the Receiver of Taxes and each tax-payer may pay the tax upon the assessment apportioned to his or its interest.

Tax a Lien on Day Due

SECTION 164. All taxes shall be liens upon and charges against the real estate affected thereby on the days and to the extent that they shall become due and payable as in this Article provided and not earlier and such taxes and all interest and penalties which shall accrue thereon shall remain such liens and charges until paid in full.

Power of Board of Aldermen to Make Regulations

SECTION 165. The Board of Aldermen may enact by ordinance regulations, consistent with the provisions of this

Act, for the preparation and correction of and additions to maps by the Department of Taxes, the assessment, levy or collection of taxes, the enforcement of liens for taxes upon real estate and proceedings for the recovery of taxes upon personal property and the conduct thereof by officials of the City and with respect to any matters as to which the Commissioner of Taxes is authorized hereby to make rules and also to fix penalties for failure by any person to perform or assist in performing any duty prescribed by this Article or otherwise with respect to the levy, collection, or payment over of taxes or the making or correction of assessments or accounting for taxes collected.

Exemptions

SECTION 166. Nothing in this Act shall affect any valid exemptions from taxation created by law with respect to property, real or personal, or authorize the creation by the City of new or different exemptions therefrom.

Dates of Taking Effect

SECTION 167. Notwithstanding anything elsewhere contained in this Act, the provisions of this Article XXII shall take effect on the first day of April, 1926, and not before. The provisions of law existing on December thirty-first, 1925, with respect to the levy, collection and payment of taxes and the making and correction of assessments therefor shall continue to apply to and govern the levy, collection and payment of taxes to be levied in March, 1926, and the making and correction of assessments therefor.

ARTICLE XXIII

Board of Review

Membership

SECTION 168. 1. **Appointment.** Prior to October first, 1926, the Mayor shall appoint three persons, residents of the City, at least one of whom shall be an attorney at law who shall have regularly practiced in the City for at least five years, who shall constitute and be known as the Board of Review. The Mayor shall designate a member of the Board of Review who shall be an attorney at law qualified as above provided to be the President thereof.

2. **Term of office.** The members of the Board of Review shall hold office for three, six and nine years, respectively, as may be prescribed by the Mayor, from the first day of October, 1926. On or before the first day of September, prior to the expiration of the term of any member of the Board of Review, the Mayor shall appoint his successor for a full term of nine years from the first day of October next ensuing.

3. **Removal on charges.** The Mayor may remove any of the members of said Board upon charges made in writing of misconduct or inefficiency in the discharge of official duties or of personal dishonesty, immoral conduct or of other unfitness to hold office under the City, but only after full opportunity to the respondent to be heard and offer evidence in his defense, either in person or by counsel. The Mayor's decision and order upon any charges which he shall require any such member of the Board to defend shall be published in full in the *City Record*.

4. **Filling of vacancies.** The Mayor shall fill vacancies in the membership of the Board promptly as they occur. Any person appointed to fill a vacancy shall hold office during the unexpired portion of the term of his predecessor.

Revision or Cancellation of Assessments

SECTION 169. 1. **Applications.** The Board shall hear all applications for the revision or cancellation of assessments for taxes upon property in the City upon any of the grounds in this Section set forth, that may be presented to it, in writing or personally, by owners of property which shall have been assessed for taxes, provided that any such application shall first have been presented to and denied in whole or in part by a tax-board and that every such application shall be presented to or filed with the Board of Review not later than the thirtieth day of April of the year in which the tax-board shall have so denied such application in whole or in part.

2. **Grounds for review.** The Board of Review shall have jurisdiction and power to review, on the merits, any decision of any tax-board and the assessments sus-

tained or corrected thereby upon the application of any such aggrieved party who shall have complied with the conditions prescribed in this Section and to cancel or correct any assessment which is the subject of any such application, upon one or more of the following grounds and none other:

(a) That the property assessed or some part thereof is exempt from taxation;

(b) That the assessment is illegal otherwise;

(c) That the assessment is erroneous by reason of overvaluation;

(d) That the assessment, if of real estate, is erroneous by reason of inequality in that the valuation assessed is proportionately higher than the assessment of other real estate of the same class in the same section or on the tax rolls of the City for the same year with the result that, in the opinion of the Board of Review, the aggrieved party will be required, by reason of such inequality, to pay more than his just proportion of the aggregate tax.

Informal Applications; No Appeal from Action On

SECTION 170. Any such aggrieved party may present his application to the Board of Review informally and without pleadings upon the record of the assessment of the property in question and such evidence, if any, as he may elect and in such case, if in its opinion the facts proved shall justify such action, the Board by order in writing may summarily cancel or reduce the assessment; otherwise it shall deny such application; but no appeal shall lie from any order made upon any such informal application.

Procedure on Formal Application for Review

SECTION 171. 1. **Presentation of application.** Any such aggrieved party may present to the Board of Review, within the period aforesaid, a formal application for the correction or cancellation of any assessment, whether such party shall have presented an informal application therefor or such informal application shall have been denied in whole or in part or such party shall not have made any previous application therefor, by filing with the Board a verified petition in writing briefly setting forth the grounds of complaint, which must be one or more of the grounds enumerated in Section 169, and the facts which the petitioner contends establish the same. In the event that an informal application for the same relief or any part thereof shall be pending and undecided, it shall be superseded by such formal application. It shall not be necessary that the City or any public body or official shall answer or defend against such petition but the same shall in every case be deemed to be at issue and the allegations thereof must be established.

2. **Proceeding of board.** The President of the Board of Review shall summarily set down said petition for hearing before the Board of Review for the earliest practicable day and shall cause the petitioner and the Commissioner of Taxes to be notified personally or by mail of the time fixed therefor. At the time so fixed or as soon thereafter as the proceeding can be heard, the Board shall hear the petitioner and his evidence, if any, and shall try the merits of such application summarily upon the law, the record of the assessment in question and the facts, as they shall appear in evidence or otherwise. The City may appear upon any such proceeding and defend the same either by the Commissioner of Taxes or an assistant commissioner or a deputy tax-commissioner authorized by him or by the Corporation Counsel, as the Commissioner of Taxes may elect. Such proceedings may be had and such evidence shall be admissible as might have been had or would have been admissible, but for this Article, had the proceeding been tried in the Supreme Court upon a writ of certiorari and the return thereto as prescribed in the Tax Law, and the Board of Review, by vote of a majority of its members, shall confirm the assessment complained of or shall make such other order as might have been made by the Supreme Court upon such proceedings by certiorari.

3. **Correction of assessment and tax rolls.** Upon the making of any such order by the Board of Review or, if the same be appealed from, upon the making of a final order by any court or upon the making of a reassessment of the property in question if directed by the Board or any such Court, the assessment and tax rolls shall, if they shall have been found to be erroneous, be corrected accordingly.

4. **Regulation of procedure.** The Board of Aldermen may provide by ordinance, or in the absence of such ordinance the Board of Review may provide by rule, but in either case consistently with the provisions of this Act, for the procedure of and before the Board of Review with respect to any matters or details which are not provided for in this Article.

Appeal to Supreme Court

SECTION 172. An appeal may be taken by the petitioner or the City from the order entered by the Board of Review to the Appellate Division of the Supreme Court for the First Department, except that in the case of an assessment of real estate such appeal must be taken to the Appellate Division of the Supreme Court for the department in which such real estate shall be situate. The record upon any such appeal shall be made and certified and the appeal shall be perfected in the same manner as appeals taken from orders entered in special proceedings of like nature at a special term of the Supreme Court, but in every such case notice of appeal shall be served by or upon the Corporation Counsel and the City shall be represented upon such appeal by him. Such appeal shall be heard and determined in like manner and with like effect as an appeal from an order entered upon a like proceeding in certiorari.

Refund of Excessive Tax

SECTION 173. In the event that it shall finally be determined that any assessment reviewed as in this Article provided is illegal or if upon correction thereof or a reassessment of the property in question directed by the Board of Review or by the final order of any court upon appeal it shall appear that the tax upon such property has been paid to an amount greater than was legal or shall be warranted by such reassessment, the tax paid to the amount of such excess with interest at the rate of six per cent. per annum upon such amount of excess from the date of payment shall be refunded in the manner provided in Section 296 of the Tax Law or in said Section as it may have been amended or by any provision of statute then in force providing for such refunding which shall have superseded said Section.

Restrictions as to Remedies

SECTION 174. No action to vacate an assessment for taxes or to remove a cloud upon title by reason thereof or to enjoin the collection or proceedings for the collection of any tax or the sale of property or of a lien upon property taxed or to recover moneys paid for or on account of taxes and no certiorari to review a determination with respect to any assessment for taxes shall be maintained after March thirty-first, 1926, with respect to any assessment or upon any claim of invalidity in any assessment for taxes made with respect to property in the City; but all parties aggrieved shall thereafter be restricted to the remedies provided in Article XXII and in this Article.

Confirmation of Assessments and Awards of Board of Assessors

SECTION 175. The Board of Review shall have jurisdiction and power to review on the merits any proposed assessment or award of the Board of Assessors and objections thereto which shall be presented to it as provided in Section 217; and to confirm or correct assessments imposing or allocating the cost of a public or local improvement upon or to property deemed to be benefited thereby, and to confirm or correct awards for damages caused by the grading of a street, other than those confirmed either by a court of record or by the Board of Assessors; and, as well, to refer any such assessment or award back to the Board of Assessors for revision and correction in such respects and in accordance with such rules as it may prescribe. The Board of Review shall have power to subpœna and examine witnesses in relation to such assessments and awards.

ARTICLE XXIV

Acquisition of Title to Real Property for Public Purposes

Definitions

SECTION 176. When used in this Article unless otherwise expressly stated or unless the context or subject-matter otherwise requires:

1. " The Court," " the Supreme Court," means a special term of the Supreme Court held in a county within the City of New York and within the judicial district in which the real property or some part thereof is situated;

2. " Days " means calendar days exclusive of Sundays and full legal holidays;

3. " Owner " means a person having an estate, interest or easement in the real property to be acquired or a lien, charge or encumbrance thereon;

4. " Real property " includes all lands and improvements, lands under water, water front property, the water of any lake, pond or stream, all water rights or privileges, all easements and hereditaments, corporeal or incorporeal, and every estate, interest, and right, legal or equitable, in lands or water, and right, interest, privilege, easement and franchise relating to the same, including terms for years and liens by way of judgment, mortgage or otherwise, and also all claims for damages to such real property;

5. " Street " includes street, avenue, road, alley, lane, highway, boulevard, concourse, parkway, culvert, sidewalk, and cross walk, every class of public road, square and place, except marginal wharf;

6. " Improvement " shall be construed as synonymous with the phrase " acquisition of title to real property pursuant to the provisions of this Article;"

7. The term "excess lands," "excess real property," " additional lands," or " additional real property " shall each be construed as synonymous with real property in addition (or additional) to the real property needed (or required) for the improvement.

Acquisition of Real Property; Application to the Court to Condemn

SECTION 177. Whenever the acquisition of real property by the City by condemnation shall have been duly authorized, the proceeding for that purpose shall be taken and conducted in the manner prescribed in this Article. The Board of Estimate and Apportionment shall cause to be prepared and shall adopt a survey, map or plan of such real property and shall cause copies thereof to be certified by the Secretary of said Board and filed as follows: one copy thereof in each office in which instruments affecting real property are required to be recorded in each county in which such real property or any part thereof shown on said map is situated; one copy thereof in the office of the Corporation Counsel; one copy thereof in the office of the President of each Borough in which the real property or any part thereof shown on such map is situated, and one copy thereof in the office of the said Board. In any case where the acquisition of additional real property in connection with any improvement has been authorized, such survey, map or plan shall show the real property to be acquired which is needed for the actual construction of the improvement and the additional real property to be acquired in connection therewith. Said Board shall also direct the Corporation Counsel to take legal proceedings to acquire such real property for the City. Thereupon the Corporation Counsel shall immediately institute a proceeding to acquire title for the use of the public to such real property and shall give notice by advertisement published in ten successive issues of the *City Record* and, in case the real property to be acquired is without the limits of the City, in two public newspapers published or circulating in each county in which such real property is located, and by causing copies of said notice in the form of handbills to be posted for the same space of time, in three conspicuous places, upon or near the real property to be acquired or affected by the intended improvement, that he intends to make application to the Supreme Court, within the judicial district in which the real property or some part thereof is situated, at a time and place specified in said notice, to have the compensation which should justly be made to the respective owners of the real property proposed to be taken, ascertained and determined by the Supreme Court without a jury, and in a proper case to have the cost of such improvement or such portion thereof, as the Board or Boards having the power to determine the same shall direct, assessed by the said Court upon such real property as may be deemed to be benefited thereby, indicating in such notice the real property to be taken by a general description by metes and bounds and by a reference to the maps on file in his office, and referring to the area of assessment if the same has been fixed by the Board of Estimate and Apportionment. The area of assessment may be described in said notice by means of a map or diagram instead of by metes and bounds.

Upon such application the Corporation Counsel shall present to the Court a petition signed and verified by him, setting forth the action had by the Board of Estimate and Apportionment and by any other Board or officer authorized to act with reference to the improvement and indicating the real property to be acquired by a general description by metes and bounds and by reference to a map which shall be attached to the said petition and to the maps on file in his office, and praying that the same be condemned by the said Court without a jury, and in a proper case to have the cost of such improvement or such portion thereof as the Board or Boards having the power to determine the same, shall direct assessed by the said Court upon such real property as may be deemed to be benefited thereby and referring to the area of assessment if the same has been already fixed by the Board of Estimate and Apportionment.

Order Granting Application to Condemn; Property Owners To File Claims; Proof of Ownership; Trial of Proceeding; Court to View

SECTION 178. At the time and place mentioned in said notice, unless the Court shall adjourn the said application to a subsequent day, and in that event, at the time and place to which the same may be adjourned, upon due proof to its satisfaction of the publication and posting of such notice and upon filing the said petition, the Court shall enter an order granting the application, which shall be filed in the office of the clerk of the county in which the real property affected is situated. Thereupon the Corporation Counsel shall file in the office of the clerk of the county in which the real property to be condemned is situated a survey or map showing such real property subdivided into parcels corresponding with the separate ownerships thereof as nearly as the same has been ascertained, and within thirty days after the entry of such order shall cause to be published in ten consecutive issues of the *City Record,* a notice containing a general description of the real property to be acquired and a statement that the map or survey thereof has been filed as hereinbefore provided, and requiring that all owners thereof shall on or before a date therein specified, at least twenty days subsequent to the first publication of such notice, file with the clerk of the Court of the county in which such real property is situated a written claim or demand, duly verified, in the manner provided by law for the verification of pleadings in an action, setting forth the real property owned by the claimant and his post-office address. The claimant or his attorney shall within the same time serve on the Corporation Counsel a copy of such verified claim. The proof of title to the real property to be acquired, in all cases where the same is undisputed, together with proof of liens or encumbrances thereon, shall be submitted by the claimant to the Corporation Counsel or to such assistant as he shall designate. The Corporation Counsel shall serve upon all parties or their attorneys, who have served on him a copy of their verified claims, a notice of the time and place at which he will receive such proof of title. In all cases where the title of the claimant is disputed it shall be the duty of the Court to determine the ownership of such real property upon the proof submitted to the Court during the trial of the proceeding. The Court shall also have power to determine all questions of title incident to the trial of the proceeding. After all parties who have filed verified claims as herein provided have proved their title or have failed to do so after being notified by the Corporation Counsel of the time and place when and where such proof of title would be received by him, the Corporation Counsel shall serve upon all parties or their attorneys who have appeared in the proceeding a notice of trial thereof, and shall file a note of issue with the clerk of the court of the county in which the trial is to be had. In case the Corporation Counsel shall fail to notice the proceeding for trial within ninety days after the entry of the order of the Court granting the application, any party in interest may apply to a Justice of the Supreme Court for an order requiring the Corporation Counsel to notice the proceeding for trial at such term of Court in which the trial may be had, as such Justice may direct, and thereupon the Corporation Counsel shall give notice of trial as such order may direct. The trial shall be had in such county within the City of New York and within the judicial district in which real property affected by the proceeding is situated as may be directed by an order of a Justice of the Supreme Court or in case no such order is made, as the Corporation Counsel in the notice of trial shall designate. The notice of trial shall be served at least ten days before, and the note of issue shall be filed at least eight days before the date for which the same is noticed for trial. The note of issue shall briefly state the title of the proceeding, the date and place of the entry of the order granting the application to condemn, the names and addresses of the parties who have filed claims, the names and addresses of their respective attorneys, and a brief statement as to the extent of the real property to be acquired. The clerk of the court must thereupon enter the proceeding upon the proper calendar according to the date of the entry of the order granting the application to condemn. When notice of trial has been served and note of issue filed the proceeding must remain on the calendar until finally disposed of. It shall be the duty of the Justice trying any such proceeding to view the real property to be thereby acquired, and if he shall deem a view of the real property in the area of assessment necessary or useful he shall also make such view.

Tentative Decree

SECTION 179. The Court after hearing such testimony and considering such proofs as may be offered shall ascertain and estimate the compensation which ought justly to be made by the City to the respective owners of the real property to be acquired; and in case a portion of the cost of the improvement is to be borne by the real property benefited thereby, it shall also make a just and equitable estimate of the assessment of the value of the benefit and advantage of such improvement to the respective owners of the real property within the area of assessment and instruct the Corporation Counsel to prepare separate tabular abstracts of its estimate of damage and of its estimate of assessments for benefit. The tabular abstract of estimated damage and the tabular abstract of the estimated assessments for benefit, respectively, shall set forth separately the amount of loss and damage and of benefit and advantage to each and every parcel of real property affected by the proceeding, and the names of the respective owners of each and every parcel of real property affected thereby as far as the same shall be ascertained, and a sufficient designation or description of the respective lots or parcels of real property acquired and assessed, by reference to the numbers of the respective parcels indicated upon the maps, diagrams or surveys which shall be attached to such tabular abstracts. The Court shall fix the area of assessment in all cases where such area has not been fixed by the Board of Estimate and Apportionment, and it shall in its estimate of assessments assess any and all real property within such area, in proportion to the amount of the benefit received. It shall be lawful if the Court shall deem it just and equitable under the circumstances to do so, but not otherwise, to assess any part not exceeding one-third of the estimated value of any building or buildings taken in the proceeding, but not of any other improvement, upon the City. Such tabular abstracts shall be signed by the Justice trying the proceeding and filed with the clerk of the court in the county in which the real property affected by the proceeding is situated and when so filed shall constitute the tentative decree of the Court as to awards for damages and as to assessments for benefit.

Notice of Filing the Tentative Decree; Filing of Objections; Awards Not to be Reduced nor Assessments Increased Without Notice

SECTION 180. Upon the filing of the tentative decree the Corporation Counsel shall give notice by advertisement in ten successive issues of the *City Record,* of the filing of such tentative decree and that the City of New York and all other parties interested in such proceedings, or in any of the real property affected thereby, having any objection thereto, shall file such objections, in writing, duly verified in the manner required by law for the verification of pleadings in an action, setting forth the real property owned by the objector and his post-office address, with said clerk within twenty days after the first publication of said notice, and that the Corporation Counsel on a date specified in the notice will apply to the Justice who made the tentative decree to fix a time when he will hear the parties so objecting. Every party so objecting or his attorney shall within the same time serve on the Corporation Counsel a copy of such verified objections. Upon such application the Justice shall fix the time when he will hear the parties so objecting and desiring to be heard. Similar notice for at least ten days shall be given of the filing of any new, supplemental or amended tentative decree, and for the filing of objections thereto. At the time fixed the Justice shall hear the person or persons who have objected to the tentative decree, or to the new, supplemental or amended tentative decree, and who may then and there appear, and shall have the power to adjourn from time to time until all parties who have filed objections and who desire to be heard shall have been fully heard. After the filing of the tentative decree or of any new, or supplemental, or amended tentative decree, no award for damages shall be diminished nor any assessment for benefit increased without notice to the owner of the real property affected or his attorney appearing in the proceeding and a reasonable opportunity given for a hearing in regard thereto before signing the final decree.

Final Decree; Preparation Thereof; What to Contain; Partial Decrees.

SECTION 181. After considering the objections, if any, and making any corrections or alterations in the tentative decree as to awards for damage or assessments for benefit, which the Court shall consider just and proper, the Justice trying the proceeding shall give instructions to the Corporation Counsel as to the preparation of the final decree, which shall consist of the tentative decree altered and corrected in accordance with the instructions of the Justice and the final awards as determined by the Court set opposite the respective parcel damage numbers in a column headed "final awards" in the tabular abstract of awards for damage and the final assessments as determined by the Court set opposite the respective parcel benefit numbers in a column headed "final assessments" in a tabular abstract of assessments for benefit, together with a statement of the facts conferring on the Court jurisdiction of the proceeding; and of such other matters as the Court shall require to be set forth; also a statement that the amounts set opposite the respective damage parcel numbers in the column headed "final awards" in the tabular abstract of awards of damage constitute and are the just compensation which the respective owners are entitled to receive from the City of New York, and that the amounts set opposite the respective benefit parcel numbers in the column headed "final assessments" in the tabular abstract of assessments for benefit constitute the sums of money to be paid to the City of New York, for the benefit and advantage derived by reason of said improvement, by the respective owners of the parcels so assessed. To the final decree shall be attached the maps, diagrams or surveys hereinbefore referred to, duly corrected, when necessary. The final decree shall set forth the several parcels taken or assessed by reference to the numbers of such parcels on the respective maps, diagrams or surveys and it shall not be necessary to describe any parcels either acquired or assessed by a description of metes and bounds. The final decree shall also set forth the names of the respective owners of the several parcels acquired and assessed for benefit as far as the same shall have been ascertained, but in all cases where the owners are unknown or not fully known to the Court, it shall be sufficient to set forth and state in general terms in the decree the respective sums to be allowed and paid to or by the owners of the respective parcels for the loss and damage or for the benefit and advantage, as the case may be, without specifying their names or their estates or interests therein, and in such cases the owners may be specified as unknown. Should any errors exist in the tentative decree or in the maps, diagrams or surveys attached thereto or should there occur between the date of the tentative decree and the time of the signing by the Court of the final decree any changes in ownership resulting in changes in the size or area, by subdivision or otherwise, of any of the parcels of real property to be acquired or to be assessed, the Court may alter and correct the respective maps, diagrams or surveys to show changes and may make an apportionment of any proposed assessment rendered necessary by any subdivision or other change in the size or area of any parcel assessed between the date of the tentative decree and the time of the signing by the Court of the final decree as to assessments so as to show such changes in such final decree.

When authorized by the Board of Estimate and Apportionment the Court may file a tentative decree as to damages embracing either the entire real property to be acquired or successive sections or parcels thereof, and ascertain and estimate the compensation to be made therefor, and make a separate final decree with reference thereto. Such separate or partial tentative and final decree shall be in the same form, and such proceedings shall be had in respect thereto, as in respect to the tentative and final decree of the Court relative to the entire real property acquired in the proceeding as herein provided for. Where partial final decrees as to awards for damages are authorized to be made the last final decree as to awards, and the last final decree as to assessments for benefit, shall be filed at the same time.

The final decree, together with all of the affidavits and proofs upon which the same is based, shall be filed in the office of the clerk of the county where the order granting the application to condemn shall have been entered and filed. The final decree, unless set aside or reversed on appeal, shall be final and conclusive as well upon the City of New York, as upon the owners of the real property mentioned therein, and also upon all other persons whomsoever.

Appeal to the Appellate Division

SECTION 182. The City of New York or any party or person affected by the proceedings and aggrieved by the final decree of the Court therein as to awards or as to assessments, or both, may appeal to the Appellate Division of the Court. An appeal from the final decree of the Court must be taken within thirty days after notice of the filing of said final decree. Except as herein otherwise provided, such appeal shall be taken and heard in the manner provided by the Civil Practice Act and the rules and practice of the Court in relation to appeals from orders in special proceedings, and such appeal shall be heard and determined by such Appellate Division upon the merits both as to matters of law and fact. The determination of the Appellate Division shall be in the form of an order. But the taking of an appeal by any person or persons shall not operate to stay the proceedings under this Act, except as to the particular parcel of real property with which the appeal is concerned; and the final decree of the Court shall be deemed to be final and conclusive upon all parties and persons affected thereby, who have not appealed. Such appeal shall be heard upon the evidence taken by the Court or such part or portion thereof as the Justice who made the decree may certify, or the parties to said appeal may agree upon as sufficient to present the merits of the questions in respect to which such appeal shall be had. An appeal taken but not prosecuted within six months after the filing of the notice of appeal, unless the time within which to prosecute the same shall have been extended by an order of the Court, shall be deemed to have been abandoned and no agreement between the parties extending the time within which the said appeal may be prosecuted shall vary the provisions hereof. When a final decree of the Court shall be reversed on appeal, the Court shall have power to make such additional awards and assessments for benefit as may be necessary.

Appeal to Court of Appeals

SECTION 183. An appeal to the Court of Appeals may be taken by the City or any person or party interested in the said proceeding and aggrieved by the order of the Appellate Division. Such appeal shall be taken and heard in the manner provided by the Civil Practice Act and the rules and practice of the Court of Appeals in relation to appeals from orders in special proceedings. An appeal taken but not prosecuted within six months after the filing of the notice of appeal, unless the time within which to prosecute the same shall have been extended by an order of the Court, shall be deemed to be abandoned, and no agreement between the parties to the appeal extending the time to prosecute the same shall vary the provisions thereof. The Court of Appeals may affirm or reverse the order appealed from, and may make such order or direction as shall be appropriate to the case. If the final decree or decrees of the Court shall be reversed by the Court of Appeals, the Court shall have power to make such additional awards and assessments for benefit as may be necessary.

Excess Lands

SECTION 184. When the acquisition of additional real property in connection with any improvement, shall have been authorized, such additional real property shall be separately described in the notice of application to condemn by the Supreme Court without a jury, and in the petition presented on any such application, and separately shown on the rule map attached to the petition and on the damage map in the proceeding, and said notice and petition shall state what part of the real property to be condemned is required for the improvement, and what part thereof is to be acquired as additional real property. The acquisition of such additional real property, when authorized pursuant to this Act shall be deemed to be for a public purpose. After the institution of a proceeding pursuant to this Article, the Board of Estimate and Apportionment may amend the proceeding by authorizing the acquisition of lands additional to those required for the improvement, provided that title shall not have vested in the City of New York to any parcel of real property to be acquired for the improvement within the block between legally existing public streets, embracing the additional lands sought to be acquired. The said Board may also amend any proceeding so as to exclude any or all additional lands being acquired in the proceeding, provided title to such additional lands shall not have vested in the City.

The Ascertainment of the Amount Properly Assessable in a Proceeding in which Excess Lands may be Acquired

SECTION 185. Where part of a parcel of real property shall be acquired for an improvement, and the remainder or a portion of the remainder of such parcel in the same ownership shall be acquired in the same proceeding as excess lands, the portion of the damages due to the acquisition of the real property required for the improvement, shall be determined and stated separately from the entire damage due to each such owner. In determining the damages due to the acquisition of that portion of such parcel, which is required for the improvement (which shall be the portion thereof properly assessable), the same rule shall be applied as would govern the determination of damages for the taking of the real property required for the improvement, in case no excess lands were acquired. Where part of a parcel of real property shall be acquired for the improvement, and the remainder or a portion of the remainder thereof in the same ownership shall be acquired in the same proceeding, as excess lands, the damages due to the acquisition of title to the real property required for the improvement (which shall constitute the portion of the owner's total damages as to such parcel, on account of the proceeding, which shall be properly assessable), shall in every case, equal the amount which would be awarded to such owner in case only that part of his real property, which shall be required for the improvement, were acquired. The aggregate of damages due to the acquisition of the real property required for the improvement shall be determined by the Court and when so determined, as aforesaid, shall be assessed by the Court upon the property deemed to be benefited by the improvement in case and to the extent that such assessment has been duly authorized. The real property acquired by the City in excess of that required for the improvement shall be subject to assessment for benefit due to the improvement, and shall bear its proper share of the cost and expense of the proceeding, which may be levied and collected with the taxes upon the real property in one or more entire boroughs. The assessment, which shall be levied in any proceeding, upon the real property acquired in excess of that required for the improvement, shall not in the case of any parcel assessed exceed one-half the fair value thereof.

Damages from Change of Grade

Section 186. In a proceeding for the purpose of opening, extending and enlarging, straightening or improving a street or part of a street, if the Court shall judge that any intended regulation will injure any building or buildings not required to be taken in the proceeding, it shall proceed to make, together with the other estimates and assessments required by law to be made by it, a just and equitable estimate of the loss and damage which will accrue by and in consequence of such intended regulation, to the respective owners, lessees, parties and persons, respectively, entitled unto or interested in the said building or buildings so to be injured by the said intended regulation; and the sums or estimates of compensation and recompense for such loss and damage shall be included by the Court in the assessment for benefit insofar as such assessment is authorized by the Board of Estimate and Apportionment.

Proceedings to Acquire Title to Real Property for Water Supply Purposes

Section 187. In any proceeding brought to acquire title to real property required by the City for the purpose of maintaining, preserving or increasing the supply of pure and wholesome water for the use of the City or for the purpose of preventing the contamination or pollution of any supply or source or sources of supply of water heretofore or hereafter acquired by the City, where such real property has been theretofore acquired or used for railroad, highway or other public purpose, the Board or Boards of the City who have authorized the acquisition of such property may direct that the persons or corporations owning such real property so to be acquired or claiming interest therein, shall be allowed the perpetual use for such purposes of the same or of such other real property to be acquired by the City as will afford practicable route or location for such railroad, highway or other public purpose. In such case such persons or corporations shall not directly or indirectly be subject to expense, loss or damage by reason of changing such route or location, but such expense, loss or damage shall be borne by the City. In case any real estate so acquired or used for such public purpose is sought to be acquired by the City, there shall be designated upon the maps referred to in this Article and there shall be described in the petition referred to, such portion of the other real property shown on said maps and described in said petition as it is proposed to substitute in place of the real property then used for such railroad, highway or other public purpose. The Supreme Court, upon the application of the Corporation Counsel to condemn the property shall either approve the substituted route or place or refer the same back to the City authorities for alteration or amendment and may refer the same back with such directions or suggestions as the said Court may deem advisable, and as often as necessary, and until the City authorities shall determine such substituted route or place as may be approved by the Court; an appeal from any order made by said Court under the provisions of this Section may be taken by any person or corporation interested in and aggrieved thereby, to the Appellate Division of the judicial department in which the real estate is situated and shall be heard as a non-enumerated motion. The Court in determining the compensation to be made to the persons or corporations owning such real estate or claiming interest therein, shall include in the amount of such compensation such sum as shall be sufficient to defray the expenses of making such change of route and location and of building said railroad or highway. The Court shall also determine, subject to revision by the Appellate Division, what reasonable time after payment of the awards to said persons or corporations shall be sufficient within which to complete the work of making such change, and the City of New York shall not be entitled to take possession or interfere with the use for the aforesaid purposes, of such real property, before the expiration of such time. This time may be subsequently extended by the Court (subject to review as aforesaid) upon sufficient cause shown. After the expiration of the time so determined or extended no use shall be made of said real property which shall cause pollution to the water supply of the City.

Claims for Compensation to Owner of Contiguous Property; When to be Presented

SECTION 188. Any owner or person interested in real property contiguous to real property taken or entered upon and used and occupied by the City for water supply purposes, which may be affected by the construction and maintenance of any aqueduct, dam, reservoir, sluice, canal, culvert, pumping works, bridge, tunnel, blow off, ventilating shaft or appurtenances thereto, if he intends to make claim for compensation for such taking, entering upon, using or occupying, shall, within three years after the Court shall enter an order granting an application to condemn the real property acquired or to be acquired for such purpose to which his property is contiguous, file with the clerk of the county in which such order has been entered, a statement of his claim duly verified in the manner provided by law for the verification of pleadings in an action, setting forth the real property owned by the claimant and his post office address, and shall within the same time serve on the Corporation Counsel a copy of such verified claim. Such claim shall be entitled in the proceeding in which such order of the Court has been entitled.

In any case where such claim is filed after the trial has been had and before the final decree has been filed in such proceeding, the claimant may apply to the Justice before whom such proceeding was tried, or in case the final decree has been filed and such Justice is unable for any reason to hear such an application, the claimant may apply to another Justice in the county in which such real property is situated, to be heard touching his claim. Thereafter such claimant shall be entitled to offer testimony and be heard before the Court touching his claim and the compensation proper to be made to him, and to have a determination made by the Court as to the amount of such compensation. Every person neglecting or refusing to present such claim to a Justice of the Supreme Court as herein provided within said period of three years shall be deemed to have surrendered his title or interest in such real property or his claims for damages thereto, except so far as he may be entitled as such owner or person interested to the whole or a part of the sum of money awarded by the Court as a just and equitable compensation for taking, using and occupying or as damages for affecting the real property owned by said person, or in which said person is interested.

Closing Streets; Sale to Abutting Owners

SECTION 189. When the Board of Estimate and Apportionment shall authorize the acquisition of real property which is or has been in the bed of any street or which has been used by the public as a street and which has been duly closed and discontinued as a street, either in a separate proceeding brought for that purpose or as excess lands in connection with an improvement, the Court in such proceeding, in case any portion of the cost of the improvement is to be borne by the real property benefited thereby, shall assess the parcels lying and being within the lines and boundaries of the closed street separately from the land not within the closed street and may assess said parcels within the lines of said closed street to the extent of the full unencumbered fee value thereof, freed of all easements, but such assessment shall not exceed the value of such respective parcels as valued by the Court for the purpose of a conveyance to the owner of the lands abutting thereon as hereinafter provided. The Court shall also appraise and determine and separately set forth and state in the tabular abstract, the value of the right, title and interest of the City in and to the fee of the land within the closed street over and above such sum as the Court may assess for benefit on the respective parcels thereof.

Whenever, in such a case as is in this Section specified, the City shall have acquired the fee title to the land within the closed street as incident to and in connection with the closing thereof, the owner of land fronting on such street so discontinued and closed at the time of such closing, or his heirs or assigns, may acquire all the right, title and interest of the City in and to such or any parcel of land lying within the lines of said street discontinued and closed as aforesaid in front of the lands owned by said person or persons respectively, upon payment to the City of the amount found by the Court as the value of such right, title and interest of the City as aforesaid, and also of the amount due on account of all assessments against the same for benefit on account of the closing of said street and a lien thereon; provided, however, that such person shall in writing apply to the Comptroller for said grant or conveyance within two years after the date of the entry of the final decree in said proceeding, and in case such application shall be so made the Comptroller shall cause to be prepared and delivered to said person or persons a conveyance or grant of the right, title and interest of the City in and to such parcel of land in such form as shall be approved by the Corporation Counsel, and when so approved said conveyance shall be executed by the proper officers of the City authorized to convey property belonging to the City.

In conveying the land within a closed street, the City shall not be obliged to convey the land within one half of the closed street to the owner of the land abutting on such half but it may convey all of the land in any such closed street to the owner of the land abutting on one side thereof, whenever in the judgment of the Board of Estimate and Apportionment it will be just and proper so to do.

In case no application for such grant shall be made as aforesaid by the owner of the adjacent property, the right, title and interest of the City therein shall be subject to sale, grant, disposal or use to any person whomsoever in such manner and upon such terms as the Board of Estimate and Apportionment may thereafter designate, provide and approve.

Real Property may be Conveyed or Ceded to the City on Such Terms and Conditions as the Board of Estimate and Apportionment may Prescribe

SECTION 190. An owner of real property which the City is authorized by this act to acquire may convey or cede the same to the City provided such real property be free from encumbrances inconsistent with the title to be acquired by the City, on such terms and conditions, including exemptions from assessments, as the Board of Estimate and Apportionment may from time to time prescribe. When a conveyance of such real property shall be accepted, the City of New York shall become vested with the title to the real property so conveyed to the same extent and effect as if it had been acquired for the improvement by a proceeding had for that purpose.

Purchase of Property under Condemnation or Awards therefor

SECTION 191. When no part of the cost of the improvement is to be assessed upon property benefited thereby, the Board of Estimate and Apportionment after the acquisition thereof shall have been authorized, may purchase the real property so authorized to be acquired or any part thereof, and may purchase the right to any award for damage caused by the taking of real property where title thereto shall have vested in the City prior to the entry of the final decree of the Court.

Vesting of Title

SECTION 192. Except in cases where the Board of Estimate and Apportionment, pursuant to the powers conferred in Subdivision 1 of Section 26, of this Act, has fixed an earlier date, title to property condemned at the instance of the City, shall vest in the City upon the filing of the final decree of the Court and the reversal on appeal of the final decree of the Court shall not divest the City of title to the real property affected by the appeal.

Whenever the Board of Estimate and Apportionment has fixed an earlier date for the vesting in the City of the title to any parcel of property being condemned, interest at the legal rate upon the sum or sums to which the owner or owners thereof are justly entitled upon the date of the vesting of title in the City, from said date to the date of the final decree of the Court, shall be awarded by the Court as part of the compensation to which such owner or owners are entitled.

In any proceeding in which excess lands shall be acquired, when title to any part less than the whole of the real property required for the street, highway, or public place in any one block thereof, between legally existing public streets, shall vest in the City, title to the remainder of the real property required for such street, highway or public place in the same block and title to the excess lands to be acquired in the proceeding abutting on such street, highway or public place in the same block, shall vest in the City simultaneously.

Upon the vesting of title in the City, the City or any person or persons acting under its authority may immediately or any time thereafter, take possession of the real property so vested in the City or any part or parts thereof without any suit or proceeding at law for that purpose.

The Title to be Acquired by the City

SECTION 193. The title acquired by the City of New York to real property required for a street shall be in trust, that the same be appropriated and kept open for, or as part of a public street, forever, in like manner as the other streets in the City are and of right ought to be.

The Board of Estimate and Apportionment may, at any time before the vesting in the City of the title to lands determine whether the fee or an easement shall be acquired and may prescribe such conditions and limitations on the title so to be acquired and as to the temporary or permanent use of the land so to be acquired as it may deem proper.

If any individual or corporation before the entry of the order granting the application to condemn, has acquired by private grant, prescription or otherwise, any easement for the purpose of laying or maintaining in the real property to be acquired for street purposes as herein provided, underground pipes or conduits for the distribution of water, gas, steam or electricity, or for pneumatic service, such easement shall not be extinguished, but the title to the real property so to be acquired for the purposes herein provided for shall be taken subject to such easement; provided, however, that nothing herein contained shall be so construed as to limit the power of the City of New York to acquire by purchase or by condemnation proceedings the entire plant or service of such individual or corporation, or to acquire such easement in such street in any other appropriate proceedings.

City Entitled to Compensation and Liable to Assessment

SECTION 194. If any real property belonging to the City of New York, or in which it may be interested, shall be acquired for or shall be benefited by any such improvement, the City shall be entitled to compensation for the loss and damage it may sustain, and shall be liable to pay for the benefit and advantage it may be deemed to acquire thereby, in like manner as other owners. The assessment against each parcel owned by the City shall be separately stated in the tentative and final decrees of the Court, and the total amount of all such assessments upon real property owned by the City shall also be stated in a gross sum in the final decree of the Court.

Contracts of Landlord and Tenant or Other Contracting Parties; How Affected

SECTION 195. Where the whole of any lot or parcel of real property, under lease or other contract, shall be taken for any of the purposes aforesaid, by virtue of this Article, all the covenants, contracts and engagements between landlord and tenant, or any other contracting parties, respecting the same or any part thereof, shall, upon the vesting of the title in the City of New York, cease and determine and be absolutely discharged; and where part only of any lot or parcel of real property, so under lease or other contract, shall be so taken, all contracts and engagements respecting the same shall upon such vesting of title cease, determine and be absolutely discharged, as to the part thereof so taken.

Corporation Counsel to Represent Interest of City before the Court and Provide Clerks and Offices; Expenses

SECTION 196. The Corporation Counsel shall furnish the Court such necessary clerks and other employees as may be required; and shall provide such suitable offices for the clerks and other employees as may be required to enable the Court to fully and satisfactorily discharge the duties imposed by law. The Corporation Counsel shall, either in person or by such assistant or assistants as he shall designate for the purpose, appear for and protect the interest of the City in all proceedings in court. All salaries of such assistants and other employees and all necessary expenses and disbursements which the City and the Corporation Counsel, on behalf of the City, shall incur under the provisions of this Article shall be paid by the Comptroller and if the Board of Estimate and Apportionment or said Board and the Board of Aldermen as the case may be, so direct, shall be borne and reimbursed and paid to the City by the parties and persons interested and entitled, as owners or otherwise, unto and in the real property deemed to be benefited, and the same shall be included in and taxed by the Court, upon due proof of the services rendered, and disbursements charged as part of the necessary costs and expenses of the said proceedings; but such expenses and disbursements shall not be included in the assessments for benefit until after the same have been taxed before a Justice of the Supreme Court in the appropriate department, and have been directed to be so included by the Board of Estimate and Apportionment, or by said Board and the Board of Aldermen, as the case may be. An amount estimated to be sufficient to cover the legally taxable costs, charges, expenses and disbursements of the Corporation Counsel which are necessary to be incurred in a proceeding, between the date to which the final bill of costs shall be made up and the date of the entry of the final decree of the Court, may be taxed by the Court and included in the assessments for benefit in the proceeding.

Board of Estimate and Apportionment to Direct Who Shall Furnish Maps, Etc.

SECTION 197. Such maps, surveys and diagrams as the Corporation Counsel or the Court shall require to initiate a proceeding for the acquisition of real property, to prepare for the trial of such proceeding, and to enable the Court to hear and determine the claims of the owners of real property affected by the proceeding, and in a proper case to assess for benefit the property deemed to be benefited by the proceeding, shall be furnished by such board, department or officer of the City as the Board of Estimate and Apportionment shall direct. The surveys and maps furnished as aforesaid shall distinctly indicate by separate numbers the names of the claimants to or of the owners of the respective parcels of real property to be taken or to be assessed for benefit by such proceedings as far as the same are known and shall also specify in figures with sufficient accuracy the dimensions and bounds of each of the said tracks to be taken or to be assessed. In all cases the lots on the benefit maps shall be designated on such maps by the same ward or block and lot numbers or other designations as shall be used to designate the said real property on the tax books and the tax maps of the City provided that in case any lot designated on such tax books shall not be assessed as a whole, but either as to a part or in separate parts there shall be added to the designation such letters, numbers or figures or other description as may be necessary in order to indicate the particular parcel or parcels comprised in such tax lot which is or are assessed. In case of an assessment for benefit upon the real property in one or more entire boroughs, it shall not be necessary to prepare benefit maps, but only to refer to the parcels assessed by reference to the block, lot and ward numbers as shown on the tax maps of the City for said borough, but all subdivisions of any such lot or parcel shall be described as aforesaid. The Court may require any board, department or officer of the City of New York, if the Corporation Counsel shall approve, to furnish such other surveys and maps and other information as shall aid and assist the Court in the trial or determination of the proceeding.

Cost of Maps, Etc., to Be Certified to the Corporation Counsel

SECTION 198. The board, department or officer of the City which has been directed by the Board of Estimate and Apportionment or by the Court to prepare surveys, maps or diagrams for a proceeding in which any part of the cost of the improvement is to be assessed upon real property deemed to be benefited thereby, shall in the preparation of such surveys, maps and diagrams make a monthly written return to the Corporation Counsel, duly verified, showing the names of persons employed, and the number of hours occupied by them in the preparation of such maps, and the date of the days of each month so occupied, their respective salaries, and the amount of such salary apportioned to each proceeding according to the time employed thereon. Such return shall be considered presumptive evidence of the correctness of the expense thereof, which, if the Board of Estimate and Apportionment or said Board and the Board of Aldermen as the case may be so determine, shall be included in whole or in part in the assessment for benefit in any proceeding after the same shall have been taxed by the Supreme Court in the manner provided for taxation of bills of costs and expenses in such proceeding.

Costs and Charges; Taxation Thereof

SECTION 199. Except as herein otherwise provided no costs or charges shall be paid or allowed for any service performed under this Article, unless the same shall be taxed by the said Court after notice given as herein provided. Upon such taxation, due proof of the nature and extent of the service rendered and disbursements charged shall be furnished and no unnecessary costs shall be allowed. A bill of said costs, charges and expenses shall be filed in the office of the clerk of the county in which the order granting the application to condemn has been entered, at least ten days before the same shall be presented for taxation. All such costs, fees and expenses or disbursements, which by law are required to be taxed, shall be stated in detail in the bill of costs, charges and expenses and shall be accompanied by such proof of the reasonableness thereof and of the necessity therefor, as is now required by law and the practice of the said Court upon taxation of costs and disbursements in other special proceedings or actions in said Court. There shall be annexed a statement of the amounts, if any, previously taxed, to whom such amounts were payable, and the date of such taxation. A notice by advertisement shall be published for ten days in the *City Record* and a copy of such notice served upon the Corporation Counsel, of the time and place of taxing said costs, charges and expenses, which shall be thereupon taxed by a Justice of the Supreme Court, or a referee under his special order, and before the final decree or decrees of the Court shall be prepared. On the taxation of the final bill of costs there may be a retaxation of any bill previously taxed in the same proceeding, if sufficient reason therefor be made to appear. The Corporation Counsel shall present to the Justice or Referee upon such taxation his certificate in writing that the items of costs, charges and expenses have been audited and examined by him, and also setting forth the result of such audit and examination. The certificate of the Corporation Counsel shall be presumptive evidence of the correctness, reasonableness and necessity of such costs, charges and expenses. Property owners appearing in proceedings instituted pursuant to this article shall not be entitled to recover counsel fees, costs, disbursements or allowances.

Damages for Real Property Taken; When to be Paid

SECTION 200. All damages awarded by the Court with interest thereon from the date of filing of the final decree, and all costs and expenses which may be taxed, shall be paid by the City of New York to the respective owners mentioned or referred to in said final decree, or to the persons and parties in whose favor such costs or expenses shall be taxed, within thirty days after the entry of the final decree of the Court. Interest shall cease to run on the sums awarded as damages six months after the date of the filing of the final decree, unless within that time demand therefor, in writing, be served upon the Comptroller. In case the person or persons legally entitled to receive a sum or a part thereof awarded as damages are unascertainable or in dispute, any person claiming to be interested in such sum or the income therefrom may serve upon the Comptroller a demand that such sum be paid into the Supreme Court, and in case the amount demanded by any person entitled to receive a sum awarded as damages exceeds the amount payable to such person, interest shall continue to run on any amount payable by the City on account of the award or awards referred to in any such demand, or any portion thereof as shall remain unpaid, from the date of said demand until the amount due with interest is paid to the person entitled thereto or in case the person so entitled is undetermined until the amount due with interest is paid into the Supreme Court. Where the amount due is in dispute the Comptroller may tender the claimant to an award a payment on account of his demand and if such tender is refused interest on the amount thereof shall cease unless and until such claimant notifies the Comptroller in writing that he accepts such tender and demands payment accordingly. If such tender be accepted it shall be without prejudice to any right which the claimant may have to an additional sum on account of principal or interest or both.

In case the City shall provide for a fund out of which to pay such damages, costs and expenses, the owners to whom an award shall be made in such proceedings, and the person in whose favor costs and expenses may be taxed, shall not have an action at law against the City of New York for such awards, costs or expenses, but the Court in which said proceedings have been had, upon the application of any such owner or person, in case of the failure of the Comptroller to pay the same within thirty days after demand therefor, shall by order require and direct the Comptroller to pay the said awards, costs and expenses from the said fund, and enforce said order in the same manner as other orders of said Court are enforced. Provided, however, that whenever the amount of damages awarded in any final decree, together with the costs, shall exceed the balance remaining in such fund after deducting all outstanding claims against said balance, the Comptroller shall and he is hereby authorized to raise, by the issue and sale of revenue bonds, such amounts as shall be necessary to pay such damages, costs and expenses, and said Court, upon the application of any owner to whom an award shall be made in such proceeding, and the person in whose favor costs and expenses may be taxed may require or direct the Comptroller to raise the money necessary to enable him to pay such awards, costs and expenses, and from such fund pay the same, except that where any sum or sums shall in said final decree be made to unknown owners, the Supreme Court shall, upon the application of said City of New York, or of any person entitled to, or claiming to be interested in the real property for which said awards have been made, or any part thereof, either direct the same to be retained by the Comptroller or to be paid into the Supreme Court, until the title thereto, or the respective estates and interests of all parties therein shall be determined by said Court, and upon such application, the said Court shall take the proof and testimony of the claimant or person interested in the real property for which said award has been made, or refer the matter to a referee for such purpose.

In any proceeding for the acquisition of title to real property by the City in which title thereto shall have become vested in the City by virtue of a resolution of the Board of Estimate and Apportionment, the said Board may authorize the Comptroller to pay to the person entitled to an award for real property acquired in a proceeding, in advance of the final determination of his damages, a sum to be determined by the Board of Estimate and Apportionment, not exceeding sixty per centum of the amount estimated as damages by the expert or experts employed by the Corporation Counsel in said proceeding, which amount shall be certified to the Comptroller by the Corporation Counsel. Before any such advance payment shall be made the Comptroller shall procure the certificate of the Corporation Counsel showing that the person to whom payment is to be made, is the person legally entitled to receive the same. In case the person entitled to an award at the date of the vesting of title to real property in the City shall have transferred or assigned his claim, such transfer or assignment made by him, or by his successor in interest or legal representative, shall not become binding upon the City of New York, unless the instrument or instruments evidencing such transfer or assignment shall have been executed and filed in the office of the Comptroller, as in this Article provided, prior to any such advance payment. When any such advance payment shall have been made, the Comptroller shall, on paying the awards made for the real property acquired, deduct from the total amount allowed as compensation the sum advanced plus interest thereon from the date of the payment of such advance to the date of the final decree and the balance shall be paid as herein provided. In case an advance payment shall have been authorized and the person entitled thereto shall have been notified by mail or otherwise that the Comptroller is ready to make such advance payment, interest on the amount so authorized to be paid in advance from a date five days after notification by the Comptroller that he is ready to make such advance payment to the time the person entitled thereto shall accept such advance payment, shall be deducted by the Comptroller on paying the awards therefor from the total amount allowed as compensation to such person.

Instruments Assigning or Pledging Awards to Be Filed in the Office of the Comptroller

SECTION 201. In case of the pledge, sale, transfer or assignment of an award by the person entitled to receive the same by virtue of the final decree, or other order of the Court, the instrument evidencing such pledge, sale, transfer or assignment, acknowledged or proved as instruments are required to be acknowledged or proved for the recording of transfers of real property, shall be filed in the office of the Comptroller, who shall indorse on the said instrument its number and the hour, day, month and year of its receipt. If an assignment of an award be contained in an instrument recorded in an office in which instruments affecting real property are by law required to be recorded, a certified copy thereof may be filed in the office of the Comptroller in place of the original. An index shall be kept in alphabetical order under the name of the pledgor or assignor and also the pledgee or assignee, stating the title of the proceeding, the time of filing of the instrument, the file number thereof, and what part of the award is assigned thereby. A memorandum of the file number of the instrument shall be made by the Comptroller on the duplicate decree of the Court opposite the place where the amount of the award so assigned is set forth. Every such instrument not so filed shall be void as against any subsequent pledgee or assignee in good faith and for a valuable consideration from the same pledgor or assignor, his heirs, administrators or assigns, of the same award or any portion thereof, the assignment of which is first duly filed in the office of the Comptroller. Payment to the assignee or pledgee shown to be entitled to the award by such record in the office of the Comptroller shall protect the City from liability to any other person or persons.

Moneys of Persons Under Disability, How Disposed of; Moneys Paid to Persons Not Entitled Thereto

SECTION 202. When an owner in whose favor an award shall have been made in a final decree is under legal disability, or absent from the City, and when the name of the owner shall not be set forth or mentioned in the final decree, or when the owner, although named in said decree or report, cannot upon diligent inquiry be found, or where there are adverse or conflicting claims to the money awarded as compensation, the City shall pay such award into the Supreme Court to be secured, disposed of, invested and paid out as the said Court shall direct and such payment shall be as valid and effectual in all respects as if made to the person entitled thereto; and in default of such payment into court the City shall be and remain liable for such award with lawful interest thereon from a date one year after the date of the final decree to the person or persons who may thereafter be found entitled to the same. Where an award shall be paid to a person not entitled thereto the person to whom it ought to have been paid may sue for and recover the same, with lawful interest and costs of suit, as so much money had and received to his use, by the person to whom the same shall have been so paid. Payment of an award to a person named in the final decree of the Court as the owner thereof, if not under legal disability, shall, in the absence of notice in writing to the Comptroller of adverse claims thereto, protect the City.

Sums Assessed to Be Liens; Provisions of Article XXV of This Act Not Applicable

SECTION 203. The sums assessed by the Court for the benefit and advantage of an improvement shall be a lien or charge on the real property specified in the final decree of the Court, but nothing herein contained shall affect any agreement between landlord and tenant or other contracting parties respecting the payment of such assessment. Nothing contained in Article XXV of this Act relating to the vacation and reduction of assessments shall apply to assessments made and levied pursuant to this Article.

Notice of Filing the Final Decree of Assessments

SECTION 204. The Corporation Counsel shall transmit to the Chamberlain or such officer as shall be charged with the collection of assessments, immediately after the filing of the final decree of the Court as to assessments for benefit, a duplicate copy thereof and if such assessment affect real property in a borough other than the Borough of Manhattan, also a triplicate copy thereof; and the Chamberlain or such other officer shall give public notice by advertisement for at least ten days in the *City Record,* as soon as practicable and within ten days after receipt thereof, that the final decree of the Court as to assessments for benefit has been filed, specifying the title of such assessment, the date of the filing of such final decree and also the date of entry in the " record of assessments confirmed," kept in the Bureau for the Collection of Assessments and Arrears, notifying all persons, owners of the real property affected by any such assessment, that, unless the amount assessed for benefit on any parcel of real property shall be paid within sixty days after the date of said entry of any such assessments, interest shall thereafter be collected thereon as provided in the following Section; and all provisions of law or ordinance requiring any other or different notice of assessments and interest thereon are hereby repealed.

Interest to be Charged on Assessments if Not Paid in Sixty Days

SECTION 205. If any such assessment shall remain unpaid for the period of sixty days after the date of entry thereof in the said "record of assessments confirmed," provided that the notice prescribed in Section 204 shall have been given, the officer authorized to collect and receive the amount of such assessment shall charge, collect and receive interest thereon at the rate of seven per centum per annum, to be calculated to the date of payment from the date of the entry of such assessments in the " record of assessments confirmed."

Assessments May Be Set Off Against Award

SECTION 206. If an owner to whom an award shall have been made in the final decree of the Court as to awards, also own real property against which an assessment in the final decree of the Court as to assessments shall have been entered for collection in the same proceeding, he may, at any time prior to receiving payment of the award, apply to the Comptroller and Collector of Assessments and Arrears to have the award set off against the assessment, and thereupon such set-off shall be made as of the date of the entry of the assessment for collection. If the award exceed the assessment, the City shall be liable for interest only on the amount of such excess. If the assessment exceed the award, the owner assessed shall be liable for interest on the amount of such excess as if no set-off had been made. If it shall appear by the final decree of the Court as to awards or otherwise, that a person entitled to an award also owns property against which an assessment in the same proceeding shall have been entered for collection, the City may, without the assent of the person entitled to the award, set off the assessment against the award. Such set-off shall be made by the

City in the same manner and have the same effect as if made on the application of the person entitled to the award.

How Notices Shall be Posted

SECTION 207. Whenever handbills are required by statute to be posted in any proceeding provided for in this Article, they shall be posted or affixed with paste or other adhesive substance in three conspicuous places upon or near the real property to be taken in such proceeding, and proof by affidavit that such notice has been posted shall be sufficient evidence that said notice remained posted during the whole of the period required by law.

Publication of Notices Where Property is Without the City

SECTION 208. In a proceeding to acquire title by the City to real property located without the limits of the City, all notices in such proceeding required to be published in the *City Record,* shall be published also in two newspapers published or circulating in the county in which such real property is located, in ten consecutive issues thereof.

Order of Court Granting Application to Condemn to be Filed in the Office Where Instruments Affecting Real Property are Required to be Recorded

SECTION 209. The Corporation Counsel shall within ten days after the entry of an order granting an application to condemn, file a copy of such order to be recorded in the office where instruments affecting real property in the county in which the real property to be acquired is situated, are required to be recorded. There shall be endorsed upon such copy order a reference to the section and block, or sections and blocks on the land map of the City of New York in and for such county which includes the real property to be taken by such proceeding or abuts thereon. The Register or County Clerk with whom such copy order shall be filed shall index in the index of conveyances on each block so endorsed on said copy order a statement giving the title of said proceeding and the date of the entry of said order.

Procedure in Case Property to be Acquired is Situated in Two or More Counties; Filing of Orders, Reports and Decrees in Such Cases

SECTION 210. If the real property to be acquired in any proceeding be situated in two or more counties, the application to condemn such real property, may be made to the Supreme Court, at any special term thereof, held in any judicial district in which any one of the said counties is situated. If the real property to be acquired in any proceeding be situated in two judicial districts, the application to condemn the same may be made in either judicial district. The order granting the application to condemn, in any such proceeding, shall be entered and filed in the office of the clerk of any one of the counties in which a part of the property to be thereby acquired is situated, as the Court shall direct, and a certified copy of the order granting the application to condemn and a certified copy of the final decree shall be filed in the office in which instruments affecting real property are required to be recorded, in the other county or counties in which any part of the property thereby acquired is situated. In all other respects the proceeding shall be conducted in the same manner as a proceeding affecting real property situated in only one county.

Discontinuance of Proceedings by Board of Estimate and Apportionment

SECTION 211. The Board of Estimate and Apportionment may discontinue any legal proceeding taken for the purpose provided for in this Article, as to the whole or a part of the lands to be acquired in such proceeding, at any time before title to the real property to be thereby acquired shall have vested in the City of New York, and may cause new proceedings to be taken for the condemnation of such real property. The resolution of the Board declaring any such proceeding discontinued shall effect the discontinuance of such proceeding or such part thereof as may be discontinued, upon the filing of an authenticated copy of such resolution in the office of the clerk of the county where the order granting the application to condemn shall have been entered and filed. But in case of such discontinuance the reasonable actual cash disbursements, necessarily incurred and made in good faith by any party interested, shall be paid by the City of New York, after the same shall have been taxed by a Justice of the Supreme Court, or by a referee under his special order, upon ten days' notice of such taxation being previously given to the Corporation Counsel, provided the application to have such disbursements taxed shall be made and presented to the Court within one year after the filing of the resolution of the Board discontinuing the proceeding in whole or in part. The amounts taxed as disbursements shall be due and payable thirty days after written demand for payment thereof shall have been filed with the Comptroller.

Discontinuance of a Proceeding by the Court

SECTION 212. In any case where all or a part of the cost of the improvement is to be assessed upon property benefited thereby, if persons appearing by the tentative decree to be the owners of a majority in amount of awards and liable for a majority in amount of assessments shall at any time before the signing by the Court of the final decree apply for the discontinuance of the proceeding, the Court, provided title to the real property being acquired shall not have theretofore vested in the City, and provided the real property being acquired be not required for a public park, parkway, public square or public place, shall order the proceedings to be discontinued, and may, in its discretion, impose as a condition that the persons so objecting or petitioning for such discontinuance shall present to the Court a certificate, signed by the Comptroller, that the City of New York has been reimbursed for the expenses incurred by it on account of such proceeding.

Amendment of Defects, Et Cetera

SECTION 213. The Court may at any time amend any defect or informality in any notice, petition, pleading, order, or decree in a proceeding instituted pursuant to this Article, or cause real property affected by such defect, informality or lack of jurisdiction to be excluded therefrom, or other real property affected by such defect, informality or lack of jurisdiction to be included therein by amendment, upon ten days' notice, published and posted as provided by this Article for the institution of a proceeding, and may permit any person having an interest therein to be made a party thereto, or to relieve from any default, mistake or irregularity, and may direct such further notices to be given to any party in interest as it shall deem proper.

ARTICLE XXV

Assessments for Local Improvements and Awards for Damages Caused by Grading Streets

Board of Assessors

SECTION 214. The Mayor shall appoint three persons who shall constitute the Board of Assessors. The said Board shall make all assessments, other than those required by law to be confirmed by a court of record, for public or local improvements for which assessments may be legally imposed in any part of the City and shall also ascertain and make awards for damages to land, buildings, and improvements by reason of the grading of streets, in the manner hereinafter provided in this Article. The said Board may compel the attendance of witnesses and the production of papers by subpoena attested by any member of the Board and may examine and administer oaths to witnesses and shall cause any testimony taken before it to be reduced to writing.

Award of Damages to Land and Buildings by Reason of Grading Streets

SECTION 215. An owner who has built upon or otherwise improved his property prior to the original establishment of the grade of any street or avenue by lawful authority and the lessee thereof shall be entitled to damages caused by the grading of the street in accordance with the grade established.

If an abutting owner has built upon or otherwise improved his property in conformity with the grade of any street or avenue established by lawful authority and if thereafter such grade is changed, such abutting owner and the lessee of such property shall be entitled to damages caused by the grading of the street in accordance with such change of grade.

The word lessee as used in this Section shall include only a person whose lease does not expire within three years from the date of the completion and acceptance of the grading by the city authorities.

Whenever any street shall have been graded to a grade which in the opinion of the Board of Estimate and Apportionment has been occasioned by an improvement other than the normal and usual street improvement, the said Board may in its discretion within sixty days after the grading shall have been completed and accepted by the city authorities in charge of the work, make a certificate that in its opinion the street in question has been graded to a special grade. Such certificate shall be transmitted to the Board of Assessors together with the plan and profile of the portion of the street affected by such special grade; upon such plan and profile there shall be shown the level which in the opinion of the Board of Estimate and Apportionment constitutes the normal grade for the street and the special grade to which the street has been graded. Each owner or lessee of the land fronting on that portion of the street affected by such special grade shall be entitled to damages caused by reason of the departure of the grade of the street from the normal grade as shown on such plan and profile.

Except as hereinabove provided there shall be no liability for originally establishing a grade or for changing an established grade of any street or avenue in the City.

The Board of Assessors shall ascertain and award damages for grading streets in the cases provided for herein, in the manner hereinafter set forth.

(a) When any street shall have been regulated and graded and the city authorities in charge of the work of such grading shall have transmitted a certificate of the completion and acceptance thereof to the Board of Assessors, said Board shall cause to be published in the *City Record* twice a week for four successive weeks a notice to all persons claiming to have been injured by the physical grading of such street, to present their claims in writing to the Board of Assessors. Said notice shall specify the place where and the time when the said Board will receive evidence and testimony of the nature and extent of such injury.

(b) After hearing and considering the testimony and evidence and after viewing and inspecting the property claimed to have been injured, the Board of Assessors shall ascertain and award the compensation, if any, which ought justly to be made to the respective owners of the real property damaged by such grading. Such awards shall be considered and acted upon by the Board of Assessors or by the Board of Review in the manner provided in Section 217 after the notice as therein provided shall have been given. Interest at the legal rate upon the sum or sums to which the respective owners of the real property damaged by such grading are justly entitled upon the date of the completion and acceptance by the City of the grading of the street, from said date to a date sixty days after the date set in the published notice for the hearing upon objections to the awards, shall be awarded by the Board of Assessors as part of the compensation to which such owners are entitled.

(c) No award shall be made in any case unless a claim in writing therefor shall have been filed with the Board of Assessors within ninety days after the grading shall have been completed and accepted by the city authorities in charge of the work, or at or prior to the time specified in the notice caused to be published by said Board as above required.

(d) The Board of Assessors shall also determine the reasonable expense incident to the making of awards for damages which have been incurred by it or by the Corporation Counsel of the City upon the hearings before said Board.

(e) The amount of such awards, together with the interest included therein and the reasonable expense of making the awards as determined by the Board of Assessors shall be included in an assessment to be levied upon the property deemed by the Board of Assessors to have been benefited by the grading of the street in question or by the improvement of which said grading forms a part.

Certificates; Description of Property

SECTION 216. All assessments shall be made by the Board of Assessors on the following certificates, to wit:

(a) The officer or head of the board or department charged with the execution of the work in question, shall certify to the Board of Assessors the total amount of all the expenses which shall have been actually incurred by the City on account thereof, excepting, however, that there shall be omitted from such expenses all charges, if such there be, for altering, removing or relocating water mains, pipes or appurtenances in actual use as part of the water distribution system of the City, or any other installations in actual use by any revenue-producing enterprise belonging to the City.

(b) The Board of Assessors shall certify the amount of any awards made for loss and damage to owners of property by reason of grading any street or by the improvement of which said grading forms a part, the interest upon such awards and the reasonable expense of making the same as determined by said Board.

(c) The Comptroller shall certify to the Board of Assessors the registration of the contract for the work in question, and shall also certify the amount of the interest, at the legal rate, upon the several installments advanced or payments made on account of such work, from the time of such payment or advance by the City, to a day sixty days after the date of such interest certificate.

Thereafter the Board of Assessors shall assess upon the property benefited the aggregate amount of such certificates or such proportion thereof as shall have been duly authorized and the said Board shall not in any way be enjoined, restrained, hindered or delayed in the performance of this duty. The property so assessed by it shall be described in the assessment by the same ward or block numbers or other designations as shall be used to designate such property on the tax books of the City, and also by the street numbers, if any, or such description as will clearly show the property assessed. The name of the owner or owners and occupant or occupants, if they be known to the assessors, shall also be indicated in the assessment, and it shall be the duty of the assessors to inquire of the Tax Commissioner and others for such information.

Notice of Completion of Assessments or Awards to Be Given

SECTION 217. When the Board of Assessors has completed any proposed assessment or award, it shall give notice to the owner or owners; such notice shall be published daily in the *City Record* for at least ten days successively. The notice shall describe the limits within which it is proposed to lay the said assessment, or, in case of awards, the block and lot numbers of the property affected, and shall contain a request that all persons whose interests may be affected thereby, and who may be opposed to the same, present their objections in writing, to the Board of Assessors, within thirty days from the date of such notice, specifying a time and place after the expiration of the said thirty days when and where the said objections will be heard and testimony received in reference thereto. If after hearing and examining such objections and testimony, the assessors shall not deem it proper to alter their assessment or award, or having altered it there shall still be objections to the same, it shall be their duty to present such objections with the proposed assessment or award to the Board of Review. If no objections shall be received, or if the Board of Assessors shall alter the assessment or award so as to satisfy the objectors, said Board shall forthwith confirm such assessment or award. An assessment or award so confirmed shall be of the same force and effect as if confirmed by the Board of Review.

Confirmation of Any Award Final and Conclusive

SECTION 218. The confirmation of any award by the Board of Assessors or by the Board of Review, as provided in this Act shall be final and conclusive upon all parties and persons whomsoever with respect to the amount of damage sustained.

Awards for Intended Regulation

SECTION 219. The Board of Assessors may, in its discretion, upon the receipt from the Comptroller of the certificate of the registration of contract for the work in question, make an award with respect to any property built upon or otherwise improved and abutting upon that portion of the street to be regulated and graded under said contract for said intended regulation. No interest shall be paid upon such awards for intended regulation, nor shall any further award be made with respect to any property for damage to which an award for such intended regulation has been made. Whenever an award shall so be made prior to the confirmation of the final assessment for the work in question, it shall, upon the confirmation of such award, be certified to the Comptroller together with a statement of the probable amount of the assessment to be levied against the property with respect to which the award has been made. If the amount of such award shall exceed the probable amount of such assessment as so stated, the excess shall be paid by the Comptroller. The balance of such award shall not be paid until after the confirmation of the final assessment for the work in question imposed upon such property.

Assessments After Registration of Contract

SECTION 220. The Board of Assessors or the Board of Review may confirm an assessment at any time after the registration of the contract for such work in the office of the Comptroller. Should such assessment be for an amount less than the total assessable cost of such work, an additional assessment may be levied for such excess. Should such assessment exceed the total cost of such work, the surplus shall be returned to those legally entitled to such surplus.

Assessments to Be Transmitted for Entry and Collection and Awards Certified for Payment

SECTION 221. All assessments immediately upon confirmation by the Board of Assessors or by the Board of Review as the case may be shall be transmitted for entry and collection to the Chamberlain or such officer as shall be charged with the collection of assessments for improvements and all awards immediately upon confirmation shall be certified to the Comptroller for payment.

Awards: When to Be Paid

SECTION 222. All awards made pursuant to the provisions of this Article shall be paid by the City to the persons entitled thereto within sixty days after the confirmation thereof, together with interest thereon at the legal rate from a date sixty days after the date set in the published notice for the hearing upon objections to the awards; provided, however, that all the provisions of Sections 200, 201 and 202 of this Act, so far as the same are applicable, shall apply to the payment of such awards and the liability of the City to pay interest thereon, except as in this Article otherwise provided.

Remedies

SECTION 223. No suit or action in the nature of a bill in equity or otherwise shall be commenced for the vacating of any assessment in the City, or to remove a cloud upon title arising from an assessment; but owners of property shall be confined to remedies in such cases to the proceedings under this Article and Article XXIII.

Comptroller's Power

SECTION 224. The Comptroller acting pursuant to the written advice of the Corporation Counsel may cancel in writing and annul any and all void assessments heretofore and hereafter confirmed, may compromise and settle claims for assessments for local improvements heretofore or hereafter confirmed and interest thereon and payments made in accordance with the terms of such settlements shall be in the nature of accord and satisfaction and no action shall be maintainable to recover amounts thus paid. The Comptroller may correct at any time after the confirmation and entry of an assessment for a public or local improvement heretofore or hereafter confirmed, any erroneous assessment due to a clerical error irrespective of whether or not such assessment has been paid and may refund any sum paid on account thereof in excess of the amount thereof as corrected.

Petition to the Supreme Court in Case of Fraud or Error; Power of Court Limited

SECTION 225. If in the proceedings relative to any assessment or assessments for local improvements, or in the proceedings to collect the same, any fraud, substantial error or irregularity shall be alleged to have been committed, the party aggrieved thereby may apply to a Justice of the Supreme Court at special term or in chambers, who shall thereupon, upon due notice to the Corporation Counsel, proceed forthwith to hear the proofs and allegations of the parties. If, upon such hearing it shall appear that the alleged fraud, substantial error or irregularity, other than such as are specified in the next Section, has been committed, such assessment shall be vacated or modified as follows:

(a) If it shall appear that the property in question could not be legally assessed for the local improvement such assessment may be vacated, and the lien created thereby, or by any subsequent proceedings, shall cease.

(b) If it shall appear that by reason of any such fraud, substantial error or irregularity the expense of any local improvement has been unlawfully increased, the Court or Justice may order that such assessment upon the lands of such aggrieved party be modified by deducting therefrom such sum as is in the same proportion to such assessment as is the whole amount of such unlawful increase to the whole amount of the expense of such local improvement.

(c) If it shall appear that by reason of fraud, substantial error or irregularity the assessment upon the lands of such aggrieved party has been increased, the Justice may order that such assessment be reduced to the extent that the same may be shown to have been in fact increased by reason of such fraud, substantial error or irregularity.

In no event shall that proportion of any assessment claimed to be excessive which is equivalent to the fair value or fair cost of any local improvement (with interest at the rate of three per cent. per annum from the date of confirmation to the date of the final order of reduction and seven per cent. thereafter) be disturbed for any cause either through the proceedings provided in this Article or through an action to recover money paid for assessments.

Any order that may be made by a Court or Justice under authority of this section shall be filed in the office of the county clerk in the county in which the lands are situated, and after the filing of a certified copy thereof with the officer having charge of the assessment, it shall be the duty of such officer to cancel or reduce the assessment as required by the order or do any other act required thereby.

Assessments Not to Be Set Aside for Certain Irregularities and Technicalities

SECTION 226. No assessment heretofore made or imposed, or which shall hereafter be made or imposed for any local improvement or other public work, already completed or now being made or performed, or which shall hereafter be made, done, or performed, shall hereafter be vacated or set aside for or by reason of any omission to advertise, or irregularity in advertising any ordinance, resolution, notice, or other proceeding relative to, or authorizing the improvement or work for which such assessment shall have been made or imposed, or for proposals to do the work, or for or by reason of the omission of any officer to perform any duty imposed upon him, or for or by reason of any defect in the authority of any department or officer upon whose action the assessment shall be in any manner or to any extent dependent, or for or by reason of any omission to comply with or carry out any detail of any law or ordinance, or for or by reason of any irregularity or technicality, except only in cases in which fraud shall be shown and in case of an assessment for repaving any street or public place, upon property for which an assessment has once been paid for paving the same street or public place; and all property in said city benefited by any improvement or other public work already completed, or now being made or performed and hereafter made, done or performed, except as aforesaid, shall be liable to assessment for such improvement or work and all assessments for any such improvement or other public work shall be valid and binding notwithstanding any such omission, irregularity, defect in authority or technicality. No assessment shall be vacated by reason of fraud or irregularity in the proceedings to collect the same by sale of the assessed premises; but, upon proof of such fraud or irregularity, such sale shall be set aside and the respective rights and liabilities of the assessed person and of the City shall become and be the same as if such sale had not been made.

Re-assessment

SECTION 227. Any lands which may be discharged from any lien for an assessment for any local improvement or as to which a sale of the tax lien thereon for such assessments has been vacated or set aside may be again assessed by the Board of Assessors, provided the same be lawfully subject to assessment, after a public hearing, notice of which said hearing shall be published twice in each week for two successive weeks in the *City Record,* for such amount as would have been justly chargeable if fraud or irregularity had not been committed; and the amount so assessed shall be a lien on said lands until paid, and shall be collectable in the manner provided for the collection of assessments, but all proceedings to make a new assessment shall be at the expense of the City.

All Claims May Be Embraced in One Proceeding

SECTION 228. Any person applying for relief under the provisions of this Article may embrace in one proceeding any or all assessments for local improvement in which he is interested.

When Proceedings to Be Brought

SECTION 229. Any proceeding to vacate or reduce an assessment in the City must be brought within one year after the confirmation thereof.

ARTICLE XXVI

Miscellaneous Provisions

Definitions

SECTION 230. As used in this Act, unless a different meaning be clearly indicated by the context:

1. The word, "City" means The City of New York;

2. The word, "person" comprehends in meaning a natural person, a corporation, association, joint stock association and co-partnership and the plural as well as the singular number;

3. The words, "now" and "existing" and any equivalent word or words shall be construed to refer to the condition existing at the time this Act shall take effect and the words "heretofore" and "hereafter" or any equivalent word or words shall be construed to refer to the time anterior or subsequent to the time when it shall come into force, as the case may require;

4. The word, "officer" means any elective officer, the heads of departments or offices not subordinate to any department, their deputies and assistants, the members of permanent boards and commissions and such other persons in the service of the City or any of the counties therein as the Board of Estimate and Apportionment may designate

as such. The words "employee" or "employees" comprehend every person employed by the City or any county therein other than officers.

5. The term "real estate" or "real property" or any equivalent term, except as used in Article XXIV, comprehends in meaning lands, improvements upon lands whether considered separately or as a part of the land, property and interests other than land or appurtenances declared by general law to be real property, lands under water, the water of any lake, pond, stream or back-water, all easements and hereditaments, corporeal or incorporeal, and every estate, interest or right in real property, including terms for years and liens by mortgage, judgment or otherwise.

6. The phrase "the time when (or "at which") this Act shall take effect" or any equivalent expression shall be construed to refer to the time when it shall become law by the Governor's approval or otherwise as provided in the Constitution of the State; the phrase "the time when (or "at which") this Act shall come into force" or any equivalent expression shall be construed to refer to the first day of January, 1926, and to a time on said day prior to the performance of any act or the happening of any event.

Inferior Courts Continued

SECTION 231. Courts of inferior local jurisdiction existing at the time this Act shall take effect, including the City Court, the Municipal Courts, the Court of Special Sessions and the City Magistrates' Courts shall continue to exist and each of said courts, the justices and magistrates thereof shall continue to possess the jurisdictions, powers, functions and duties then prescribed by law. The justices and magistrates of said courts shall be elected or appointed in the manner and receive the compensation so provided.

City Record

SECTION 232. The paper heretofore published known as the *City Record* shall continue to be published by or under contract with the City in such manner and under such management and supervision as the Board of Estimate and Apportionment may determine or authorize. Contracts for the publication thereof shall be such and shall contain such terms and conditions as the Board of Estimate and Apportionment shall determine or approve. The *City Record* shall contain all messages, budgets, statements, reports, lists, advertisements, notices and other official matters or information required by law or ordinance to be published by the City, any county therein or any officer, board, department, bureau or commission of any thereof and all such other matters of official concern to the City or any county therein or to any official, board, department, bureau or commission or corporation sustained in whole or in part out of appropriations made by the City as the Board of Estimate and Apportionment may direct to be published or as may be directed to be published by its authority. The Board of Estimate and Apportionment shall determine the number of copies of supplements of the *City Record* containing lists of registered voters and supplements containing records of the assessed valuation of real estate, respectively, that are to be published, as provided in Sections 233 and 234 and the prices at which the same shall be sold, but all moneys received for any of the same shall be paid into the City Treasury.

Preparation of Registry of Voters; Publication in City Record

SECTION 233. It shall be the duty of each captain or other officer of police, immediately upon receiving from the Board of Elections any list of registered voters, to deliver the same to the supervisor or other person in charge of the *City Record*, who shall arrange the same by Assembly Districts and by Election Districts of Assembly Districts in such manner that the names of all registered voters residing at any given house-number shall appear together and those of each street in each Election District shall appear arranged by house-numbers in consecutive order, each street separately. As soon as any registry of voters shall be completed and arranged as aforesaid, and in any event within 108 hours after the close of each annual registration, the same shall be printed and published in the *City Record*. The registry of each Assembly District shall be printed separately as a supplement to the *City Record* and each supplement, containing the registry of one Assembly District, shall be sold separately to persons wishing to purchase the same.

Publication of Record of Assessed Valuation of Real Estate in City Record

SECTION 234. It shall be the duty of the Commissioner of Taxes and the supervisor or other person in charge of the *City Record* to cause the annual record of the assessed valuation of real estate to be printed and published in the *City Record* in type not smaller than nonpareil, as promptly and expeditiously as possible after the completion of the same, and the opening thereof for public inspection, and in any event within such time as the Board of Aldermen may prescribe by ordinance or resolution. The annual record of the assessed valuation of real estate of each section, district or ward shall be printed separately as a supplement to the *City Record*. On each such supplement shall be printed the designation of the section, district or ward the record whereof is therein contained, its boundaries or an outline map thereof and the name of the borough in which it is situated. Each supplement, containing the record of the assessed valuation of real estate of one section, district or ward, shall be sold separately to persons wishing to purchase the same.

Expense Limited to Unexpended Balance

SECTION 235. No expense shall be incurred, to be met either presently or in the future, by any officer, board, department, commission or employee of the City or any county therein unless there shall be an unexpended balance in an appropriation authorized to be applied thereto sufficient to meet such expense at the time and no liability of the City shall result from any attempt to create the same in excess of the amount so appropriated and available to meet the same.

Officer or Employee Not to Have Interest in Transactions with the City; Penalty

SECTION 236. No officer or employee of the City or any county therein shall be interested, directly or indirectly, as contracting party, partner, stockholder or otherwise in any purchase, lease, contract, business or work or the execution, performance or conduct thereof, the price, consideration or expense whereof is payable by the City or any such county or out of any assessment made by the City or under authority of any act of any board, officer or other City or county authority or in any sale or lease made by the City or at its instance or for taxes or assessments and any such officer or employee who shall knowingly be so interested, except by will or succession, shall be guilty of a misdemeanor, shall forfeit his office or employment and all of the pay and emoluments thereof and shall be disqualified to hold any office or employment under the City or any county therein. All contracts and transactions in which any officer or employee shall have any such interest shall at the election of the Board of Estimate and Apportionment be absolutely void or terminable as it may determine.

Officer or Employee Not to Influence Election or Appointment to Office; Penalty

SECTION 237. Any officer or employee of the City or any county therein who shall give or promise or offer to give to any person any consideration whatsoever, actual or contingent, in consideration or upon condition of the nomination, election or appointment to any office or employment of the City or any county therein of any person or of the exercise or promise to exercise influence to procure any such nomination, election or employment shall be guilty of a misdemeanor and shall forfeit his office or employment and all of the pay and emoluments thereof and shall be disqualified to hold any office or employment under the City or any county therein.

Officer Not to Appoint or Retain in Any Office or Employment any Person Dismissed on Charges; Penalty

SECTION 238. The appointment or reappointment to or retention in any office or department of the City or any county therein or in the police force or fire force, of any person who shall have been lawfully dismissed upon charges, if the officer making such appointment or any officer permitting such retention shall know or shall have had notice of such disqualification, shall constitute conclusive ground for the removal from office of the officer making such appointment or permitting such retention and any officer or employee of the City who shall audit, pay or direct or procure the payment of any compensation or emolument to any person so disqualified, if he shall know or have had notice of such disqualification, shall be personally liable to the City for all sums whatsoever which shall be so paid with interest from the dates of all such payments respectively.

Penalties to this Act in Addition to Other Penalties

SECTION 239. Every disqualification, forfeiture and penalty imposed or provided for in this Act shall be in addition to and not exclusive of any other penalty or punishment in such case prescribed by law.

Court to Compel Testimony Required by City Official

SECTION 240. In the event of non-compliance with any subpoena issued by any officer, board or commission as authorized by this Act, or of refusal to be sworn or to testify or to answer any question propounded to any witness in the course of any investigation conducted by any officer, board or commission as so authorized, application may be made to any Justice of the Supreme Court for an order compelling the witness or proposed witness to obey the subpoena or submit to be sworn or to testify or to answer any such question and such Justice, in case he shall decide that the person in question has not the constitutional right to refuse to appear, produce such evidence, be sworn or testify as the case may be or to answer any question which such Justice shall decide to be pertinent to such authorized inquiry, shall order such person to appear, be sworn, testify or answer each such pertinent question, as the case may require, and in event of failure to obey such order may punish such person for comtempt in the same manner and to the same extent as if such person had been subpoenaed as a witness in a civil action tried before such Justice and a like order or direction had been made or given by such Justice during the course of such trial and had not been obeyed; but no testimony or evidence obtained by compulsory process as aforesaid shall be received or offered in evidence upon the trial of any criminal action.

Access of Public to Books, Accounts and Papers

SECTION 241. 1. **Copies to be furnished.** All officers of the City and of every county therein and the chief executive officer of each and every bureau of any department or office, except district attorneys, the Police Commissioner, the Corporation Counsel and bureaus of the Police and Law Departments, shall with all reasonable promptness furnish to any tax-payer desiring the same a true certified copy of any book, account or paper kept by such officer or by any office, board, department, bureau or commission of which he shall be chief executive officer or such part of any thereof as may be demanded, upon payment in advance by the person demanding the same, of such fee, if any, as shall have been prescribed by the Board of Estimate and Apportionment.

2. **Open to inspection.** All such books, accounts and papers, except those of district attorneys and the Police and Law Departments, respectively, shall be open at all times to the inspection of any tax-payer, subject to reasonable regulations with respect to the time and manner of inspection.

3. **Court order to compel compliance.** In case such inspection, or a copy of any such book, account or paper shall be refused to any tax-payer, such tax-payer on his sworn petition describing such particular books, accounts and papers as he desires to inspect, or of which he desires copies, may, upon notice of not less than twenty-four hours to the chief executive officer of the office, board, department, bureau or commission refusing such inspection or copy, apply to any Justice of the Supreme Court of any county in the City for an order directing that such inspection be permitted or such copy be furnished, and if the petitioner be entitled to such inspection or copy under the provisions of this Section, such Justice shall make such order and therein shall specify the time and manner of compliance therewith; provided, that if the district attorney of any county within the City or the Corporation Counsel shall certify under oath to the Justice to whom such application shall be made that in his opinion the granting of such application will be detrimental to the public interest and in his certificate shall state the grounds for such opinion, such Justice in his discretion may deny such application or he or any other Justice may vacate or modify any order granting the same that may have been made. An order granting any such application may be enforced and refusal to obey the same punished as in the case of an order of mandamus.

Court Order for Examination of Public Officer

SECTION 242. 1. **Ground for issuing order.** Any officer of the City or of any of the counties therein, including any member of the Board of Aldermen, any head of a department or of any bureau, any member of any permanent board or commission, or any executive officer of any revenue-producing improvement maintained by the City, and any deputy or assistant of any thereof, if a Justice of the Supreme Court for any county within the City shall so order, may be summarily examined upon an order, to be made by such Justice on an application for such examination based on an affidavit of the Mayor, the Comptroller, the Commissioner of Inquiry, any five members of the Board of Aldermen or any five citizens who are taxpayers, directing such examination to be made publicly, at a time and place fixed in such order, with respect to any alleged wrongful diversion, misapplication or misuse of moneys or property of the City or any violation of law or incompetency, neglect or misfeasance in connection with any conduct or inspection of public work or any delinquency in the conduct of office or any neglect of duty of which the person to be examined is alleged in such affidavit to have been guilty or to have knowledge or information.

2. **Procedure.** Any person so to be examined shall answer such pertinent questions and produce such books and papers under his control relative to the subject of inquiry as the Justice shall direct. The examination may be continued from time to time before the same Justice or any other Justice in the same judicial department as may be ordered. Other witnesses, and as well the parties making such application, in the discretion of the Justice, may be compelled by his order to attend and be examined touching the subject of inquiry. Such Justice may punish any refusal to attend or to answer questions pursuant to his order as for contempt of court with the same power and authority which he would possess to enforce obedience or to punish contempt in like circumstances upon the trial of a civil action, but testimony given in the course of any such examination shall not be admissible in any criminal proceeding against the person giving the same. Such examination shall be reduced to

writing and filed in the office of the county clerk for such county within the City as the Justice directing the examination shall direct and notice of the same shall be given to the Comptroller and to the Corporation Counsel.

3. **Costs.** A Justice who shall have directed any such examination may impose costs upon the party or parties applying for such examination, not exceeding two hundred and fifty dollars, if he is of the opinion that there was no probable cause for making the application.

Taxpayer's Suits Against Officers

SECTION 243. All officers, boards, commissions and employees are trustees of the properties, estates, rights and funds of the City to the extent that they shall manage or control or ought to manage or control the same and any person who shall pay or be under obligations to pay taxes to the City is a *cestui que* trust with respect thereto and any co-trustee or *cestui que* trust, as against any such trustee or trustees, shall be entitled to and may enforce all of the rights and remedies provided by law for any co-trustee or *cestui que* trust and to maintain an action to prevent the entering into or carrying out of any illegal or unauthorized contract or transaction or waste of or injury to any property, estate, interest, right or funds subject to such trust.

Suits Against the City

SECTION 244. 1. **Service of papers.** All process and papers for the commencement of actions or legal proceedings of any description against the City shall be served upon the Mayor, the Comptroller or the Corporation Counsel.

2. **Place of trial.** All actions wherein the City is a party defendant shall be tried in that county within the City in which the cause of action arose or in the County of New York, subject only to the power of the court to change the place of trial in cases provided by law.

3. **Execution on judgment.** No execution shall be issued upon any judgment recovered against the City until after ten days' notice in writing of the recovery of such judgment shall have been given to the Comptroller.

Unexecuted Contracts to be Performed

SECTION 245. Every contract existing and unexecuted in whole or in part on the first day of January, 1926, made by any officer, board or department whose functions with respect to the subject-matter of such contract are transferred by this Act or shall be transferred as authorized hereby to any other officer, board or department, before the complete execution of such contract, shall be executed by the officer, board or department to which such functions are or shall be so transferred and nothing contained herein shall affect the obligation or enforceability of any contract.

Seals of City and its Departments

SECTION 246. The common seal of the City shall be of the form heretofore in use or of such other form and shall be kept in such custody as may be prescribed by the Board of Estimate and Apportionment and shall be used only by officers and upon conditions authorized, either specially or generally, by the Board of Estimate and Apportionment. Each department shall have a seal, which shall be the common seal of the City with the name of the department incorporated therein and its officials shall use the same whenever authorized to use a seal; and all courts of this State shall take judicial notice of the common seal of the City and of departmental seals.

Acts Repealed

SECTION 247. The Act known as the New York City Consolidation Act, being Chapter 410 of the Laws of 1882, and the acts amendatory thereof and supplemental thereto and the Greater New York Charter, as re-enacted by Chapter 466 of the Laws of 1901 and the acts amendatory thereof and supplemental thereto, and all other acts and parts of acts now in force relating to or affecting the City of New York or its government or affairs, in-so-far as any of the provisions of said Consolidation Act or the Greater New York Charter or of any such other acts are inconsistent with the provisions or manifest intent of this Act or in-so-far as the subject matter thereof is in substance re-enacted or covered by this Act are hereby repealed. Said Consolidation Act and the Greater New York Charter and any of said other acts or parts of acts, insofar as any of the provisions of any thereof shall be inconsistent with any action or resolution which may be taken or adopted by the Board of Estimate and Apportionment, or any action or resolution taken or adopted by the Board of Aldermen and the Board of Estimate and Apportionment, conjointly, or any ordinance which may be enacted by the Board of Aldermen, as authorized hereby, or insofar as the subject-matter thereof shall in substance be re-enacted or covered by any such action or resolution of the Board of Estimate and Apportionment or of said two boards, acting conjointly, or any such ordinance of the Board of Aldermen, as authorized hereby, shall be deemed to be repealed from and after the taking effect of such action or resolution of the Board of Estimate and Apportionment or of said two boards acting conjointly or of such ordinance of the Board of Aldermen, and thereafter the same, to the extent aforesaid, shall be without force. In-so-far as this Act is or such action or resolution of the Board of Estimate and Apportionment or of said two boards acting conjointly or such ordinance of the Board of Aldermen shall be the same in terms, substance or effect as said Consolidation Act or the Greater New York Charter or any other of the acts or parts of acts last mentioned or referred to or acts in force relating to or affecting any of the municipalities or public bodies heretofore united or merged in The City of New York, this Act is intended to be, and such action or resolution of the Board of Estimate and Apportionment or of said Board and the Board of Aldermen, acting conjointly, or such ordinance of the Board of Aldermen, as the case may be, shall be deemed to be, a continuation of such enactment and to apply the provisions thereof as modified hereby or thereby. Nothing contained in this Act shall be deemed to repeal any of the provisions of the Rapid Transit Acts, viz., Chapter 4 of the Laws of 1891, as amended, except to the extent, if any, to which the same shall conflict herewith. No right or remedy shall be lost or impaired nor shall any action, proceeding or prosecution pending in any court or any act done or right or obligation accrued or penalty, forfeiture or punishment incurred prior to the time when this Act comes into force, whether the same depend for its virtue upon any laws repealed or modified hereby or otherwise, be abated or affected by reason of this Act. All ordinances of the City of New York, all resolutions of the Board of Estimate and Apportionment and all departmental rules or regulations in force at the time this Act comes into force shall remain in force, except to the extent to which they shall conflict with the provisions or intent of this Act, until the same shall be repealed or modified by action of the board, boards or other authority having jurisdiction of the subject-matter thereof as provided herein.

Constitutionality

SECTION 248. The invalidity of any provision of this Act shall not operate to invalidate the Act as a whole nor any other provision thereof.

Time of Taking Effect

SECTION 249. This Act shall take effect when it shall become law as provided in the Constitution of the State, but the question of the acceptance thereof by the City, although the same may have been accepted by act of the Mayor or without such acceptance shall again have been passed by the Legislature, shall be submitted to the electors of the City at the general election to occur in November, 1923, and this Act, except this Section, shall not come into force unless a majority of all of the votes cast by such electors in favor of and against the acceptance thereof shall be in favor of its acceptance. In the event of its acceptance by action of the electors of the City the entire Act, with the exception of Articles XVI, XX, XXII and XXIII, shall be in force on and after January 1, 1926. Said excepted Articles shall be in force on and from the following dates, respectively, viz.:

Article XVI, at midnight on the thirty-first day of March, 1926;

Article XX, from and after the acceptance of this Act by the electors of the City;

Article XXII and Article XXIII, at midnight on the thirty-first day of March, 1926, but only with respect to assessments made and taxes levied after said thirty-first day of March, 1926.

Act a Public Act

SECTION 250. This Act is a Public Act and judicial notice thereof shall be taken by all courts and in all places.

TABLE OF SOURCES

Showing the Derivation of the Sections of the Proposed Charter or, where Changes in Form or in the Method of Granting Power under the Proposed Charter Make It Impossible to Show a Direct Derivation, Citing the Related Provisions of Present Law.

ABBREVIATIONS.

Amd.—Amended by.
Art.—Article.
C.—Present Greater New York Charter, L. 1901, ch. 466, as amended.
C. A.—New York City Consolidation Act, L. 1882, ch. 410, as amended.
Cf.—Compare.
Ch.—Chapter.
Consol.—Consolidated.
G. C. L.—General City Law; G. C. L. (amd. L. 1913, ch. 247)—General City Law as Amended by Municipal Empowering Act.
G. M. L.—General Municipal Law.
L.—Laws.
L. 1897, ch. 378—First Greater New York Charter.
Subd.—Subdivision; Subds.—Subdivisions.
Tit.—Title.

ARTICLE I.

§ 1. Cf. C. § 1.
§ 2. C. §§ 1, 3, 1617.
§ 3. C. § 2.
See also, for details, C. A., § 1.
§ 4. Introductory Paragraph—New; see, however, G. C. L. (amd. L. 1913, ch. 247) §§ 19, 20, subd. 13; C. §§ 44, 1586.
Subd 1. Cf. C. § 43.
See also G. C. L. (amd. L. 1913, ch. 247), § 20, subd. 22.
Subd. 2.
(a) Cf. C. § 889.
(b) Cf. G. C. L. (amd. L. 1913, ch. 247), § 20, subd. 4, but provision regarding differing rates on differing classes is new.
(c) Cf. C. §§ 894a (added 1906, ch. 207), 895, 896, 897, 898.
(d) New.
(e) Cf. C. § 914; also §§ 1017, 1027-1051, incl.
Subd. 3.
(a) Cf. C. §§ 247 (added L. 1911, ch. 679) and 972 (added L. 1915, ch. 606).
(b) Cf. C. § 436.
(c) Cf. C. § 970; also §§ 436, 951, 972, 1001.
(d) Cf. C. § 970; also §§ 958, 959, 960, 962, 978, 1002, 1003, 1017-1051, especially, particularizing procedures here generalized upon.
(e) C. § 1001 (added L. 1915, ch. 606).
(f) Cf. C. §§ 425-430, 432-437.

§ 4. Subd. 4. Cf. C. §§ 884-1053, incl.; 942-964; 1004-1016, etc., for present prescriptions.

Subd. 5.

(a) New; but see C. §§ 230, 237.
(b) C. 149; also §§ 149-a (added L. 1906, ch. 190), 151, subd. 4.
(c) Cf. C. §§ 173, 174, 181, 188.

Subd. 6.

(a) G. C. L. (amd. L. 1913, ch. 247), § 20, subd. 1.
See also C. § 419.
(b) G. C. L. (amd. L. 1913, ch. 247), § 20, subd. 1.
See also C. § 225, in connection with § 149.

Subd. 7.

(a) Cf. G. C. L. (amd. L. 1913, ch. 247), § 20, subd. 2.
See also C. §§ 1431–1453, incl. (added L. 1915, ch. 596); 969, 970, 970*a* (all added L. 1915, ch. 606).
(b) Cf. G. C. L. (amd. L. 1913, ch. 247) § 20, subd. 3.
(c) Constitution, Art. I, § 7 (as amd. Nov. 4, 1913); C § 970*a*.
(d) Cf. C. § 218*a* (added L. 1916, ch. 494); also § 971*a* (added L. 1915, ch. 523) and § 971*b* (added L. 1920, ch. 715).
See also G. M. L., § 210.
See also C. A., § 1633.

Subd. 8.

(a) C. §§ 47, 818, 824*a*, 826; also G. C. L. (amd. L. 1913, ch. 247), § 20, subd. 8.
Cf. C. §§ 46, 178, 472, 483-518, incl.; L. 1905, ch. 724.
Cf. C. § 530; G. C. L. (amd. L. 1913, ch. 247) § 20, subd. 7.
Cf. C. §§ 47, 835.
Cf. C. § 541; also G. C. L., sec. 17.
Cf. C. § 401.
(b) Cf. C. § 448.
(c) New; see, however, C. § 47.
(d) Cf. C. § 419; see also, for example, C. §§ 469, 539, 618; but see C. § 471.

Subd. 9. Cf. C. §§ 47, 50, 320, 691a (added L. 1911, ch. 69), 713, 834, 1565.
See also G. C. L. (amd. L. 1913, ch. 247), § 20, subd. 11.
See also G. C. L., § 140; G. M. L., § 121.

Subd. 10.

(a) Cf. G. C. L. (amd. L. 1913, ch. 247), § 20, subd. 16.
Cf. (schools, etc.) C. §§ 47, 1055, 1057, 1058, 1065, 1066, 1152-1156, incl., 1127-1133, incl., 1139-1145, incl., 1157. But see L. 1917, ch. 786, amending Education Law (Consol. L., ch. 16).
Cf. (libraries) C. §§ 47, 623; also G. M. L., § 79.
Cf. (museums and art galleries, etc.) C. §§ 230, 613, 621, 622, 624-626, incl.; G. M. L., § 79.
(b) See citations under (a).
(c) See citations under (a).

Subd. 11.

(a) Cf. C. §§ 976, 1435 (both added L. 1915, ch. 596).
(b) Cf. G. C. L. (amd. L. 1913, ch. 247), § 20, subd. 2 and subd. 3.
The charter provisions, empowering particular agencies to hold property, are too numerous for citation here.
(c) C. §§ 205, 402 (added L. 1911, ch. 834).
(d) New.
(e) Cf. C. § 76; see also §§ 151, subd. 1, 205, 205*a*, 220.
(f) Cf. C. § 205.
(g) Cf. C. §§ 47, 821, 827, 836, 970.
(h) Cf. C. § 83; also §§ 432, 439, 499, 818, 818*a* in connection with 205, 819, 820, 832.
See also G. C. L. (amd. L. 1913, ch. 247) § 20, subd. 8.

§ 4. Subd. 11.
(i) C. § 71; G. C. L. (amd. L. 1913, ch. 247) § 20, subd. 2. But, regarding exceptions, see L. 1895, ch. 1006; also C. §§ 205, 205*b*; G. C. L. (amd. L. 1913, ch. 247) § 20, subd. 7.
(j) C. § 205; but see § 220.

Subd. 12.
(a) Cf. C. §§ 47, 438-449.
(b) Cf. C. §§ 1575*a*, 1575*b*, 1575*c* (all added L. 1916, ch. 514).
(c) New.
(d) Cf. C. §448.
(e) Cf. C. §§ 47, 50, 205, 205*a* (added L. 1907, ch. 302), 444 in connection with 396, 837.
See also G. C. L. (and L. 1913, ch. 247), § 20, subds. 7 and 9.
(f) New; but see G. M. L., § 120 *et seq.* (added L. 1917, ch. 709.)
(g) Cf. L. 1895, ch. 1006.

Subd. 13. Cf. C. §§ 242*a*, 242*b* (added L. 1916, ch. 497).
See also terms of G. C. L. (and L. 1917, ch. 483), § 20, subds. 24, 25, 26.

Subd. 14.
(a) New. See, however, partial power conferred by C., § 1543, regarding consolidation of bureaus by heads of departments; also application of principle in connection with Department of Plant and Structures under C., § 595, subd. 2 (amd. L. 1916, ch. 526).
See also Optional City Government Law (L. 1914, ch. 444), § 37.
(b) Cf. C. § 255.
(c) New, as an express grant in charter. See G. C. L. (amd. L. 1913, ch. 247), § 20, subd. 19.

Subd. 15. Cf. C. § 56; see also § 1543. See L. 1910, ch. 659, § 104, and L. 1915, ch. 581, amending C. § 1373.

Subd. 16. Cf. C. §§ 72, 73, 74.
See also G. C. L. (amd. L. 1913, ch. 247), § 20, subd. 10.

Subd. 17. New Cf. C. § 73.

Subd. 18. New. But Cf. C. §§ 73, 469, 819, 821, 824*a*, 826.

Subd. 19.
(a) Cf. C. § 169; also § 47, and, on particular phases, §§ 182, 189.
See also G. C. L. (amd. L. 1913, ch. 247), § 20, subd. 5.
(b) Cf. C. §§ 205, 206; but see § 211.
See also G. C. L. (amd. L. 1913, ch. 247), § 20, subd. 5.
(c) Cf. C. § 169 (as amd. L. 1916, ch. 615), but note exceptions, including those added by L. 1920, ch. 589, L. 1921, ch. 618, and L. 1922, ch. 517.
Cf. (regarding assessment bonds) C. § 181.
Cf. (regarding general fund bonds) C. § 222.
Provisions regarding consolidated pension fund deficiencies new.
(d) Cf. C. §§ 169, 187, 188, 189.
(e) New.
(f) New; but note principles implicit in C. § 169, as amended.
(g) Cf. C. § 169.
(h) Cf. C. § 169.
(i) Cf. C. § 169.
(j) Cf. C. § 222, although much of paragraph is new.

Subd. 20.
(a) Cf. G. C. L. (amd. L. 1913, ch. 247), § 20, subd. 20.
Cf. C. §§ 165, 166; see also C. §§ 351-357, incl.; 548-558, incl. (added L. 1911, ch. 839); 789-792, incl.; 1092 (amd. L. 1917, ch. 303); 1130*a* (added L. 1902, ch. 604); 1146 (added L. 1918, ch. 584); 1319-1324, incl., L. 1920, ch. 427.

§ 4. Subd. 20.
(b) New; but as a partial example see C. § 351.

Subd. 21.
(a) New; but see C. § 149.
(b) Cf. C. §§ 419.
(c) Cf. C. § 246; also G. C. L. (amd. L. 1913, ch. 247), § 20, subd. 5.
(d) Cf. G. C. L. (amd. L. 1913, ch. 247), § 20, subd. 5.
(e) C. § 241.

Subd. 22. Cf. C. § 49, subd. 11, §§ 1175, 1528, 1545, 1575*a*-1575*e*, incl. (added L. 1916, ch. 514).

Subd. 23.
(a) Cf. G. C. L. (amd. L. 1913, ch. 247), § 20, subd. 13. Cf. C. §§ 271, 292, 315, 316; and special assignments of police, §§ 312, 313, 314, 350, 1202*a*.
(b) Cf. C. § 695; see also § 338.
(c) Cf. C. §§ 331-335, incl.
(d) Cf. G. C. L. (amd. L. 1913, ch. 247), § 20, subd. 12. Of the Charter provisions, too numerous for citation, see especially C. §§ 724, 775.
(e) Cf. C. §§ 43, 49, subd. 16, 718*a*, 760-773, 775, 778*c*.
(f) Cf. C. §§ 1172, 1178; also §§ 1170, 1219, 1220; but note § 1168.
(g) Cf. C. §§ 1204, 1539*a*.
(h) Cf. C. §§ 49, subd. 4, 353, subd. 7, 524-529*a*, incl., 766, 771, 1169, 1171, 1176.
(i) Cf. C. §§ 50, 534, 540, 880, 881, 1205, 1223; see also C. § 383. Cf. G. C. L., § 17.
(j) Cf. C. §§ 1481, 1535.
(k) Cf. C. §§ 50, 315; see also C. §§ 1454, 1455.
(l) New; but cf. C. §§ 49, subd. 8, 50, 776.
(m) Cf. C. § 51; see also §§ 347, 349, 529*a*, 1472-1474, incl.
(n) Cf. C. §§ 242*a*, 395, 407, 411*a*, 415, 524, 754, 775, 780, 1176, 1299, 1300.
(o) Cf. C. § 1236. Domestic Relations Law, Consol. L., ch. 14, § 11*a*.
(p) Cf. C. §§ 1236-1241, incl. See also G. C. L. (amd. L. 1913, ch. 247) § 20, subd. 14. See also Domestic Relations Law.
(q) New, as a general grant; see, as illustration of present grant of power to administer oaths, C. § 895.
(r) Cf. C. § 305.
(s) Cf. C. § 49.
(t) Cf. G. C. L. (amd. L. 1913, ch. 247) § 20, subd. 15. Cf. C. §§ 660, 663, 682.
(u) C. § 664; see also C. § 683 (added L. 1921, ch. 204) and § 684 (added L. 1919, ch. 537).
(v) Cf. G. C. L. (amd. L. 1913, ch. 247) § 20, subd. 15. Cf. also C. § 673.
(w) Cf. G. C. L. (amd. L. 1913, ch. 247) § 20, subd. 13. Cf. also C. § 661.

Subd. 24. New.

Subd. 25.
(a) G. C. L. (amd. L. 1913, ch. 247), subd. 20, § 23; see also G. C. L., §§ 6-8, incl. Cf. C. § 54.
(b) Cf. C. § 1526; see also C. §§ 74, 161, 182, 205, 419, 442, 486, 491, 495, 498, 541, 544, 545, 618, 675, 704, 821, 826, 829, 853, 892, 898, 914, 950, 951, 1018, 1027, 1028, 1035.

Subd. 26.
(a) Cf. C. § 44; also G. C. L. (amd. L. 1913, ch. 247) § 19.
(b) Cf. C. § 44; also G. C. L. (amd. L. 1913, ch. 247) § 19.

§ 4. Subd. 26.
(c) New. But note earlier partial uses of this kind of repeal under the Greater New York Charters: L. 1897, ch. 378, § 647 (building laws); C. "section three," referring to schedule two (46 designated sections subjected to supersession by the enactment of ordinances). See also C. § 56 for an application of the same underlying principles.
(d) New.
§ 5. New; but see C. §§ 4, 42, 43.

ARTICLE II.

§ 6. Cf. C. §§ 18, 94, 97, 382.
§ 7. C. § 226.
§ 8. Cf. C. §§ 18, 94, 97, 382.
§ 9. Cf. C. § 19 (as last amended by L. 1921, ch. 670).
§ 10. Cf. C. § 19.
§ 11. Cf. C. § 18.
§ 12. New.
§ 13. New.
§ 14.
Subd. 1. New.
Subd. 2. C. §§ 97. 122; but note § 382.
Subd. 3. Cf. C. § 27.
§ 15.
Subd. 1. Cf. C. § 23.
Subd. 2. C. § 97.
Subd. 3. Cf. C. § 23.
Subd. 4. Cf. C. § 18, 382.
§ 16. Cf. C. §§ 18, 94, 149, 382.

ARTICLE III.

§ 17. Cf. C. § 27.
§ 18. C. §§ 18, 23.
§ 19. C. § 23.
§ 20. Cf. (regarding city clerk) C. §§ 28-33, incl.; also (regarding journal) C. § 35; and (regarding opening of proceedings) C. § 27.
§ 21. Cf. C. §§ 18. 22, 37.
§ 22. C. § 35.
§ 23. New, but see C. § 30; also, for application of principle, see Constitution, Art. III, § 5.
§ 24. Cf. C. § 40.
§ 25. Cf. C. §§ 18, 25.

ARTICLE IV.

§ 26. Preliminary—New.
Subd. 1. See provisions cited, *supra*, under § 4, subds. 11, 12, 17.
Subd. 2. Cf. C. § 47; also 434, 1433, 1434.
Sub. 3. Cf. C. §§ 970*a* and 970*b*, (added L. 1915, ch. 606; re-enacted, after repeal by inadvertence, L. 1916, ch. 112).
Subd. 4. Cf. C. § 247 (added L. 1911, ch. 679).
Subd. 5. See provisions cited, *supra*, under § 4, subd. 13.
Subd. 6. See provisions cited, *supra*, under § 4, subd. 14.
See also (regarding Board of Water Supply), L. 1905 ch. 724.
Subd. 7. Cf. C. § 74.
Subd. 8. Cf. C. § 246; also G. C. L. (amd. L. 1913, ch. 247), § 20, subd. 5.
But see C § 255.
See also C. § 241.

§ 26. Subd. 9. Cf. C. § 237.
Subd. 10. Cf. C. §§ 47, 169.
Subd. 11. See provisions cited, *supra*, under § 4, subd. 19; especially C § 222; also §§ 47, 169, 205. 206, 213.
§ 27. New.
§ 28. (a) Cf. C. § 442.
(b) Cf. C. § 247 (added L. 1911, ch. 679).
(c) Cf. C. § 247 (added L. 1911, ch. 679).
(d) L. 1905, ch. 724, § 3; see also C., §§ 472, 484, 485, 486.
(e) Cf. C. §§ 242*a*, 242*b*.
(f) Cf. C. § 74 (superseding Railroad Law, § 173—formerly § 92).
(g) New.
§ 29. C. § 226; except requirement that six votes of majority be of those entitled to cast three each.
§ 30. C. § 226.
§ 31. New.
§ 32. New. See, however, C. § 226.

ARTICLE V.

§ 33. New, in most part, but based upon an existing system of conjoint powers. See especially C. §§ 47, 242, 436 (improvements generally), 56 (salaries), and 226 (budget). But, as regards the powers of the Board of Estimate alone, see C. §§ 247 (added L. 1911, ch. 679) (improvements) and 45, 50, 74 (franchises).
§ 34. New.
§ 35. New.
§ 36. New.

ARTICLE VI.

§ 37. Cf. C. § 94.
§ 38.
Subd. 1. Cf. C. §§ 118 (appointments) and 95 (removal), except as regards express prohibition against judicial review and following provisos, which are new.
Subd. 2. New, but see C. § 115.
Subd. 3. Cf. C. § 115, subd. 4.
Subd. 4. Cf. C. § 37 (Board of Aldermen, but note required number changed); but new as regards Board of Estimate; see C. § 226.
Subd. 5. C. § 115, subd. 2.
Subd. 6. Cf. C. § 115, subd. 1.
§ 39. C. § 116.

ARTICLE VII.

§ 40. Cf. C. § 97. in connection with § 149.
§ 41. Cf. C. § 149, but, as regards designation of depositaries, see C. § 196.
§ 42. C. §§ 149, 149*a* (added L. 1906, ch. 190), the reference to revenue-producing improvements being new, however.
§ 43.
Subd. 1. New; but for a suggestion of terms, see C. § 149*a*.
Subd. 2. New; but see C. § 161.
§ 44. Cf. C. § 149.
§ 45. Cf. C. §§ 149, 422.
§ 46. C. § 149.
§ 47. Cf. C. § 149; but see also C. § 261.
§ 48. New, as express provision; but see C. § 149.
§ 49. Cf. C. § 149.
§ 50. Cf. C. § 261.
§ 51. New, as express requirement.

§ 52. C. § 149.
§ 53. Cf. C. § 255.
§ 54. Cf. C. § 169; see also C. § 182.
§ 55.
Subd. 1. C. § 187.
Subd. 2. Cf. C. § 188.
Subd. 3. Cf. C. § 189.
§ 56. Cf. C. § 161.
§ 57. Cf. C. § 150.

ARTICLE VIII.

§ 58. C. § 18.
§ 59. C. § 23.

ARTICLE IX.

§ 60. Cf. C. § 383.
§ 61. Cf. C. § 383.
§ 62. Preliminary. New.
Subd. 1. C. § 383, subds. 1, 2, and 3.
Subd. 2. C. § 383, subd. 6.
Subd. 3. C. § 383, subd. 12.
Subd. 4. C. § 383, subd. 4.
Subd. 5. C. § 383, subds. 5, 7, in part.
Subd. 6. C. § 383, subd. 8.
Subd. 7. C. § 383, subd. 9.
Subd. 8. C. § 383, subd. 10.
Subd. 9. Cf. C. § 383, subd. 12.
Subd. 10. C. § 383, subd. 5.

ARTICLE X.

§ 63. New; contrast with C. § 96. See, as regards department headships and term "executive officer," C. §§ 97-110, 1179.
§ 64. New, but see C. §§ 99 (police) and 107, 885 (taxes).
§ 65. New, but see C. §§ 98 (corporation counsel), 195 (chamberlain) and 119 (as amd. L. 1916, ch. 517, § 1) (commissioner of inquiry).
§ 66. Subd. 1. New, but see C. §§ 150 (finance), 270 (police), 452 (water supply, gas and electricity), 640 (licenses), 659 (public welfare), 694 (corrections), 720 (fire), 816 (docks), 1327 (tenement house).
Subd. 2. Cf. C. § 1543.
§ 67. Cf. C. § 1543.
§ 68. Cf. C. § 1544.
§ 69. Cf. C. §§ 1545, 1546; also G. M. L., § 51.

ARTICLE XI.

§ 70. C. § 255; but note reference to Board of Estimate is new.
§ 71. Cf. C. § 255; but note minimum is new.

ARTICLE XII.

§ 72. Cf. C. § 195. See also C. §§ 151, subd. 5, 196, 197, 1587.
§ 73.
Subd. 1. Cf. C. § 151, subd. 2; see also C. §§ 152-156, incl., 158, 160.
Subd. 2. Cf. C. § 151, subd. 3; see also C. §§ 152-156, incl., 158, 160.
Subd. 3. Cf. C. § 151, subd. 1.
Subd. 4. New.
Concluding clause. New.

ARTICLE XIII.

§ 74. C. § 119 (as amd. L. 1916, ch. 517).
§ 75.
Subd. 1. C. § 119.
Subd. 2. C. § 119.
Subd. 3. Cf. C. § 119.
Subd. 4. New.
Subd. 5. Cf. C. § 119.

ARTICLE XIV.

§ 76. Cf. C. § 270.
§ 77.
Introductory clause. Cf. C. §§ 271, 300.
Subd. 1.
(a) Cf. C. § 270.
(b) New.
(c) Cf. C. §§ 276, 288.
(d) C. § 290.
(e) Cf. C. § 292.
(f) New in part, but see C. §§ 272, 292, 300.
Subd. 2.
(a) Cf. C. §§ 283, 284, 292, 300, 302; see also 355.
(b) New; see C. §§ 276, 283 and (regarding promotions) 288.
(c) C. § 339.
(d) New; but see C. §§ 308; also 276, 283, 289.
See (park police) C. §§ 275, 313. But note C. A., § 690 (repealed by L. 1897, ch. 378).
(e) Cf. C. §§ 320, 324.
(f) Cf. C. § 305.
(g) Cf. C. § 315; but new as regards aerial traffic.
Cf. (as regards parades, etc.) G. C. L., § 5; C. § 1547; Code of Ordinances, ch. 24.
Cf. (as regards fire-arms) C. §§ 49, 353; Code of Ordinances, ch. 11.
(h) Cf. C. §§ 315, 316, 317, 1486. But note C. §§ 640, 641 (added L. 1914, ch. 475).
(i) C. § 301.
§ 78. Cf. C. § 290, for suggestion.
§ 79. Cf. C. § 288.
§ 80. C. § 315; also Cf. 741 (fire cooperation), 310, 311, 312, 1264 (health cooperation);
§ 81. C. § 337; Cf. also C. § 340. See also C. § 315.
§ 82. Cf. C. § 303.
§ 83. New. But see C. §§ 300, 301.
§ 84. New. Cf. interim clauses C. §§ 273-275, incl., 276b, 277-282, incl.
§ 85. C. § 341.

ARTICLE XV.

§ 86. New.
§ 87. New.
§ 88. New.
§ 89. New. But see C. §§ 351-357, incl. (police).
C. §§ 789-792 incl.; also 808-812, incl. (fire).
C. §§ 548 (added L. 1911, ch. 839); also 549-558 (street cleaning).
C. §§ 1319-1324, incl. (health).
C. §§ 1092 (amd. L. 1917, ch. 303), 1130a (added L. 1902, ch. 604), and 1146 (added L. 1918, ch. 584) (educational institutions).

§ 89. New. But see L. 1911, ch. 855; amd. L. 1912, ch. 486; L. 1913, ch. 138; L. 1914, ch. 497; L. 1916, ch. 480; L. 1920, ch. 758; L. 1921, ch. 324 (Supreme Court).
L. 1918, ch. 645 (Special Sessions).
L. 1920, ch. 741 (Kings County).
L. 1920, ch. 427 (City Employees Retirement System).

§ 90. New.

§ 91. New. But see (subd. 1) C. §§ 351; 550; 789, subd. 7; 1092, E. subd. 1; 1146, B, subd. 13; 1319. See also for suggestion (subd. 3) C. §§ 1092, C. 7; 1146, B. 7.

§ 92. New.

§ 93. New. See C. §§ 351, 550, 789, 1319.

§ 94. New. See, for present stipulations regarding appropriations, etc., C. §§ 789; 1092, F. subd. 1; 1146, E, subd. 1; 1130 A.
See also, for present stipulations regarding contributions, C. §§ 353, subd. 9; 549; 792; 1092, F, subd. 5; 1146, E, subd. 5; 1320.

§ 95. New. See C. §§ 351, 550.

§ 96. New.

§ 97. New.

§ 98. New.

§ 99. New. See C. §§ 165, 166. 167.

ARTICLE XVI.

§ 100.
Subd. 1. Cf. C. §§ 884, 885.
Subd. 2. Cf. C. § 887; also (b) C §§ 891, 891*a*, 891*b* (added L. 1916, ch. 491).
Subd. 3. Cf. C. § 890.

§ 101. Cf. C. §§ 888*a* (added L. 1913, ch. 324), 895.

§ 102. Cf. C. § 887.

§ 103. Cf. C. § 898, but note important difference and fact that latter part of section is new.

§ 104. New.

ARTICLE XVII.

§ 105. Cf. C. § 123.
See also Civil Service Law (L. 1909, ch. 15) §§ 11, 18, 95.

§ 106. Cf. C. § 123, but note new provisions regarding vote necessary to act.

§ 107. C. § 123; also cf. C. §§ 124, 125, 126.

ARTICLE XVIII.

§ 108. C. § 718 (added L. 1916, ch. 503).

§ 109. C. § 718*a*.

§ 110. C. § 718*b*, subd. 1.

§ 111. C. § 718, subd. 4.

§ 112. C. § 718*c*.

§ 113. C. § 718*b*, subd. 2.

§ 114. C. § 718*d*; clauses regarding applications for buildings on streets laid out on official map and temporary permits are new.

§ 115. C. § 718*d*.

§ 116. C. § 719, subds. 1, 2.

§ 117. C. § 719, subd. 3.

§ 118. C. § 719, subd. 4.

§ 119. C. § 719, subd. 5.

§ 120. C. § 719, subd. 6.

§ 121. C. § 719*a*, subd. 1.

§ 122. C. § 719*a*, subd. 2.

§ 123. C. § 719*a*, subd. 3.

§ 124. C. § 719*a*, subd. 6, except provision regarding election cases.
§ 125. Cf. C. § 719*a*, subd. 5, except last phrase.

ARTICLE XIX.

§ 126. Cf. Education Law (Consol. L. , ch. 16), § 300, and see Ackley *v.* Board of Education (1916), 159 N. Y. S. 249. See also Education Law, § 873 (added L. 1917, ch. 786). But see C. § 96. Constitution, Art. IX, § 1.
§ 127. Cf. Education Law, § 866, subd. 2 (added L. 1917, ch. 786, § 1).
§ 128. Cf. Education Law, § 877, subd. 7, § 880 (added L. 1917, ch. 786, § 1).
§ 129. Cf. C. §§ 1127-1133, incl.; 1139-1145, incl.

ARTICLE XX.

§ 130. New.
§ 131. New.
§ 132. New.
§ 133. New.
§ 134. Cf. C. § 1167; also (a) C. §§ 1168, 1169; (b) 1169, 1170, 1247-1251, incl.; (c) 1178, 1219, 1220, 1222, 1225, 1226; (d) 1169, 1171, also 1204-1212, incl.; (e) 1169; (f) 1176, also 1171, 1229, 1287-1300, incl.; 1304-1318, incl. But see 1340; (g) 1169, 1175; (h) 1236-1241, incl., also 1179; (i) 1257-1259, 1275-1280, 1287-1300.
§ 135. New.

ARTICLE XXI.

§ 136. Cf. C. § 226. See also Education Law, § 877 (added L. 1917, ch. 786), subds. 1, 7. See also C. § 1102.
§ 137. Cf. C. § 226.
§ 138.
Subd. 1. New.
Subd. 2. New.
Subd. 3. New.
Subd. 4. New.
§ 139. New. See, however, C. § 226.
§ 140. New. Cf. General Education Law, § 877, subd. 7.
§ 141.
Subd. 1. Cf. C. §§ 206, 222, 226, 228, 229; (b) 222, 229; (c) 187; (d) 187; (e) 187, 189; (f) new.
Subd. 2. Cf. C. § 226; also 186.
Subd. 3. New; but see C. § 226; also C. § 230.
Subd. 4. Cf. C. §§ 226, 230; but largely new. See C. § 1583, as amd. L. 1922, ch. 58.
Subd. 5. C. § 230, subd. "four."
Subd. 6. C. § 230, subd. "eight."
Subd. 7. Cf. C. § 978 (added L. 1915, ch. 606).
Subd. 8. Cf. C. § 248.
Subd. 9. New.
Subd. 10. New. See C. § 230.
§ 142. New Cf. Education Law, § 877, subd. 1.
§ 143.
Subd. 1. C. § 226.
Subd. 2. C. § 226.
Subd. 3. New.
Subd. 4. C. § 226.
§ 144. Cf. C. §§ 204, 205, 205*a*, 205*b*, 210, 211, 215. See C. § 216.
See also C. §§ 352, 549, 789, 808-812, incl.; 1092, 1130*a*, 1320.
§ 145. New.

ARTICLE XXII.

§ 146.
Subd. 1. C. § 889.
Subd. 2. C. § 889.
Subd. 3. C. § 889.
Subd. 4. Cf. C. § 889.
Subd. 5. New.
§ 147. C. § 892.
§ 148. Cf. C. § 899; see also C. §§ 887, 892.
§ 149. C. § 892.
§ 150. Cf. C. 898.
§ 151. Cf. C. § 896; also 894*a*.
§ 152.
Subd. 1. C. §§ 907, 913, 914.
Subd. 2, Cf. C. § 916. See Tax Law (Consol. L., ch. 60), § 48.
Subd. 3. Cf. C. § 909.
Subd. 4. C. § 907.
Subd. 5. Cf. C. § 907.
Subd. 6. C. § 907.
§ 153.
Subd. 1. Cf. C. § 910.
Subd. 2. C. § 910, but new in part. See C. §§ 892, 892*a*, 894.
Subd. 3. Cf. C. § 910.
§ 154. C. § 900.
§ 155. C. § 900.
§ 156. Cf. C. § 902; but note amendment thereof by L. 1922, ch. 58.
§ 157. C. § 907.
§ 158. Cf. C. § 910.
§ 159. C. § 911.
§ 160. New.
§ 161.
Subd. 1. C. § 914, but note change of dates.
Subd. 2. C. § 916, but note change of dates. See also C. § 917. The concluding sentence new.
§ 162. Cf. C. § 922.
§ 163. C. § 920.
§ 164. Cf. C. § 1017.
§ 165. New.
§ 166. Cf. C. §§ 904, 905.
C. A., §§ 824, 826.
Tax Law, § 4.
§ 167. New.

ARTICLE XXIII.

§ 168. New. See, as regards this whole Article, C. §§ 906, 944, and, as regards pleading, Tax Law (Consol. L., ch. 60), § 290; also ch. XIII thereof, *passim*, on supplementary procedural points.
§ 169. New; see note under § 168.
§ 170. New; see note under § 168.
§ 171. New; see note under § 168.
§ 172. New; see note under § 168.
§ 173. Tax Law (Consol. L., ch. 60, § 296).
§ 174. New; see note under § 168.
§ 175. New; see note under § 168.
§ 176. C. § 969 (added L. 1915, ch. 606).
Also C. § 485, as regards concluding clause in subd. 4; C. § 970*a*, as regards subd. 7.
See also L. 1905, ch. 724, § 25.
§ 177. C. § 999 (added L. 1915, ch. 606).
See also C. § 1432 (added L. 1915, ch. 596). L. 1905, ch. 724, § 8.
§ 178. C. § 1000 (added L. 1915, ch. 606).

§ 179. C. § 1001 (added L. 1915, ch. 606).
§ 180. C. § 1002 (added L. 1915, ch. 606).
§ 181. C. § 1003 (added L. 1915, ch. 606).
§ 182. C. § 995 (added L. 1915, ch. 606, amd. L. 1917, ch. 259).
§ 183. C. § 996 (added L. 1915 ch. 606).
§ 184. C. § 970*a* (added L. 1916, ch. 112).
§ 185. C. § 970*b* (added L. 1916, ch. 112).
§ 186. C. § 980, before repeal by L. 1915, ch. 606.
§ 187. C. § 485.
§ 188. Cf. C. § 502.
§ 189. Cf. C. § 205; L. 1895, ch. 1006, § 17.
§ 190. C. § 971 (added L. 1915, ch. 606).
§ 191. C. § 1434 (added L. 1915, ch. 596).
§ 192. Cf. C. §§ 976 (added L. 1915, ch. 606, amd. L. 1917, ch. 631), 970*a* (added L. 1916, ch. 112).
§ 193. C. § 976 (added L. 1915, ch. 606, amd. L. 1917, ch. 631).
§ 194. C. § 978 (added L. 1915, ch. 606).
§ 195. C. § 979 (added L. 1915, ch. 606).
§ 196. C. § 977 (added L. 1915, ch. 606).
§ 197. C. § 974 (added L. 1915, ch. 606).
§ 198. C. § 975 (added L. 1915, ch. 606), but note lodgment of discretion with Board of Estimate.
§ 199. C. § 980 (added L. 1915, ch. 606).
§ 200. C. § 981 (added L. 1915, ch. 606); also C. § 1438 (added L. 1915, ch. 596).
§ 201. C. § 982 (added L. 1915, ch. 606), 1438 (added L. 1915, ch. 596).
§ 202. C. § 983 (added L. 1915, ch. 606).
§ 203. C. § 985 (added L. 1915, ch. 606).
§ 204. C. § 986 (added L. 1915, ch. 606).
§ 205. C. § 987 (added L. 1915, ch. 606).
§ 206. C. § 988 (added L. 1915, ch. 606).
§ 207. C. § 989 (added L. 1915, ch. 606).
§ 208. Cf. L. 1905, ch. 724, § 8.
§ 209. C. § 990 (added L. 1915, ch. 606).
§ 210. C. § 991 (added L. 1915, ch. 606).
§ 211. C. § 992 (added L. 1915, ch. 606).
§ 212. C. § 993 (added L. 1915, ch. 606).
§ 213. C. § 994 (added L. 1915, ch. 606); also C. § 1440 (added L. 1915, ch. 596, to same effect).

ARTICLE XXV.

§ 214. C. § 943.
§ 215. Cf. C. §§ 950, 951.
§ 216. C. § 946; also §§ 949 (amd. L. 1915, ch. 516), 950.
§ 217. Cf. C. § 950.
§ 218. New: but see C. § 950.
§ 219. C. 951.
§ 220. C. § 946.
§ 221. Cf. C. § 950.
§ 222. Cf. C. § 981.
§ 223. C. § 958.
§ 224. C. § 958.
§ 225. C. §§ 959, 962.
§ 226. C. § 960.
§ 227. C. § 964.
§ 228. C. § 961.
§ 229. C. § 963.

ARTICLE XXVI.

§ 230. New.
§ 231. Cf. C. §§ 1345, 1373.
§ 232. Cf. C. § 1526; also §§ 1527, 1558.

§ 233. C. § 1527.
§ 234. C. § 1527.
§ 235. Cf. C. § 1542; also C. §§ 149, 419, 1541, 1541*a*.
§ 236. C. § 1533. See also G. C. L., § 3.
§ 237. C. § 1533.
§ 238. Cf. C. § 241.
§ 239. New, as explicit provision.
§ 240. Cf. C. § 1534.
§ 241. Cf. C. § 284.
Subd. 1. C. § 1545; also C. § 1175. See also G. M. L. § 51.
Subd. 2. C. § 1545.
Subd. 3. C. § 1545.
§ 242.
Subd. 1. C. § 1534.
Subd. 2. C. § 1534.
§ 243. C. § 59.
§ 244.
Subd. 1. C. § 263.
Subd. 2. C. § 262.
Subd. 3. C. § 264.
§ 245. New.
§ 246. Cf. C. §§ 3, 31, 169. See also, regarding departmental seals, §§ 730, 830.
§ 247. Cf., as regards repeal of inconsistent or covered provisions, and construction of Act as continuation of latter, C. § 1608.
Cf., as regards displacing of statutory provisions by joint resolution, C. "section three" and also L. 1897, ch. 378, § 469, as partial precedents.
Cf., as regards Rapid Transit Act, C. § 45.
Cf., as regards protection of existing actions, C. § 1614.
Cf., as regards ordinances, C. § 41.
§ 248. New.
§ 249. New.
§ 250. C. § 1620.

INDEX OF CHARTER

C.

D.

I.

N.

O.

APPENDIX B

OPINION

Concerning the Possibility

OF A

System of Proportional Representation

UNDER THE

Existing Constitution of the State of New York

Submitted to the Commission,

By F. W. M. Cutcheon,
Counsel.

CONCERNING THE POSSIBILITY

of a

System of Proportional Representation

under the

Existing Constitution of the State of New York

To the New York Charter Commission:

No attempt will be made in this memorandum to determine the abstract question whether a system of voting for aldermen involving proportional representation ought logically to be held constitutional under the Constitution of this State as it now exists. The utmost that can profitably be accomplished is to appraise, to such extent as is possible, the probability of a favorable or an unfavorable decision of the question by the Court of Appeals.

"Proportional representation," as I shall consider it, will be understood to mean any system under which, whether by means of a system of cumulative, restrictive or preferential voting and counting or of a division of offices in proportion to the votes cast for lists of nominees, minority groups are permitted to elect candidates in multiple districts, despite the possibility that, if every elector were to have his vote counted as cast, all candidates of such groups would be defeated.

I shall not attempt to differentiate between systems under which every voter may vote once, and once only, for a candidate for every office, although by apportionment of offices among parties or lists effect is given to votes for only a certain proportion of the candidates voted for, and systems, like the so-called Hare system, under which votes may be cast, or, if cast, may be counted, for less than all of the officers to be elected, or systems, like the cumulative system, under which more votes may be cast or counted for one candidate than for another. In my opinion, the courts will not decide the question of constitutionality upon mere technical consistency with such constitutional restrictions as may exist, but will assume as axiomatic the proposition that if the Constitution entitles every voter to vote once for a candidate for each office to be filled, it contemplates the counting of the votes as cast and the election of at least those candidates who receive majorities. I shall not concern myself with those systems which provide methods of ascertaining majorities, as distinguished from pluralities, except as decisions with respect to them bear upon the constitutionality of proportional representation, properly speaking.

At the outset, it should be said that, in the absence of any provision of the Constitution which expressly or by plain implication limits its power, the Legislature would be competent to provide for any system of voting for city officers which would not be subversive of the system of popular government which exists in this State, and that to justify a court in declaring void an act of the Legislature the court, theoretically at least, must be able to point out a specific provision—or specific provisions—with which the law assailed conflicts; for, subject to the restraints of the Constitution, the entire legislative power of the State resides in the Legislature. (*Constitution,* Sec. 1, Art. III; *Bertholf* vs. *O'Reilly,* 74 N. Y. 509; *Cleveland* vs. *Watertown,* 222 N. Y. 159.)

There exists no provision of the Constitution which bears directly upon the question, unless it be (1) Section 1 of Article II, which provides that "every citizen * * * shall be entitled to vote at such election" (presumably any election at which "he or she may offer his or her vote") "in the election district of which he or she shall at the time be a resident * * * for all officers that now are or hereafter may be elective by the people and upon all questions which may be submitted to the vote of the people," etc., or (2) provisions of Section 2 of Article X, the material sentences of which read:

> *"All city * * * officers, whose election or appointment is not provided for by this Constitution, shall be elected by the electors of such cities * * *, or of some division thereof, or appointed by such authorities*

> *thereof, as the Legislature shall designate for that purpose.* All other officers, whose election or appointment is not provided for by this Constitution, and all officers, whose offices may hereafter be created by law, shall be elected by the people, or appointed, as the Legislature may direct."

As the office of alderman is a city office and, in substance, existed before the adoption of the present Constitution and even before the Constitution of 1846 in which this provision appeared in substantially its present form, the last sentence of Section 2, Article X, is not material to this discussion, unless it be intended that the powers and functions of aldermen shall be so changed that, by reason of the addition or subtraction of authority and duty, the office may be said to be created now for the first time. It will be assumed that this is not intended, even if practicable.

Section 3 of Article XII provides that the election of all city officers (i. e., all elective city officers) "shall be held on the Tuesday succeeding the first Monday in November in odd-numbered years and that the term of every such officer shall expire at the end of an odd-numbered year." Despite this provision and although the existence of aldermen or like city officials is recognized in the Constitution (e. g., in Section 5 and in Section 26 of Article III), it may be doubted whether they are "constitutional officers" except possibly in the sense that it is contemplated that every city shall have authorities which are vested with local legislative powers. (But see *Rathbone* vs. *Wirth,* 6 A. D., 277; *People* vs. *Hogan,* 214 N. Y., 216.) Certainly the Constitution does not specify whether aldermen shall be elected or shall be appointed by other local authority and it must result that, if not so appointed, they must be "elected by the electors" of the city, "or of some division thereof."

Some doubt has been raised as to the applicability of Section 1 of Article II to city elections. *In Matter of Carrick,* 183 A. D., 916, the court said broadly that the provisions of the section with respect to voting upon questions submitted to voters apply only to propositions which "relate to the general governmental affairs of the State and not to local affairs of municipalities." This, however, I think should be considered as a statement inadvertently phrased too broadly or as a misinterpretation of the decision in *Spitzer* vs. *Fulton,* 172 N. Y., 285, upon which it avowedly is founded. In the last-mentioned case, the Court of Appeals, as I understand it, merely read together Section 1, Article II, and Section 1, Article XII (prescribing that the Legislature shall provide for the organization of cities and villages and restrict their power of taxation, etc.), and held that a statute in effect limiting to taxpayers the right of suffrage with respect to a proposition to establish water-works and issue bonds therefor was constitutional because justified by the constitutional provision authorizing regulation of the financial affairs of municipalities. At least, the decision *does not require* a broader interpretation. Nevertheless, it must be conceded that the language of the court is both broad and vague and that it is impossible to determine how much weight it intended to give to the provision of Section 1, Article XII, that the Legislature shall provide for the "*organization*" of cities and villages. This provision alone, of course, might conceivably be held to confer power to prescribe the method of election of officials and the qualifications of voters in the broadest sense.

On the other hand, the Court of Appeals assumed, in *People* vs. *Clute,* 50 N. Y., 451 (pp. 459 and 60), and indeed expressly declared, that Section 1 of Article II applies to elections of town officers (classed with city officers in Section 2, Article X) and it was clearly the view of the Appellate Division in *Rathbone* vs. *Wirth,* 6 A. D., 277, that the section applies to elections of city officers.

Whether or not it should be assumed that Section 1 of Article II applies directly to elections of city officers, the evidence of policy which it affords undoubtedly would be accorded great weight in construing the language of Section 2 of Article X and thus in determining whether provisions for the election of city officers which fail to apply the rule prescribed by Section 1 of Article II are valid.

It has been suggested that the provision really does not mean just what it says but was intended merely to establish manhood suffrage and to prohibit limitations upon the suffrage other than such as are implied by its requirements of qualifications and that the phrase "for all officers * * * elective by the people" should be understood as if it read "for all elective officers for whom he or she may by law be entitled to vote." But as a fact the phrase reads "for all officers that now are or hereafter may be elective by the people." It may be true that the assumed evil which occasioned the incorporation of this provision in the Constitution was the practice of requiring property and educational qualifications for voting, but it hardly seems to follow that the framers of the Constitution may not have thought wise, while engaged in curing that evil, to provide also that every qualified elector should have a right to vote for every officer for whom electors of his community should have the right to vote. That certainly is the literal sense of the provision.

It must be borne in mind that it has generally been considered that one purpose of popular voting is to enable the electorate to reject bad or unacceptable candidates and that this purpose has been regarded as only a little less important than the right to elect acceptable officials. A system of plurality voting such as that ordinarily in use permits the ballot to be used with full effectiveness in single representative districts and very effectively in multiple districts to accomplish the purpose of defeating any unacceptable candidate and it is easily conceivable that the framers of the Constitution deliberately intended that every elector should possess the right to express his preference as between all candidates for every given office in order not only that the office should be filled by those preferred by a majority or plurality, but that every candidate unacceptable to the major portion of the electorate should be excluded. In any event, that reflection furnishes a sufficient and a plausible reason for assuming that Section 1 of Article II of the Constitution should be taken literally.

But advocates of proportional representation argue that even if Section 1 of Article II is to be literally construed when we are dealing with State elections, it may reasonably be given a different construction or ignored when we deal with city elections, because Section 2 of Article X provides that "all city officers * * * shall be elected by the electors of such cities * * * *or of some division thereof,* or appointed by such authorities thereof as the Legislature may designate * * *", and they assert: (first) that there is no apparent reason why the "division" mentioned should not be a division of voters actuated by common preferences rather than a territorial division; and (second) that if the Legislature may provide that all officers of a given class shall be appointed by some local authority, there seems to be no reason of substance why they should not be elected by such sections of the electorate as the Legislature may determine.

The first argument seems to me to be over-refined. Certainly, the meaning which the ordinary reader would spontaneously ascribe to the word "division" is "geographical district." Such, historically, has been its meaning and such therefore is the meaning which naturally we ascribe to it. Such, too, I think, is the meaning which grammatical construction compels us to assign to it. What is the significance of the entire phrase, "or of some division thereof"? The elided words of the earlier portion of the phrase which must be supplied are "by the electors," and the complete phrase (for the moment disregarding the word "thereof") would read, "or by the electors of some division thereof." But it now becomes apparent that "thereof" must refer to cities, etc., and that the entire phrase, all elisions supplied, would be, "or by the electors of some divisions of any such city," etc. This conclusion is reinforced by the succeeding phrase, "or appointed by such authorities thereof"—that is, necessarily, authorities of a city or village. No one, I think, has ever suggested that this last phrase could intend "authorities of the *electors*." Now a division of a city in any except a figurative sense means a geographical division.

Moreover, when one speaks of an *election* by a division even of persons, he ordinarily means a division within which there *may* exist differences of preference. An election in the abstract sense presupposes opposing candidates representing different interests or purposes between whom the voters may exercise an election, and the word as used in Section 2 of Article X must, I think, be supposed to refer to some defined division, ascertainable in advance of an election by applying a statutory description or definition. It seems inappropriate to speak of a candidate's being elected by the voters of "some division," when the division defines itself only by the act of certain voters in voting in common and which cannot be ascertained at all until the votes have been cast. One might speak of divisions of voters such as exist under the Soviet system as divisions of a city, although in a somewhat figurative sense. All of the unskilled laborers or mechanics or shop-keepers or professional men would constitute a defined constituency which might be called a division—perhaps even a division of a city when speaking colloquially—but to say that an officer shall be elected from "some division" of a city and that the division shall be deemed to be those who vote for him provided they be such or such a proportion of the qualified electors seems merely to beg the question.

The second proposition of the advocates of Proportional Representation seems to possess greater substance. It does seem somewhat contradictory to contend that, although no obligation exists to permit an officer to be voted for at all, he must, if elected, be chosen in a particular way. This, however, may be an attack upon the logic of the constitutional provision rather than a guide to its construction.

The contention that the Legislature may determine *at will* the manner in which city officers shall be chosen is merely another way of saying that Section 1 of Article II does not apply at all to city elections, and, to say the least, it may well be said that Section 1 of Article II and Section 2 of Article X impose reciprocal qualifications. But, even assuming that we may disregard Section 1 of Article II altogether, Section 2 of Article X does in fact say that *all* city officers shall be elected by "*the electors*" of the city or of some division thereof or shall be appointed by authorities of the city to be designated and there does not seem to be a great deal of difference between saying that every elector shall be entitled to vote for all elective officers and saying that all city officers shall be elected by the electors of the city or its appropriate subdivisions, which, certainly, seems to mean *all* of the electors thereof. And does not the language of Section 1 of Article II (the only definition of electors to be found in the Constitution) make fairly plain what is meant by Section 2 of Article X, where the latter speaks of "electors"? If so, must not Section 2 of Article X intend that every officer shall be elected by all of the electors of the appropriate territorial district?

It must be remembered, too, that only a particular species of *appointment* is permitted. The appointment cannot be made by individuals—whether electors or not—in their individual capacities (*Rathbone* vs. *Wirth*, 150 N. Y. 459)—it must be made by some of the city authorities as such. If, then, the Constitution defines the method of appointment, why should it not be supposed that it also defines the method of election?

It seems, therefore, that in the election of city officers, the Legislature is commanded by Section 2 of Article X to choose between providing for an election of the same sort would be necessary in the case of a State official or providing for appointment by some city authority.

There is nothing in this conclusion which conflicts with the construction which I have given to *Spitzer* vs. *Fulton*, for Section 2 of Article X does not deal with voting upon propositions.

Despite all that I have said, it is quite true that an election of aldermen of a district by a system of proportional representation would be literally an election of all of them, taken together, by all of the electors of the district, taken together, and that if Section 1 of Article II be left out of consideration—which is possible—and the historical argument be deemed not to be controlling, the application of proportional representation to municipal elections might conceivably be sustained under a narrow interpretation of the language and a broad interpretation of the purpose of Section 2 of Article X.

It remains briefly to review such of the authorities as bear or have been claimed to bear upon the question under consideration.

In New York there has been no decision which can be said to assist in any definite way to a solution of the question. At most, it can be said: on the one hand, that the Court of Appeals has had several opportunities to dispose of a closely analogous question by holding constitutional a law for restrictive voting and has refused to avail itself of the opportunity to pass upon that question, since to have held the law unconstitutional would not have affected the result which it reached; and on the other, that the court has been careful to say that its assumption, *arguendo*, of the possibility of the unconstitutionality of the law must not be deemed to indicate its view and that the question of the constitutionality of minority representation was not presented.

People ex rel. *Woods* vs. *Crissey,* 91 N. Y. 616, involved the validity of the election by the Common Council of the City of Troy of two police commissioners under a statute which provided that each alderman should vote for only one person, although two offices were to be filled, thus making it possible for less than a majority of a quorum to elect one commissioner. The court refused to pass upon the constitutionality of the arrangement but held that even if it were assumed to be unconstitutional, the incumbents had been lawfully elected. The court (in refusing to consider the question of constitutionality, said (p. 622):

> "Two of them, Magill and Craig, claim to have been appointed by the common council, under the provisions of chapter 328 of the Laws of 1880, which act the respondent asserts to be unconstitutional, and so raises the first question which has been argued before us. We ought not to decide it. It has a possible importance beyond the issues here involved. It touches the question of minority representation upon which has been founded very much of legislation, and about which there is room for difference and debate. It respects also the power of the legislature to put restraint upon the action of city authorities, and to guide and limit their modes of procedure. We do not at all mean to intimate or suggest a doubt; but to follow a rule long and wisely adopted by the courts, not to decide a constitutional question unless directly involved in the determination of the case presented, nor without clear and apparent necessity for so doing. In the present case its determination is not essential to the decision, nor even to the general purposes for which this litigation was instituted."

This quotation fairly represents the court's attitude toward the similar question presented in each of the three cases next referred to.

People ex rel. *Augerstein* vs. *Kenney,* 96 N. Y., 295, of several cases in which was raised the title to their seats of aldermen of New York City. The Act (of 1873) under which the respondents had been elected provided that three aldermen should be elected from the senatorial district in question and that each voter should vote for but two names.

The respondents had received a large majority of all of the votes cast, which had been cast as provided in the law. The arrangement, however, was attacked as unconstitutional because prohibiting electors from voting for candidates for all three of the offices to be filled. It was held that, as the voters might have voted for three but in fact voted for only two, and this without protest, their votes were valid and the question of constitutionality was not presented by the case.

People ex rel. *Augerstein* vs. *Kenney,* 96 N. Y., 295, arose under the same law that had been attacked in the *Perley* case. The law was assailed in this case upon the particular ground that it contravened Section 1 of Article II of the Constitution. The Court of Appeals refused to consider the question because it did not appear that voters had offered to vote for candidates for all offices to be filled and that the respondents had clearly received a majority of the votes cast. The court also seems to have regarded the case as presenting a moot question since the term for which aldermen had been elected at the two contested elections had expired and the law providing for minority elections had been repealed (in 1882). The court spoke of the constitutional question as "grave and interesting."

Demarest vs. *The Mayor,* 147 N. Y., 203, was an action to recover salary alleged to be due the plaintiff, who claimed to have been elected an alderman of New York City, although another person claiming to have been elected under and in accordance with the Act of 1873 had been declared elected, had served as alderman and been paid the salary attaching to the office. The court once more declined to pass upon the constitutionality of the Act of 1873.

Rathbone vs. *Wirth,* 150 N. Y., 459 (affirming 6 A. D., 277), involved the constitutionality of an act of the Legislature (L. 1896, Ch. 427) under which the members of the Common Council of Albany were threatening to proceed in the election of police commissioners. The act provided that such members of the Council as should attend for the purpose of electing commissioners should be sufficient to constitute a quorum; that four commissioners should be elected; that each member of the Council attending the election might vote for two persons and no more; that the four persons receiving the highest votes should be the police commissioners, provided that no person should be eligible unless a member of the political party having the highest or of the party having the second highest representation in the Council; and that vacancies should be filled by the Mayor's appointment upon recommendation of a majority of the members of the Council belonging to the same political party as the commissioner whose office should have become vacant. The court affirmed the Appellate Division in holding the act unconstitutional. It held (1) that the act struck at the principle of local self-government established by Section 2 of Article X of the Constitution; (2) that it denied the principle of majority rule, in that a majority of the electors could not directly or indirectly control the choice of a majority of the commissioners; (3) that it delegated the power of appointment not to the Common Council, as a body and as constituted by law, but to members thereof authorized to assemble in any number and act in a way unknown to the law of its being and that such delegation was not to an authority of the city such as the Constitution authorized; (4) that the provision which limited the choice of commissioners to the two principal parties was an unconstitutional restraint upon the right of the majority freely to choose their own representatives and an unauthorized addition to and qualification of the power of appointment which could not be so restricted if delegated; and (5) that the delegation, in effect, to majority and minority members of the Council of the power to fill vacancies was not a delegation to municipal authorities such as was authorized by the Constitution. Perhaps the view of the court can best be summed up by saying that it regarded the act in substance not as a delegation of power such as the Constitution authorizes or contemplates, but as in effect an attempt upon the part of the Legislature itself, by indirection, to make the appointments in question—a proceeding clearly violative of the letter and spirit of the Constitution.

The Court followed the Appellate Division in expressly disavowing an intention to pass upon the principle of minority representation.

The Court of Appeals, however, has sustained acts providing for the appointment of non-partisan boards which, while leaving the power to appoint unqualifiedly in the hands of the municipal authorities, have prohibited the choice of more than a certain number from a single political party.

> *Rogers* vs. *Common Council of Buffalo,* 123 N. Y. 173;
> *Pearce* vs. *Stephens,* 153 N. Y. 673.

In other States, we find a number of authorities which are more directly in point.

The leading case condemning proportional representation as unconstitutional is *Wattles* vs. *Upjohn,* 179 N. W. 335 (1920); same case, 211 Mich. 514.

The provisions of the Home Rule Charter of Kalamazoo providing for proportional representation under the Hare system were declared unconstitutional, principally upon the ground that, under the provisions of the Michigan Constitution declaring that " in all elections " (every qualified voter) " shall be an elector and entitled to vote " and another provision prohibiting cities, in adopting Home Rule charters, to abridge the right of elective franchise, every voter had the right to vote for a person for every office to be voted for in his district. Some weight is put also upon the point that the precise destiny of any voter's indicated choice cannot be definitely determined. The court seems to have been influenced largely by the conviction that the framers of the Constitution must have had in mind the traditional method of plurality election. The tone and reasoning of this decision leave much to be desired but the decision is by the highest tribunal of an important State and is the only decision, so far as I know, in which the Hare system has been directly passed upon under a constitution resembling that of New York. The provision of the Michigan Constitution quoted above is not more express in its terms than Section 1 of Article II of the New York Constitution.

It should be observed that the Michigan court (and the observation applies to other courts which have dealt with constitutional provisions such as Section 1 of Article II) does not treat the expression " all elections," or an equivalent term, as having reference merely to general or annual elections—that is to say, to fixtures—but as referring to the process of electing each separate officer; " all elections " being assumed to mean all votings for any officer, whether or not other officers are voted for. This seems a proper assumption and probably it would be indulged with respect to Section 1 of Article II of our Constitution, if the meaning of the expression "all officers" should be considered to be ambiguous.

In *Maynard* vs. *Board of District Canvassers,* 47 N. W. Rep 756 (Mich.), it was held that a law providing for cumulative voting for members of the Legislature was unconstitutional on several grounds, one of which was that it violated the provision of the Constitution that every elector shall be entitled to vote at all elections, which, it was held, entitled each elector to vote for a candidate for each office and by implication forbade any elector from casting more than one vote for any candidate. This was held to have been the practical construction of the Michigan Constitution from the date of its adoption. It was also held that inasmuch as there could be no cumulative voting in districts where only one representative was to be chosen, the act was also void because it destroyed the uniformity of a substantial right among the electors of the State.

And see the concurring and dissenting opinions in *State* vs. *Thompson*, 131 N. W. R. 231 (N. Y.), a case which was decided upon an extremely doubtful construction of a statute which the court held not to provide for cumulative voting.

Farrell vs. *Hicken,* 147 N. W. Rep. 815 (Minn.), involved the constitutionality in certain aspects only of the home-rule charter of Duluth, by which a system of preferential voting for city commissioners was prescribed, providing for the expression of first, second and additional choices and, in the absence of a majority of first choice votes for any candidate, then for the addition of secondary choices to first choices in order to determine full majorities, which only were to decide the election of candidates. It was also provided that no vote should be counted unless the voter had marked as many first choices as there should be commissioners to be elected. It was held that the requirement that votes must be cast for all commissioners did not contravene the Minnesota Constitution, which provided that every elector should have the right to vote for all officers "that are now or hereafter may be elected by the people," nor the provision of the General Election Law that he should have the right to vote for persons other than regularly nominated candidates. (Candidates in that case were to be nominated solely by petition.)

But in *Brown* vs. *Smallwood,* 153 N. W. R. 953, (Minn.), it was held that the provision of the Duluth charter outlined above was unconstitutional, under the provision of the Minnesota Constitution above quoted (which is similar to Section 1 of Article II of the New York Constitution) upon the ground that the Constitution must be deemed to contemplate one vote and only one by each elector for each officer to be elected. Traditional practice seemed to have been influential in leading the court to its decision. In *State* vs. *Portland,* 133 Pac., 62 (Ore.), in which provisions of the charter of the City of Portland (similar to those of the City of Duluth just referred to) for the expression by the voter of as many first, second and third choices as there are offices to be filled were upheld but under a constitutional provision reading: "Provisions may be made by law for the voter's direct or indirect expression of his first, second or additional choices among the candidates for any office." The method of choosing city officials was held to be a matter of local concern, properly dealt with in the charter, and, therefore, the provision in question of the charter to be a law within the meaning of the constitution.

In re Opinion of Judges, 41 Atl. 1009 (R. I.), the Supreme Court of Rhode Island condemned as unconstitutional a proposed act of the General Assembly providing that in electing the five members of the Town Council of the Town of Cumberland, each elector should vote for one person only and that the five receiving the highest number of votes should be declared elected. The judges were of the opinion that the proposed act would violate provisions of the Rhode Island Constitution conferring upon qualified electors, with certain immaterial exceptions, "the right to vote in the election of all civil officers * * * in all legal town or ward meetings."

In *McArdle* vs. *Mayor,* 49 Atl. Rep. 1013 (N. J.), the Court of Errors and Appeals held void an act requiring that in cities of the first class a Board of Excise Commissioners consisting of four members should be elected in pairs of two each, an elector to vote for only one candidate and the two candidates receiving the highest votes to be deemed elected. This was held to be unconstitutional as in conflict with a provision of the New Jersey Constitution substantially identical with Section 1 of Article II of the Constitution of this State.

The New Jersey Supreme Court made a similar decision in *State* ex rel. *Bowden* vs. *Bedell,* 53 Atl. Rep. 198.

The same conclusion was reached by the Supreme Court of Ohio in a similar case, *State* vs. *Constantine,* 42 Ohio St. 437, the court founding its opinion upon a provision of the Ohio Constitution to the effect that each elector shall be "entitled to vote at all elections," which was said to have been universally understood to confer upon each elector the right to vote for a candidate for each office to be filled at an election.

But in *Orpen* vs. *Watson,* 93 Atl. Rep., 853 (N. J.), a statute of New Jersey providing for a commission form of government, which had been adopted in the City of New Brunswick and under which five commissioners had been elected pursuant to provisions substantially identical with those of the Duluth charter, referred to above, was sustained The Supreme Court conceded that a provision of the New Jersey Constitution, practically identical with Section 1 of Article II of our Constitution, was intended to give to each elector one vote for each officer to be elected and no more, but concluded (because, as it said, no vote could be effective to elect more than one candidate) that the system prescribed did not conflict with the constitutional guaranty.

And in *Commonwealth* vs. *Reeder,* 33 Atl. Rep., 67, (Pa.), the Supreme Court of Pennsylvania decided that the provision of the Constitution of that State that every elector shall be entitled to vote at all elections was not violated by an act providing for the election at one time of seven judges of the Superior Court, but declaring that no elector may vote at any election for more than six candidates. In that case, the court placed emphasis upon a constitutional provision somewhat similar to (but not identical with) Section 2 of Article X of the Constitution of this State, that "all officers whose election is not provided for under this Constitution shall be elected or appointed as may be directed by law."

In a case which involved the constitutionality of the Hare system of proportional representation which had been adopted in the Freeholders' Charter of the City of Sacramento, California (a copy whereof, but lacking the title of the cause, has been furnished to me), it was held by the Superior Court of Sacramento County that provisions of Article XI of the California Constitution, which declared that it should be competent for any city, "and plenary authority is hereby granted, subject only to the restrictions of this Article, to provide therein (i. e., in a Freeholders' Charter) or by amendment thereto, the manner in which, the method by which, the times at which and the terms for which the several * * * municipal officers and employees whose compensation is paid by said city * * * shall be elected or appointed, etc." and that it should likewise be competent to provide "for the manner in which * * * any municipal election shall be held and the result thereof determined * * *," (Section 8½, Article XI), authorized and justified the adoption of the system of proportional representation which had been provided for in the charter.

Recently the decision of the Superior Court was reversed by the District Court of Appeals, Third Appellate District, in *People* ex rel. *Devine* vs. *Elkus and others*, 39 Cal. App. Dec., 279. The Court, in an elaborate opinion, holds in effect that the provisions of Section 8½ of Article XI of the California Constitution (of which the salient clauses have been quoted) are controlled by Section 1 of Article II thereof, which provides that every qualified elector "shall be entitled to vote at all elections which are now or may hereafter be authorized by law." The court expressly holds that the right to vote "at all elections" includes the right to vote for a candidate for every office to be filled and that each member of the Sacramento City Council must be deemed to hold a separate and distinct office. It holds further that to justify a conclusion that the provisions of Section 8½ of Article XI were intended to alter the fundamental rule of Section 1 of Article II, such intention must appear with "irresistible clearness" and that such intention does not indubitably appear; that the words of Section 8½, conferring power to determine "the manner in which" and "the method by which" municipal officers shall be elected, should be held to refer to the ordinary and necessary details of conducting elections and not to authorize the prescription of qualifications of electors; that, as municipalities are not authorized to prescribe the qualifications of electors, they cannot be deemed empowered to deny the right of electors to vote at any election (meaning any election of any officer). Moreover, the court holds that the power to make municipal officers appointive does not carry with it the authority to alter the general constitutional rule as to the right of electors to vote, if election be the form of selection adopted. The decision contains a fairly comprehensive survey of such decided cases as may be said to have a direct bearing upon the questions discussed. The court reaches the conclusion that the provision of the Sacramento charter for the employment of the Hare system of proportional representation was violative of the electors' constitutional right to vote at all elections. I am informed that the California Supreme Court has denied an application to carry the case to that Court for review of the decision of the District Court of Appeals.

In the Fall of 1821, the City of Cleveland adopted a charter under the assumed authority of a "home-rule" provision of the Ohio Constitution. The Ohio Court of Appeals (Eighth District) in a decision rendered May 6, 1922, in the case of *Reutener* vs. *Cleveland* (not yet reported) held that notwithstanding other and perhaps conflicting provisions of the Ohio Constitution, the Home Rule provisions (Article XVIII) authorized the electors of the City to exercise their own discretion in determining the method of election of city officials and that the provisions of the Cleveland charter for proportional representation were constitutional. In that case, the particular provision of the Constitution relied upon as inimical to the provisions for proportional representation was the provision that every qualified elector shall "be entitled to vote at all elections," and the question primarily considered and determined was the narrow question whether under the Hare system adopted by the Cleveland charter the limitation of the vote in a multiple district to one candidate for membership in the City Council, although several councilmen were to be elected in the district, was a valid limitation.

Neither the Superior Court decision in the Sacramento case nor the decision of the District Court of Appeals in the Ohio case seems to be entitled to any substantial weight in the determination of the question under discussion in this opinion, inasmuch as the Constitution of this State contains no provisions in the least degree similar to those upon which the courts of California and Ohio relied, respectively.

For completeness, I refer also to *State* vs. *Nichols*, 97 Pac. R., 728 (Wash.), and *Adams* vs. *Landson,* 110 Pac., 280 (Idaho), which, however, are primary election cases.

In addition to the foregoing, attention should be called to two historical facts (1) that two previous New York Charter Commissions have refrained from proposing charter provisions for elections under some system of proportional representation on account of the doubts which they entertained concerning the constitutionality of the proposal if adopted; and (2) that proposals to incorporate provisions for proportional representation in the State Constitution have been urged upon at least two Constitutional Conventions and have failed of adoption. I think these occurrences may fairly be said to indicate the state of opinion of the bar of New York with respect to the question under consideration. Some slight confirmation of this assumption, perhaps, may be gathered from a statement made by Mr. Justice Herrick, in his opinion in *Rathbone* vs. *Wirth,* 6 A. D., 277, where (commenting on the failure of the Constitutional Convention of 1894 to approve proposals for minority representation) he says that he has before him, at the time of writing, the opinions of distinguished constitutional lawyers to the effect that a proposed law providing for divided representation upon the Board of Police Commissioners of this City would not be constitutional under the State Constitution, as it then existed. The law in question, however, was open to other and more evident objections than that to minority representation.

My conclusion as to the question under discussion is this: It seems to me probable, but not certain, that the New York Court of Appeals, in a case squarely presenting the question for decision, would hold unconstitutional any system of proportional representation which, like the Hare system, requires the elector to vote at an election for only one candidate for alderman, although several aldermen are to be voted for throughout the aldermanic district of which the voter's election district is a part, and permits additional choices to be expressed and to be utilized (contingently) in the event that the voter's first choice shall have been defeated or shall have been elected without the aid of his vote. In my opinion, the court probably would hold that the language of Section 2 of Article X, particularly when read in the light of the generally recognized practice of the past with respect to the election of officers and interpreted. if not directly affected, by Section 1 of Article II, contemplates a system under which each elector may vote directly and definitely for one candidate for every office to be filled by the voters of his territorial district, or of that district and others, and that he may so vote not only with a view to assisting, if possible, to elect to any given office a candidate whom he prefers, but also of assisting to defeat, if possible, any candidate for any office to whom he is opposed. I do not see how such a decision can be placed upon the ground that such a system as the Hare system is not democratic or does not substantially accomplish the aims of a popular form of government or that it could operate to defeat the will of the majority, but my impression is that the court's decision would be grounded upon an interpretation of Section 2 of Article X, and perhaps an application of Section 1 of Article II of the Constitution, regard being had for tradition and an assumption being indulged that the Constitution had been framed in the light of that tradition.

I concede that an opportunity exists to make a contrary ruling. The court could (1) hold that Section 1 of Article II is not applicable to city elections; (2) confine the interpretation of Section 2 of Article X strictly to its literal phraseology; (3) distinguish cases in other jurisdictions upon the ground that in those jurisdictions the Constitutions do not contain provisions precisely like Section 2 of Article X; (4) argue that as (a) the manifest intent of the latter section is to permit the Legislature wide latitude in determining the method of selecting local officers, (b) no elector can claim an absolute right to vote for any, except so-called "constitutional officers" (since the Legislature may provide for the appointment of all others), and (c) the result of voting under a proportional representation system must be the choice by the electors of the district of all aldermen to be elected, all electors voting freely and equally, the voice of the majority indubitably prevailing, such a system of voting and counting votes—which is not subversive of our system of popular government and does not, with absolute necessity, conflict with the language of Section 2 of Article X, literally regarded—should be upheld; and finally (5) sustain the law as a salutary reform adapted to attain the true objects of democratic government. All this is possible but I regret to say that I cannot believe that such a result can be counted upon with any degree whatever of confidence.

In my judgment, the Commission, if it desires to recommend the adoption of a system of proportional representation in city elections, should submit a proposed amendment of the Constitution, which will permit its use and should urge that, if the amendment be adopted, the Legislature provide for its employment or give permission for its adoption in New York City. If the Commission desires, I will prepare and submit an appropriate form of amendment.

Respectfully submitted,

F. W. M. CUTCHEON,
Counsel.

New York, December 16, 1922.

M. B. Brown Printing & Binding Co.,
37-41 Chambers Street, N. Y.

www.ingramcontent.com/pod-product-compliance
Lightning Source LLC
LaVergne TN
LVHW010200110826
845151LV00002B/562

* 9 7 8 1 4 2 5 5 3 6 0 9 1 *